In praise of

MARILYN: A WOMAN IN CHARGE

" . . . A THRILLING and transformational journey into the life of one of the most powerful, unsung trusted advisors of our time. I finished the book inspired and with a deeper appreciation for all she achieved on behalf of women in business. This book is relevant today for any woman, at any age, in any profession."

—*Cheryl Procter-Rogers, APR, Fellow, PCC; senior public relations consultant and executive coach*

"One of the closest insider views ever written of the essential role public relations plays in a large organization. . . . An important read for everyone in the field—men and women—especially those just starting careers in public relations. Martin's recounting of crises Marilyn faced is done in GRIPPING detail. There is much to be learned from his important book."

—*Bill Nielsen, former corporate vice president of Public Affairs, Johnson & Johnson*

"Martin's description of how Marilyn handled reputational crises, complex situations, sudden reversals, self-inflicted wounds, prickly personalities, conflicting stakeholder interests, and uncooperative leaders, should be required reading for anyone aspiring to hold a similar corporate role. Martin has done a fine job of showing us the qualities that enabled her to be the first breakthrough female corporate communications leader with the AUTHENTICITY only an insider can deliver."

—*John Onoda, senior corporate counselor, Gagen MacDonald*

"Those in search of lessons in leadership have hit the jackpot. This book offers a TREASURE TROVE of insights—in leadership, diversity, inclusion and representation, and crisis communications. I'm better for the read."

—*Del Galloway, APR, Fellow PRSA; former AT&T executive; vice president, communications, Wells Fargo*

"Martin offers a deeply researched, ENGAGING account of Marilyn Laurie's rise to upper management in the context of events with global implications—from the first Earth Day to AT&T's divestiture of the Bell operating companies. I gained a better understanding of Laurie, of women in public relations history, and the role of public relations in corporate America.

—*Karen Miller Russell, associate professor, Henry W. Grady College of Journalism and Mass Communication, University of Georgia*

"Martin has written a RIVETING book that shows us the backbreaking and heartbreaking work it took for Marilyn to achieve the pinnacle of our profession. She was fearless, outspoken, demanding, intense, a critical thinker, totally trustworthy, and not thin skinned when experiencing gender discrimination."

—*Patrice Tanaka, founder & Chief Joy Officer, Joyful Planet LLC*

"Dick Martin brilliantly captures the energy, spirit, and quest for change that embodied Marilyn's life in public relations. Marilyn was a PR leader at a time when few women carried a senior title. [She was] deeply rooted in purpose and passion, change agentry and business problem-solving. Whether you're in the field of PR or not, Martin writes a MUST-READ book that draws you in from page one, and keeps your attention the whole way through. I kept saying to myself as I read the chapters, 'I wish I had met Marilyn.'"

—*Deirdre Breakenridge, author, and CEO of Pure Performance*

MARILYN: A WOMAN IN CHARGE

MARILYN
A WOMAN IN CHARGE

*Marilyn Laurie's Life
In Public Relations*

DICK MARTIN

PRMuseumPress

Marilyn: A Woman In Charge
Marilyn Laurie's Life In Public Relations

By DICK MARTIN

First edition, 2020

ISBN 978-0-9990245-6-0
Library of Congress Control Number: 2020909347

10 9 8 7 6 5 4 3 2

To all
the women
I've worked with
and worked for,
with deep affection
and boundless
gratitude.

Marilyn

1939 – 2010

"Experience is not what happens to you;
it is what you do with what happens to you."

—Aldous Huxley

CONTENTS

ACKNOWLEDGEMENTS

Because so much of my career was intertwined with Marilyn Laurie's, especially from 1991 to 1998, parts of this book appeared in different form in my own memoir, *Tough Calls: AT&T and the Hard Lessons Learned from the Telecom Wars*, published by the American Management Association in 2004. To keep the focus on Marilyn, however, this book is told largely in the third person, from the perspective of an interested observer. After the Introduction, I don't change voice to the first person until the final pages when I can speak of what she meant to me personally.

All the direct quotes in this book were taken from personal interviews or from contemporaneous documents. For example, many of the quotes attributed to Marilyn come from oral histories she recorded for the AT&T Corporate Archives and for the Arthur W. Page Center at Penn State. Other quotes are drawn from notes I took of our personal conversations, speeches she gave, papers she wrote, and her voluminous office files in the AT&T Archives. Even in her final days, Marilyn recorded her thoughts on lined note paper. Her family found them after she was gone and published many in a memorial booklet, from which I have quoted.

I'm indebted to Marilyn's sister Lois Gold Schauber for sharing early memories of growing up in the Bronx. Marilyn's daughters Amy Laurie and Lisa Laurie Potts generously shared stories about their mother's home life, and Lisa gave me copies of such material as the Sunday newspaper supplement Marilyn and her husband Bob created for the second celebration of Earth Day in 1971. I also profited from the memories of Eve Preminger, a close friend of Marilyn's when she was a young mom wheeling a carriage in Central Park and, later, when she was a neighbor on Manhattan's Upper West Side.

Meredith Mann at the New York Public Library kindly gave me access to the records of the Environmental Action Coalition, which organized the first New York City Earth Day celebration in 1970 and of which Marilyn was a founding member. Sarah Badgley of the Fifth Avenue Association dug through the organization's archives to confirm its stance on closing Fifth Avenue to cars. Fred Kent, the "coordinator" of that first Earth Day in New York, provided a first-hand account of Marilyn's role in planning and executing the celebration. Sheldon Hochheiser and Melissa Wasson of the AT&T Archives were tireless in retrieving 29 file boxes of Marilyn's AT&T papers for me.

I am grateful for the perspectives a number of Marilyn's AT&T colleagues shared, including Marge Boberschmidt Barpal, Henry Bassman, Jane Biba, Dave Boyce, Bruce Brackett, Hal Burlingame, Kathy Fitzgerald Cocca, Adele Donohue, Carole Howard, Barry Johnson, Bob Kavner, Reynold Levy, Shelly London, Gail McGovern, Esther Novak, Al Partoll, Jack Shultz, Randy Tobias, Bill Weiss, Burt Wolder, John Zeglis, and others who prefer to remain anonymous. Unless indicated otherwise, all quotes attributed to these people are from interviews I conducted with them.

I also want to thank my wife Ginny, our son Christopher, and our daughters Elizabeth and Teukie, who have educated me over the years on a host of issues raised in these pages, from gender stereotyping and work-family balance to precarious manhood (once known as toxic masculinity), and the feminization of certain occupations. I will be forever grateful for their loving counsel.

Finally, I want to acknowledge the seminal role Shelley and Barry Spector played in this book's publication. As founders of the Museum of Public Relations, they have helped shape the practice's future by drawing lessons from its past. This book was their idea, and their enthusiastic support never flagged. I'm honored they entrusted its research and writing to me.

Among the many sayings attributed to baseball legend Yogi Berra is, "It's tough to make predictions, especially about the future." Well, it turns out it's just as tough to produce an accurate record of the past. Oral histories, diaries, even memoirs are, like newspapers, only a rough first draft of history. In the moments after an event, we all have selective memories and a tendency to make ourselves look better than we were. Years later, those initial memories are embellished a bit in every subsequent retelling until they become what we honestly believe really happened.[1] Marilyn was not immune to this phenomenon; nor am I. So I have done my best to confirm the key events described in this book with multiple sources, even when I was one of the participants.

I make no claim the story told in this book is "objective." Writer and literary critic Judith Thurman maintains that's impossible anyway. "There is no objective biography," she has written. "The trick is to be conscious of your subjectivity, just present the evidence, and leave the judgments to the reader." I've tried to follow that admonition as well as Thurman's second warning. "It's easy to judge people with the benefit of historical hindsight, but at the time, who's to say what you'd do?"[2]

Still, I confess to feeling like the unfortunate writer assigned to review John Updike's lifework, "standing tiptoe on the balance beam

---

[1] As psychologist Elizabeth Loftus put it in a 2013 Ted talk, "Our brains are Wikipedia pages, subject to continual revision, prompted either by ourselves or the suggestions of others." See: http://bit.ly/2S6d35e.

[2] "The Secret Life of Biographers: A Conversation with Judith Thurman and Jean Strouse," New York Times on the Web, Oct. 17, 1999. See: https://nyti.ms/2vcLXjV.

of *objectivity* and *fair assessment*."[3] I leave it to you to judge if and where my balance faltered.

Of course, unless otherwise noted, the conclusions drawn from the events described in the following pages are solely my own, as are any errors of fact or omission.

Dick Martin,
September 2020

---

[3] Patricia Lockwood, "Malfunctioning Sex Robot," *The London Review of Books*, Vol. 41, No. 19, Oct. 10, 2019.

INTRODUCTION

AT&T's media relations director sat behind a mahogany desk the size of a small aircraft carrier. At least that's how it looked from the edge of the straight-backed chair on which Marilyn Laurie was perched. He was her boss, and they were locked in disagreement. He rocked back and forth in his swivel chair as she made her argument. She wouldn't remember the specifics of their dispute for long. But how it ended would stay with her the rest of her life.

She had left her home in the Edgemont[4] section of Scarsdale, New York, that summer morning for the long, uncomfortable train and subway ride to AT&T headquarters at 195 Broadway in downtown Manhattan. She was clad as usual in a practical skirt, hanging just below her knees, flats—even though, at five feet, two inches tall, she could have used the extra lift of heels—and a demure long-sleeved blouse with a keyhole neck, which is to say it was a round collar held together by a thin, fabric bow. Untied, it fell into a V, no deeper than a man's shirt collar with the top button undone. And that's the way she was wearing it that morning.

She was in mid-sentence, when her boss sprang out of his chair, circled over to her side of the desk and tied the strings of her blouse into a bow. It was one of few times in her career she was speechless. There was nothing sexual about it. But more than two decades later, she still described it as "the most aggressive male-to-female action" she had ever been subjected to.

She put it aside and attributed it to that one individual. It wasn't anything she felt was generic. God knows, it didn't hurt her career. In fact, the guy who did that eventually reported to her. And if she ever felt an urge to tighten his tie then, she resisted it.

---

4 Edgemont is an unincorporated area in the town of Greenburgh, but most of its homes have a Scarsdale ZIP Code.

She claimed she remembered the incident because it was so uncharacteristic of her interactions with the men she worked with and to whom she reported. She often said she didn't feel the personal impact of working among so many men. Even when she found herself in conflict with her male colleagues, she never felt it was because she was a woman and they were men. She felt it was usually because she was a liberal New Yorker and they were conservative Midwesterners. They represented the values of the country's heartland, and she represented bicoastal values that had not reached the heartland yet.

It may have been the one time this ears-to-the-ground public relations woman failed to hear the rumbling under her own feet. If the #MeToo movement is solely about sexual harassment, there's no evidence Marilyn could claim the hashtag. But if it's about a more subtle form of sexism whose engine is gender stereotyping, she could have been its poster child.

Robert Caro, whose books about Robert Moses and Lyndon B. Johnson run more than 3,500 meticulously researched pages—with a fifth concluding volume on Johnson to come—does not consider himself a biographer, but a reporter. "I never thought of the books as the stories of Moses or Johnson," he wrote. "I never had the slightest interest in writing the life of a great man. I thought of writing biographies as a means of illuminating the times of the men I was writing about and the great forces that molded those times—particularly the force that is political power."[5]

I would no more compare Marilyn Laurie to Robert Moses or Lyndon Johnson than liken myself to Robert Caro. But I see his point. I knew Marilyn personally, worked with her as a colleague, reported to her, and ultimately succeeded her as the AT&T Corporation's chief communications officer. I was an admirer and—

---

[5] Robert A. Caro, *Working* (New York: Alfred A. Knopf, 2019), p. 3.

as she knew well—an occasional critic. And I have come to believe Marilyn's story can teach us a lot about the times and forces that shaped her—and continue to shape our own stories today.

If Caro's focus was power, my focus in these pages is "meaning." Both the personal meaning we all strive to understand—who am I, do I matter? And "meaning" as the craft Marilyn practiced for her entire career—active participation in the social construction of meaning, what we sometimes call branding, public relations, corporate communications, or to be unkind, "flackery." She fought valiantly to rid the latter from her organization, as well as from the expectations of her internal clients. That's part of her story too. But most of all, to the extent she strived to find her meaning in a career, rather than in domestic life, she was swimming against strong currents that might have carried her to a different shore. And that may help answer the question she so often posed to herself, "How did a little Jewish girl from the Bronx get here?"

The philosopher Agnes Callard maintains that life's greatest challenge isn't to figure out what you want to do, but who you want to be.[6] Marilyn aspired to be someone who made a difference on a grand scale. She started, almost by accident, as an environmentalist and ultimately came to see her role as steward of a great company's character, which she defined as the value an organization creates and the values it stands for. In other words, the purpose it pursues and the way it pursues it. She spent much of her career trying to nail that meaning down. She drove plenty of her C-suite colleagues up the wall with her regular insistence that they join the search, until she learned to disguise it as an exploration of corporate "mission" or "brand values," which sound more marketing-ish.

---

[6] Agnes Callard, *Aspiration: The Agency of Becoming* (Oxford University Press, 2019).

But her AT&T career was hardly an academic exercise. She once confessed that, by the time she got into the position to make a real difference in the company, "you could hear the cracks splitting the foundation under you." She spent most of her time in the trenches with her C-suite colleagues. Vietnam-era Defense Secretary Bob McNamara spoke of the "fog of war" as kind of an all-purpose excuse for bad calls. Marilyn was never at war in a literal sense, but AT&T's hallways and conference rooms were often filled with the smoke of friendly fire, the debris of turf wars, and the clash of competing agendas. She was never asked to flat-out lie. But she needed the grit of a coal miner to find the truth, which was scattered across the company and jealously guarded.

Marilyn was more than her gender, much as many think it defined her. Her life story was knit from three strands: the family into which she was born in 1939, the place and times in which she grew up, and a company that no longer exists, save in name.

To start, Marilyn was a second-generation immigrant. Her father Abraham Gold was born in what is now Poland, but was then Austria, and was brought to America by his parents in 1907, when he was just four years old. Her mother Irene's parents were born in Kiev, then part of Russia, and immigrated to America in 1904, the year before she was born.

Both families were fleeing antisemitism, but even more, they were forward-looking, optimistic people, focused on opportunity. They were not tethered to the past, but secure in the belief they could change their lives and make something of themselves. They were entrepreneurial—one grandfather owned a trucking company; the other was a jeweler. And although their first language was Yiddish, they had an abiding faith in education as the great leveler and key to bettering their lives.

Marilyn's father Abraham graduated from college with degrees in both law and accounting. His wife Irene, who had been in the small minority of women to graduate from high school in the 1920s, was active in many local civic organizations. By dint of outspokenness and simply showing up, she became a big fish in the small pond represented by the neighborhoods along their stretch of the Grand Concourse in the Bronx.

Known as the Park Avenue of the middle class, the Grand Concourse was "the" neighborhood in the Bronx. Unlike other streets in the borough, it is a wide boulevard with multiple roadways, separated by verdant dividers and, back then, lined by grand apartment buildings, synagogues, theaters, and restaurants. Modeled on Paris's Champs Élysées, only bigger, it stretches four-and-a-half miles from the New York Thruway at 138th Street in the south to the Mosholu Parkway in the Bronx's northern reaches around 208th Street. Imitation or not, people who lived on the Grand Concourse were considered a tad more affluent and successful than those just one block to either side.

When the Gold's first daughter Lois was about to enter junior high school in 1947, and Marilyn was eight, they moved from their two-bedroom apartment on Creston Avenue, one of those lesser streets parallel to the Grand Concourse, into an elevator apartment building on the boulevard, just north of the present Bronx Museum of the Arts. The building stretched more than halfway up the block from McClellan Street to 167th Street in four interconnected yellow brick towers, six floors high with light courts in between.

When the Golds moved in, there were lots of Art Deco touches, like curving walls, wrap-around corner windows, a terrazzo-floored lobby, sunken living rooms, and yellow-tiled bathrooms. But the feature that gave the building its nickname, the "Fish House," was a seven-foot-high glass-tile mural of tropical fish and water plants that curved across the building's entrance facade in iridescent swirls of orange, gold, green, and blue.

As we will see, Marilyn inherited her mother's social conscience and outspokenness, her father's intelligence and analytical skills, and the streetwise independence of her neighborhood. But most of all, her grandparents' optimism and resolve to be the heroes of their own lives were knit into her DNA. From a young age, Marilyn was determined to be in charge of her own life. When she did well, she always wanted to do better; when she fell short, she always bounced back. Nowhere was that more evident than in her career at AT&T.

Marilyn's story is tightly intertwined with nearly three decades of AT&T's history, from the early 1970s to the late 1990s. To understand her, one must know the company. And to know the company, one must understand the people who ran it. So you will read a lot in these pages about AT&T and its leaders.

When Marilyn started at AT&T, it was the country's largest and richest corporation, bigger than General Motors, Ford, General Electric, IBM, Xerox, and Coca-Cola combined. And she was there when regulation and changing technology condemned AT&T to increasing irrelevance. The company from which she retired in 1998 was acquired by one of its former subsidiaries just seven years later. The brand she had endowed with so much meaning turned out to be one of its greatest assets. And the subsidiary quickly adopted it.

Marilyn drew personal meaning from AT&T's period of greatness—not particularly from its size or prominence, but rather from its sense of mission. She joined the company in its 94th year, when it was literally "The Telephone Company," handling more than nine out of ten phone calls in the United States. Since the beginning of the 20th century, its mission had been "universal service," to bring telephone service to every household in the United States, a task that was essentially completed around the time she joined the company.

AT&T's service ethic was supported by its own romantic mythology and heroic symbols. One was a golden statue on the peak of its headquarters building in lower Manhattan where Marilyn worked early in her career. The Spirit of Communications,[7] more informally known as "Golden Boy," was a 24-foot tall gilded statue of a lithe young man holding a bundle of lightning bolts overhead and a coil of thick cables over his shoulder to show how telephone service would tie the world together. The other was an oil painting of Angus MacDonald, a 23-year-old telephone lineman who snowshoed through the Blizzard of 1898 to repair lines carrying calls between New York and Boston. Known as "The Spirit of Service,"[8] prints hung proudly in company buildings across the country. Both Golden Boy and Angus MacDonald were featured in advertisements and on the cover of telephone books for many years, propagating the corporate folklore.

But the company's service ethic wasn't all smoke and mirrors. In its first incarnation, AT&T "was built on a trade-off of public trust in return for being allowed to operate as a monopoly, so we had a service ethic built into our DNA," Marilyn wrote. "I can remember as a kid in the PR department, we were given a list of objectives, and the number-one objective was to be a company worthy of trust—not a

---

[7] When the statue was commissioned by AT&T president Theodore Vail in 1914, it was to be called "The Genius of Telegraphy." However, by the time it was completed in 1916, AT&T had spun off its telegraph business, so it was renamed "The Spirit of Communications." It was sculpted by a woman, Evelyn Beatrice Longman, following a nationwide contest. Originally installed on the roof of AT&T headquarters at 195 Broadway, it has since followed the company to subsequent headquarters in New York, New Jersey, and Texas.

[8] MacDonald posed for the portrait months after the March Blizzard of 1898. Despite his and his colleagues' efforts, service was not actually restored until May. The original drawing by Frank T. Merritt was commissioned by AT&T's PR department, which later had Ernest Hamlin Baker turn it into an oil portrait.

company *perceived* as worthy of trust, but a company worthy of trust. When we came to work in the morning, we knew why we were there."

She was also there, as one of the company's most senior officers, when AT&T's greatness faded. After AT&T settled a government antitrust suit by spinning off its local telephone companies in 1984, the company was left with only the competitive part of its traditional business, telephone calls between distant cities or "long distance" service. It lost its footing in the chaos that followed—brutal price wars, relentless market share declines, perennial cost-cutting, draconian downsizing, abrupt management changes, endless reorganizations, and successive acquisitions, divestitures, and balance sheet write-offs. In those turbulent decades, she drew meaning from trying to help the company regain its balance by redefining its purpose or mission.

Many senior public relations people describe their role as kind of a check on top management's crasser instincts. Marilyn was no exception. She had a lofty conception of her job. The difference, I think, is that, for better or for worse, she actually lived that kind of career, especially in its last decade. She had a quick mind, but she was measured in her thinking and in her delivery. She was not a bad typist, but she preferred to gather her thoughts on lined paper in clear, cursive script that swaggered across the page in columns of tidy phrases. And she signed her correspondence "Marilyn" in a careful stroke of her fountain pen. No illegible scribbles for her.

Marilyn was not the first woman to practice public relations at a high level. Many had come before her. But Marilyn was the first woman at a major company to lead public relations as a "policy-making executive officer," as defined by the Securities and Exchange Commission. When she became chief communications officer of AT&T in 1987, she was the highest-ranking woman in the company's history and one of its highest-paid employees.

She was, in some sense, an anomaly. She rose through the ranks of AT&T at the same time that others of her gender were just entering the practice of public relations in greater numbers. Less than a quarter of public relations specialists were women in 1970;[9] today, women represent more than two-thirds of public relations practitioners.[10] Yet, when Marilyn became chief communications officer of AT&T, she had very few peers at PR agencies or in the corporate world. That situation has changed somewhat since then, but industry leaders are quick to admit more needs to be done.

Although AT&T was popularly known as "Ma Bell" for decades, it was in fact a very patriarchal company, as were most of its corporate peers. And it was not the easiest place for women to advance. Marilyn was athletically trim and had a radiant smile. But perhaps out of habit from always being the youngest person in the room, at work she usually adopted a facial expression intended to telegraph, "I'm serious." Unfortunately, the message received was often, "I'm smarter than you." And her naturally direct and assertive style conflicted with stereotypical notions of her gender, generating a backlash among her peers,[11] who thought her coldly ambitious. So she not only had to deal with misogyny baked into the system, but also with peers who were trapped in their own expectations of how women should behave.

Nevertheless, at the end of her career, she still maintained, "As for being a woman, I have to tell you I never saw myself through that lens." Maybe. But others certainly did. She may not have felt the

---

9 U.S. Bureau of Labor Statistics, "Occupational Outlook for College Graduates, 1972–1973, *Bulletin 1730*, p. 26.

10 U.S. Bureau of Labor Statistics, "Labor Force Statistics from Current Population Survey," 2018.

11 From Marilyn Laurie's oral history kept at the Arthur W. Page Center, Donald P. Bellisario College of Communications, Penn State University. Recorded Oct. 27, 2007. See: http://bit.ly/39izPwI.

resultant sting, but she had few other illusions about her career. In May 2008, when she may have first begun to suspect her memory was failing, she sent this email to her former PR colleagues at AT&T:

> Hi All:
>
> For a private and personal project (not writing a book), I'm seeking anecdotes from my 25 years at AT&T: the good, the bad, the ugly, the passionate, the political -- perceptions and memories as a friend, colleague, supervisor, distant boss. Just be honest (not that you have to say that to this crowd). Pls send directly to me, unless you want to bore the group. Many thanks.
>
> -- Marilyn

The first reply she received probably reminded her why she missed working with this particular set of characters:

> Oh, Marilyn, just fess up! Which VP slot or cabinet post are you being considered for? ;)
>
> -- Brian

Marilyn was not writing a book, but I'm glad I was asked to. I approached Marilyn's story as I think she would have—documenting the good, the bad, the ugly, the passionate, and the political. With a bit of the personal thrown in for context.

She retired from AT&T in 1998 and passed away in 2010. Both dates qualify as ancient history in today's fast-changing world. When she retired, Facebook, Twitter, and YouTube had not yet been invented. Smartphones were not widely available.[12] When she died,

---

[12] Facebook was introduced in 2004; YouTube, in 2005; Twitter, in 2006; the iPhone, in 2007.

Donald Trump had not entered the White House, Brexit had not entered the lexicon, and feminism had not entered its fourth wave.[13] But the technological, political, and social changes she did live to see reinforced her belief that the practice of public relations was more valuable than ever.

"Institutions are struggling with the profusion of professional and consumer-generated media. They're struggling to deal with the fact that everybody knows everything about them. They're struggling to understand how to fit into a multicultural world," she said. "This is what we do. This is what we bring to the table. As I look at the expertise we've developed in crisis planning, when people fall into crisis every Tuesday and Thursday now because of the way media works . . . When I look at the explosion—and the fragmentation—of media and citizen journalism . . . When I look at the skills we are developing in how to use the new tools, in how to deal with transparency, in how to measure reputation and the impact of what we do . . . I think, 'Hey we're about to be in the Golden Age.' The past was truly just prelude."[14]

In Marilyn's final days, when she knew the end was near, and the cancer ravaging her brain stole much of her vision, wreaked havoc with her balance, and wiped out memory after memory, she still found the strength to sort through her thoughts and feelings and commit them to paper as a kind of closing argument for her life. She wrote:

> Someone told me that one of the theories of
> Malcolm Gladwell's Outliers is that the
> difference between being a music teacher in

---

[13] "Fourth Wave Feminism" is thought to have begun in 2012 and is characterized by a focus on intersectionality and empowerment of women through use of the internet.

[14] Arthur W. Page Center oral history.

Riverdale and a concert pianist can be as simple
as putting in 10,000 hours of practice. Well, I
put in the 10,000 hours and did it gladly.
Starting with the lousy commute [by train and
subway] from Scarsdale and tolerating the
searing hatred by my neighbor because I couldn't
and wouldn't carpool children, working my way
through the housekeepers, [my husband] Bob's
problems with my being so engaged, my less than
skillful motherhood capacities . . . but when
all was done, I put in the time because we were
going to change the world . . . and we did. I
wasn't sorry for a minute then, and I wouldn't
do it any other way now.

CHAPTER ONE

GROWING UP IN THE BRONX

The neighborhood in which Marilyn was brought up is now one of the poorest in the country. Ninety percent of its residents are economically disadvantaged. Most of its schools are middling caretakers at best.[15] But back in the 1940s and 1950s, the Bronx was in its heyday, economically and culturally. Those were simpler, more innocent times to be sure, but the Bronx was clearly a special place to live. Residents took pleasure in their colorful, teeming neighborhoods; outsiders thought of it as a social and cultural attraction, a place to shop, eat out, or simply stroll and be seen.

Marilyn's father Abraham was a white-collar professional, who went to his office in Midtown Manhattan every day. After a brief stint practicing law, he became a certified public accountant. Specializing in the garment trade, he could communicate with his clients in Yiddish, the language his parents spoke at home, as easily as he could parse the tax code in English legalese. And many of his clients always had free samples on hand for his wife and young girls.

Marilyn's mother Irene was actively engaged in the social and political life of her neighborhood's tight-knit Jewish community. At that time, there were more Jews in the Bronx—650,000—than in the new state of Israel. The leading Jewish civic organization was the American Jewish Congress, which had included women in its leadership ever since its founding in 1918. Mrs. Gold was an officer of its Bronx chapter in the 1940s and '50s. She organized volunteers to sew clothing for new immigrants to Israel. And in keeping with

---

[15] On the Great Schools rating scale in 2019, 94% of the 341 public district schools assessed in the Bronx are considered "below the state average." See http://bit.ly/39gE4bR.

the organization's progressive politics, she assumed a position on the front lines of the fight to secure equal rights for all Americans regardless of race, religion, or national ancestry.

Like many women back then, she seldom left their apartment on Creston Avenue without her hat and gloves, even to walk less than a block to her older daughter Lois's school, P.S. 79. When Marilyn turned four and a half in September of 1943, her mother decided she was ready for kindergarten. She was already counting and not only knew her ABCs, but was teaching herself to read. So began Marilyn's lifelong pattern of always being the youngest person in the room.

P.S. 79 was a hulking five-story red brick building on the corner of Creston Avenue and East 181st Street. While it was a short walk from the family's Creston Avenue apartment, it was a 15-minute subway ride, bracketed by a three-minute walk at both ends, from the apartment they moved into on the Grand Concourse when Marilyn entered fourth grade.

Elementary school was punctuated by drills; not only in reading, writing, and arithmetic, but also in civil defense. During World War II, every New York City school was expected to schedule periodic air raid drills. The war didn't end until 1945, so in the first half of kindergarten, Marilyn was undoubtedly told to gather with the other children in a cloakroom or closet as a defense against attacks from the air. In the 1950s, during the Cold War, New York City school kids were issued stamped metal Civil Defense identification tags and were taught to get under their desks with their hands over their heads for protection from the broken glass that would follow an atomic bomb blast. While the Soviet Union was a common, consistent threat, the subway, bus lines, and city sidewalks were considered relatively safe. School kids negotiated all three with their friends and without adult chaperones.

"Somewhere along the line, they administered intelligence tests in the primary grades," Marilyn later recalled. "Who knows what the standards [were], or the accuracy of what I was told, but I have a clear memory of Mom telling me I scored 155. That was smart. It wasn't as smart as someone else she referred to who scored 160, but there was a level of expectation in the house after that test that infected every interaction about school."[16]

From then on, every obstacle was met with "of course you can do whatever you want to do, just try." That included the year she brought home a report card with all 99s and "caught hell" for not bringing home any 100s. Marilyn said it wasn't "pressure," but just the "Jewish cultural belief" that education was the road to a good living and a good life. Marilyn's life would turn out to be a long-running argument with that younger version of herself—was she trying as hard as she could, was she as fearless as she could be, was she as successful as she *should* be?

Even in elementary school, Marilyn was on a fast track. Those were the days when school administrators believed bright students who were capable of doing work at the next grade level should simply skip to it. Marilyn remembered skipping through P.S. 79, spending half a year in one class, then moving on to the next. She joked that she "never absorbed" long division, but she claimed to have read her way through "shelf after shelf of library books."

When not in school, Marilyn's life was typical of young people in that era. Looking back on her youth, she recalled playing with boys more than girls. Her sister was six years older and had her own group

---

16 New York City schools administered the Stanford-Binet test which calculated students' "intelligence quotients" (IQs) by dividing their "mental age" by their chronological age and then multiplying by 100. So an IQ of 155 indicated Marilyn's mental age—or the average age one would expect her to be based on her math, reading, and reasoning capabilities—was 50% higher than her chronological age. If she was 8 years old when she took the test, her mental age was about 12-and-a-half.

of friends. Other than that, "There were very few girls in my neighborhood," she said.

"I grew up with boys." In those pre-pubescent days, she played stickball and kick the can with them on the local side streets. When someone had to run an errand for his mother, she raced him to the kosher butcher or live chicken market. "I competed with the boys all through [elementary] school," she remembered.

Marilyn thought it "ironic" that her mother sent her to Elizabeth Barrett Browning Junior High, which was an all-girls school. The school's initials—E. B. B.—reportedly stood for "Everything But Boys." Mrs. Gold may have had a secret hope that her daughter would trade games that resulted in skinned knees for more feminine pursuits. Irene Gold was all about appearances and felt that her younger daughter seemed oblivious to her natural beauty. But Marilyn's college yearbook photo was of a typically pretty coed, nothing like the tomboy in coveralls who knocked around the side streets and alleyways of the Grand Concourse.

Marilyn said her high school English teacher "forced my mother to enroll me in Barnard College." Displaying the independence that would characterize her life, Marilyn had already enrolled herself in New York University. Whether Mrs. Gold wanted to fan the flame of writing talent Marilyn's teacher had seen or had motives of her own, she told her daughter, "If I'm paying your tuition, you're going to Barnard." End of story.

Tuition at Barnard was $1,500 a year, and there was no financial aid. According to Internal Revenue Service records, the average net profit for sole proprietorships in accounting was $3,800 a year. Even assuming New York salaries were higher than average, and Mr. Gold took home more than an average New York salary, paying college tuition was likely still a stretch for her family.

Marilyn commuted to Barnard with four guys who went to Columbia and who she described as "friends." She dated, of course, but it doesn't seem she was ever serious about anyone in particular. In fact, decades later, someone thought it would be a great idea to surprise her at one of her annual all-staff meetings by bringing in one of those old boyfriends. She was not amused. And the frosty handshake she gave the poor guy suggested she barely remembered him and silently hoped he'd keep any memories he had to himself.

To Marilyn, the best thing about Barnard was that it was "fully integrated with Columbia University." She wasn't referring to the boys. Barnard students could enroll in courses at both schools, though the male Columbia University students had first dibs on the more popular courses. Although Marilyn took a few courses at Columbia, her major in English suggested she hadn't fixated on a particular career. But Barnard turned out to be the perfect place for her. And it wasn't because she could slip into a course or two on the Columbia campus.

When Marilyn was there, Barnard College was very unlike its sister schools—Smith, Wellesley, Bryn Mawr, Vassar, Radcliffe, and Mount Holyoke. Few of Barnard's students were the daughters of alumnae; they were more likely to be the daughters of first- and second-generation American families. Most were commuters who lived within the five boroughs of the city or in adjacent areas, and three-quarters of its incoming students graduated from public high schools. As the college's then president Millicent Carey McIntosh put it, "We are blessed with a student body as varied and as interesting as New York itself."[17]

Mrs. Mac, as she preferred to be called, was the first married woman and mother to lead one of the seven "sister" colleges. In a day

---

[17] Mrs. McIntosh made this remark at her inauguration ceremony in October 1947.

when many coeds hoped to get engaged before graduation and marry quickly after, Mrs. Mac saw education as a way to prepare young women for the complicated balancing act of life. She urged Barnard women to take their time after college, to get started on a meaningful career that might prove to be a rewarding alternative to married life and motherhood, or for those who did marry, something to return to when family obligations permitted.

It was the path Mrs. Mac herself had followed. She had married at 33, seven years after earning her PhD at Johns Hopkins and just two years into a stint as headmistress of the Brearley School, New York City's most exclusive girls' school. She and her husband wasted no time in building a family—four boys, two of whom were twins, and a daughter who was just seven when Mrs. Mac started at Barnard.

But she also conceded that, while it was possible to have both a satisfying professional and family life, it wasn't common. She was not Everywoman. She had resources not available to all: enough family income to employ domestic help; and a supportive spouse who was a prominent pediatrician and hospital administrator. Women should not expect to have it all—certainly not right away, and not without help. Nevertheless, as one alumna later put it, "Mrs. Mac was a pioneer in telling us all that we might have both a career and be a wife/mother."[18] In that, Mrs. Mac anticipated the women's revolution of the next decade.

Marilyn's stay at Barnard from 1954 to 1959 was a period of relative calm before the political and social storms of the 1960s. Much of what captured the public's attention in her college years—from Elvis Presley's gyrations and Grace Kelly's marriage to Prince

---

[18] Alumnae interviews on the occasion of the college's 125th anniversary, "Vivian Gruder, Barnard College '57 Interview," Sept. 15, 2015, http://bit.ly/376DOuD.

Rainier of Monaco, to the invention of the Frisbee and of the hula hoop—now seems rather mundane.

Other events in the late '50s were even more significant in hindsight than when they occurred, igniting a fuse that wouldn't detonate until the following decade. The Supreme Court declared segregation in public schools unconstitutional; Rosa Parks refused to give up her seat to a white man on a bus in Montgomery, Alabama; the U.S. government agreed to train South Vietnamese troops; construction on the Interstate Highway System began; Russia launched the first satellite to orbit the earth; and the United States chose the first astronauts for its space program.

In 1957, a journalist named Betty Friedan[19] was asked to survey her college classmates for the 15th anniversary of their graduation. Her survey revealed what she called "a problem that has no name"— a deep melancholy that afflicted so many of her former classmates and, she suspected, most women of her generation. Four years later, she gave it its full due in her book *The Feminine Mystique:*

> The problem lay buried, unspoken, for many years in the minds of American women. It was a strange stirring, a sense of dissatisfaction, a yearning [that is, a longing] that women suffered in the middle of the 20th century in the United States. Each suburban [house]wife struggled with it alone. As she made the beds, shopped for groceries . . . , she was afraid to ask even of herself the silent question—"Is this all?"[20]

For Friedan, the "feminine mystique"—the image of woman as mother and wife, living through her husband and children, and giving up her own dreams—was the underlying cause of the "problem with no name." Women who had dreams of their own, outside the family

---

[19] Betty Friedan, (1963). "The Problem That Has No Name," Chapter One, *The Feminine Mystique* (New York: W. W. Norton & Company, 1963), p. 15.

[20] Friedan, *The Feminine Mystique*, p. 15.

home, felt frustrated and unfulfilled. The solution, Friedan concluded, was "for a woman, as for a man, to find herself, to know herself as a person, by creative work of her own."[21]

Friedan wasn't simply prescribing a job. In fact, she warned that taking any old job "to help out" could be a trap in itself. It had to be a job a woman could take seriously as part of her life plan, serving a human purpose larger than herself.

While some found Marilyn somewhat inscrutable, no one ever questioned whether she had a firm grasp on who she was as a person. One suspects that was as true when she was in college as in later life. She may not have had a fully articulated life plan, but she clearly had a sense of mission in life, the need to apply her full capacities to meaningful tasks outside herself.

That's where philosophers have traditionally found the source of meaning—serving some ideal larger than self.[22] Although it is inherently an individual subjective experience, research suggests women are more likely than men to find meaning in "family." Men are more likely to find meaning in their careers.[23] But these are averages that reveal the way things are at a particular point in time, not the way things must be. Some men consider their work satisfying, but find true meaning in their families, while some women love and serve their families, but discover real meaning in their work. Even in college, Marilyn found herself in the latter category.

---

[21] Friedan, *The Feminine Mystique*, p. 472.

[22] Philosopher and psychologist William James said that meaning is found in tireless struggle on behalf of some sacred ideal. Ethicist Susan Wolf said meaning is found in active engagement in important projects. Sociologist Arthur Brooks wrote that what makes work meaningful is a sense you are earning your success and serving others.

[23] See for example, "Where Americans Find Meaning in Life," Pew Research Center, (Nov. 20, 2018). https://pewrsr.ch/37a7GpS.

Marilyn was attractive enough to do some modeling for one of her father's clients who manufactured women's hats and gloves. It gave her a little walking around money while in college. But she didn't see that—or any jobs that depended on her appearance—as a meaningful career. After graduation, she took a job as a "gal Friday" in a small film syndication company. As she herself put it, "Coming out of Barnard when I did in 1959, going out into the world of work was not usual. It would have been considered more conventional to go on into graduate work or teaching. But I was determined to go out and *do* something." If her initial position was typical of the office jobs new female college graduates were getting in the late '50s, her career path was quite different.

Within a few weeks, she was promoted to take over the job of the man who hired her. Then the company she was working for bought another company, and then another. Each acquisition brought another promotion until she was handling advertising, promotion, and merchandising—what today we would call small business communications. "I almost literally reached the point where I was beyond my own capabilities," she later recalled. "It was at least 25 years later before I realized I was probably being paid half the salaries of the guys I replaced. But boy, was I having a good time."

Work in that small but growing company had other attractions. It's where Marilyn met her husband Bob Laurie, who was one of the company's art directors. Bob was a talented artist and photographer; a good-looking man, with a quiet personality, more comfortable in one-on-one conversations than in large groups. While she was methodical, he was impulsive. "Marilyn has always written, often to clarify issues that didn't lend themselves to quick and easy interpretation," he wrote. "Seldom in haste to make a judgment, she examined an issue on all sides, which she recorded. She also, apparently, never threw any of it away." Long after she had said "yes" to his marriage proposal, Bob discovered a list she had written of the "pros" and "cons" of marrying him.

Although he was ten years older than Marilyn, he shared a similar background. They were both second-generation Jewish immigrants, her father from what is now Poland, his from Hungary; they were both raised in one of the New York City boroughs, she in the Bronx, he in Brooklyn; and as kids they both went to a Jewish summer camp in the Catskills, though a decade apart and on opposite sides of the same lake. They shared an interest in art, music, travel, and good food. Politically, she was a Kennedy Democrat; he, a Woody Guthrie socialist. But while Marilyn's father was a successful accountant, Bob's was a serial entrepreneur whose financial difficulties led him to kill himself when Bob was still in his teens.

Such an experience is bound to leave its mark on anyone, particularly someone as sensitive as Bob. One of the ways he coped was by joining the Art Students League in 1948, when he was only 19. Immersing himself in art gave him an outlet for his emotions even before he realized it could be a career. He remained an active member of the League until his death in 2014.

In 1961, Marilyn moved on to another job, doing promotional work for *Popular Science* and *Outdoor Life* magazines, which were owned by the same company. She left when the company would only give her five weeks' vacation to get married and she wanted six. "Since I'd only worked there a year," she later recalled, "it shows how dumb I was that I didn't realize that was extremely generous of them." She and Bob were married in 1962 and, after their honeymoon, she did freelance work until her first daughter Amy arrived in 1964, followed by Lisa in 1967.

Meanwhile, Bob had also left the film syndication company to start his own business, Bob Laurie Studios, at 42nd Street and Fifth Avenue. He designed promotional material for major corporations and non-profits, editorial matter for magazines, and book jackets for publishers. He even persuaded Marilyn to pose on a picnic blanket with their girls to illustrate an ad for plastic drinking cups. The new business was successful enough to allow them to buy an 800-acre weekend farm outside Hudson, New York, in 1969, a year that would prove significant in their family's life for other reasons.

CHAPTER TWO

EARTH DAY AND THE DAY AFTER

At 10:20 p.m. on the evening of August 20, 1969, a bomb exploded on the eighth floor of the Marine Midland Bank building at 140 Broadway in Manhattan. It blew windows out on three sides of the building and collapsed the eighth floor into the seventh. Miraculously, only two of the 150 late-shift employees on duty required medical treatment. It was the second of what would be eight bombings in New York to protest the Vietnam War that year.

What had begun as a straightforward training mission in the late 1950s had blossomed into a full-scale war that made little sense to the very people who were expected to fight it. And they were significant enough in number to challenge the government and corporate powers they believed were driving the war, along with a long series of other injustices they saw—from inequality based on race, gender, and sexual orientation, to environmental pollution and systemic poverty.

A similar story played out across the United States and in other developed countries. The students didn't always get their way, but they controlled the public agenda more than ever before. Their numbers alone gave them power. More than 76 million children were born during the post-World War II "baby boom." These young people spent more years in school and were more affluent than previous generations. And they stayed with their peers for a longer period than in the past, when most older teenagers were full-time workers. In 1920, only one in five people graduated from high school; by 1960, three out of four did, and half of them went on to college. College students of the late 1960s not only questioned the status quo, they also took direct action to force social and political change in an unprecedented way.

Marilyn couldn't see the protests from her apartment on West 58th Street in Manhattan. But she read about them in newspapers and saw clips of the most dramatic incidents on the evening news. History seemed to be passing her by. While her contemporaries were in the streets protesting the Vietnam War and fighting for racial and gender equality, she found herself the stay-at-home mom of a five-year-old and a toddler. While she loved her daughters, tending to her home and children didn't give her the abiding sense of purpose she needed to feel fulfilled. Something was missing.

Her ennui was so profound that her mother made a special trip "into the city" to see her and, after listening to her complaints, encouraged her to get out of the apartment and "do something." She was pushing through an open door, but the question remaining was "do what?" Marilyn had little interest in joining a club or serving on some committee, as her mother had. She wasn't looking for a "mother's hour off." She wanted a mission of significance— something that would define her as more than a homemaker, something with greater meaning.

Meanwhile, Bob's business was doing well enough that he needed more staff and placed a help wanted ad in the *Village Voice*. So Marilyn found herself one Saturday morning sitting at the kitchen table, paging through the *Voice*, looking for his ad and spooning cereal into her toddler's mouth. There among the ads for barmaids and go-go dancers, she saw a small notice inviting people to a planning meeting for what would become Earth Day. The first meeting was scheduled to take place that afternoon at her alma mater, Barnard College, almost ten years to the day after she graduated. It all seemed somehow like a calling. She had worried about the effect of air pollution on her children's health, but it hadn't occurred to her she could do anything about it until that moment. She had found a cause.

So she told her husband Bob, "Watch the kids" and trotted off to the subway.

*   *   *

Earth Day was the brainchild of Senator Gaylord Nelson, who had been known as Wisconsin's two-term "conservation governor." He brought his concern for the deteriorating environment to Washington, D.C., but found it difficult to get his colleagues' attention. In September 1969, he happened to be thumbing through a copy of *Ramparts* magazine, when he ran across a story about the campus "teach-ins" that had mobilized so many students against the Vietnam War.

Suddenly, it dawned on him that the same technique could be used to force the environment into the country's political dialogue and mobilize students against threats to our water, air, and quality of life. He enlisted a Republican colleague, Representative Paul McCloskey of California, to help him form a non-profit and raise money to conduct "environmental teach-ins" nationwide. In a series of speeches that September, they announced it would all happen on April 22, 1970—between spring break and final exams.

On November 9, 1969, a long, front-page article in the *New York Times* made it official. "Rising concern about the 'environmental crisis' is sweeping the nation's campuses with an intensity that may be on its way to eclipsing student discontent over the war in Vietnam," the *Times* wrote. "A national day of observance of environmental problems, analogous to the mass demonstrations on Vietnam, is being planned for next spring, when a nationwide environmental 'teach-in' . . . coordinated from the office of Senator Gaylord Nelson is planned. . . . "[24]

Denis Hayes, a Harvard graduate student, read the *Times* article and traveled to Washington to get involved. He had been student body president and a campus activist at Stanford University, which happened to be in McCloskey's district. He thought he might be asked to organize a teach-in in Boston. Instead, Nelson asked Hayes to drop out of Harvard, assemble a staff, and direct the effort to organize the teach-in across the United States.

Hayes pulled together a D.C. staff of 75 idealistic 20-somethings to get information out to all the colleges, schools, and community groups that had responded to the same *Times* article. But first they had a hurdle to jump—"environmental teach-in" was at best boring and at worse a serious turn-off to people who wanted to change things, not debate them.

Hayes called Julian Koenig, creative director at one of the hottest shops on Madison Avenue. He had volunteered to help if the group ever wanted to do some ads. "I candidly described the problem and said we really needed a new name," Hayes said. "Something that could comfortably include moderates and political newbies while not alienating the seasoned activists we needed to enlist across the country to actually build the events."[25] In just a few days, Koenig sent over several mock-ups of newspaper ads, each tagged with a different name, but as Hayes recalled, "He made it quite clear that we would be idiots if we didn't choose Earth Day."

Over beer and pizza that same evening, Hayes and his staff agreed, and quickly placed one of Koenig's ads in the January 18,

---

[24] Gladwin Hill, "Environment May Eclipse Vietnam as College Issue," *New York Times*, Nov. 9, 1969.

[25] As quoted in the Wikipedia biography of Julian Koenig. See http://bit.ly/2H1JMCs.

1970, *New York Times*. The opening lines read: "A disease has infected our country. It has brought smog to Yosemite, dumped garbage in the Hudson, sprayed DDT in our food, and left our cities in decay. Its carrier is man. On April 22 we start to reclaim the environment we have wrecked."

It closed with a coupon asking for donations to support the effort and, more importantly, the reader's name and address to receive information on what they could do locally. Hundreds of people responded, some representing groups with classic 1960s names like SLOP (Student League Opposing Pollution), YUK (Youth Uncovering Crud), and SCARE (Students Concerned about a Ravaged Environment).

One group called itself the Environmental Action Coalition of New York. It had been organized by four students who had earlier heard Hayes speak about plans for Earth Day. They hoped to fold as many New York City area groups as possible into a single, coordinated celebration of Earth Day in the nation's media and financial capital. It was their small help wanted ad that captured Marilyn's eye that Saturday morning.

She remembered the meeting in Barnard College's Lehman Auditorium as "a madhouse with 500 people talking at once."[26] Almost everyone volunteered to help and left their contact information. But fewer people came to the second meeting and fewer still to the third and subsequent meetings. By March, the five people remaining became the Environmental Action Coalition's Policy Committee, led by Fred Kent, a Columbia University graduate student, as "coordinator."

A young Rutgers University law student named Pete Grannis was treasurer, charged with raising money to fund the events. Kristin

---

[26] This is likely hyperbole. Lehman Hall has a capacity of only 227.

Hubbard (now Alexandre) took responsibility for lining up speakers. William Hubbard, who was then her husband and a practicing lawyer, handled permits and legal matters. And when the group discovered that Marilyn was an English major with experience in advertising and promotions, they asked her to handle community relations and communications. Kent still remembers Marilyn more than 50 years later. "She was a very creative person, who got things done," he says. "She didn't know what she couldn't do, so she just did it." As we will see, that could have been her life's motto.

Kent, who was also working at Citibank, took a leave of absence and convinced the bank to let the coalition use empty office space on East 49th Street as its operations center. From there, the staff worked 12-hour days, from 9:00 a.m. to 9:00 p.m., seven days a week. They contacted potential supporters, from scientists and academics, to celebrities, politicians, and willing volunteers from all walks of life. They also called every group they could think of that might join in celebrating Earth Day. Marilyn worked from her apartment when she didn't have a babysitter and headed to the operations center when Bob got home.

"Even then, environmentalists represented a broad spectrum of interests—from those who wanted to turn back the clock to a simpler era to sophisticated technologists who saw alternative means of producing the economic goods needed by contemporary consumers," Marilyn remembered. "There were those preoccupied with the forests, parks, and wildlife; dedicated recyclers who were battling urban trash; and scientists who took a good deal of scorn for predicting a 'greenhouse effect' and global warming." And of course, every group the coalition spoke to had its own ideas about how to celebrate Earth Day.

The Columbia University chapter of Students for Democratic Action wanted to run down Manhattan streets turning over trash barrels. Some school kids wanted to sweep Union Square Park. Convincing the former to abandon their idea and the latter to schedule it for maximum media coverage took exquisite diplomatic skills given the coalition's decentralized and ad hoc decision-making process. Plus, coordinating and scheduling more than 200 different groups and thousands of volunteers in the days before electronic spreadsheets and email all had to be done by hand on large sheets of paper and over the phone. Cards posted on a bulletin board listed tasks to do, and whoever had time, took the card down and did it.

Marilyn had one of the biggest challenges. In addition to writing and supervising all communications, it was her job to get the president of the Fifth Avenue Business Association to agree to shut the avenue to traffic on April 22. "Young lady," he told her, "the sidewalks are for people, the streets are for cars and buses. And I'll fight this to the end." Apparently, some of the avenue's luxury retailers and property owners were alarmed by the prospect of ordinary New Yorkers congregating in the street outside their doors. So running out of time, Marilyn drafted a series of letters to be sent to New York City's Mayor John Lindsay from Fred Kent, supporters in the business and non-profit community, and even the pastor of the Mayor's church.

Luckily, unknown to the coalition, it had allies on the Mayor's staff. In 1968, Lindsay had created a new environmental superagency "to coordinate environmental initiatives . . . so solving one problem didn't inadvertently create another."[27] And he staffed it with people like Jerome Kretchmer,[28] a young lawyer who wasn't tied to tradition

---

[27] A 1974 New York City Environmental Protection Agency news release described the agency's mission this way.

[28] Kretchmer had been a New York State assemblyman when Lindsay appointed him head of the New York City EPA. He stayed for three years before moving back into state politics. In the 1980s, he became a housing developer and restauranteur.

and more willing to try new approaches like setting up neighborhood recycling centers. Kretchmer thought Earth Day was a great idea and convinced the Mayor to close parts of Fifth Avenue and 14th Street to traffic in addition to making Central Park available as an event site. A long, boisterous cheer went up when word reached the coalition's offices on 49th Street on March 18, just a little more than a month before the big day. From then on, the Mayor's staff became an extension of the coalition. Mayoral assistants Sid Davidoff[29] and Jeffrey Katzenberg[30] gave the coalition one-stop shopping for whatever they needed.

The next step was to let the world know what was planned. Marilyn discovered she was part of something bigger than magazine promotions when she organized the group's first press conference to announce Earth Day events. *Time* and *Life* magazines showed up, along with all the local TV stations and newspapers. An impressive list of bold face names had pledged their active participation, including Mayor Lindsay, Congressman Ed Koch, Margaret Mead, Pete Seeger, Kurt Vonnegut, Leonard Bernstein, Paul Newman, Barbra Streisand, and the entire cast of *Hair*.

There were a few naysayers. The John Birch Society pointed out that April 22 was Vladimir Lenin's birthday, proving that the whole Earth Day stunt was a communist plot. New York City's all-news radio station WINS suggested the whole event would be more appropriately staged in Central Park and urged the mayor to make "more down-to-earth arrangements." Marilyn was suddenly thrust

---

[29] As young as most of the people on the coalition's policy committee, Davidoff was Lindsay's top administrative assistant and troubleshooter. He later formed one of New York's top lobbying firms.

[30] Katzenberg was a 14-year-old volunteer on Lindsay's mayoral campaign in 1964 and wormed his way into a job at City Hall despite being a teenager. After seven years, he left politics for the entertainment business which made him a very rich man.

into damage control—a position that would become increasingly familiar to her in later life. She ignored the Birch Society, which had little credibility in New York City and was peddling a story that had already been refuted by Senator Nelson's office. The date of Earth Day had more to do with college school calendars than Russian history. But she had an immediate response issued to the radio station's editorial. "WINS misses the purpose of Earth Day," she rejoined. "Nothing is more down-to-earth than taking the answers [to pollution] to where the people and the problems are—the streets of New York City."[31]

April 22 in New York City dawned with a mix of sun and clouds in gently breezy skies. Temperatures would top out at 67 degrees, four above average. It was a picture-perfect day to save the Earth. On NBC's *Today* show, a group of schoolchildren from across the boroughs broom-swept Union Square Park to the enthusiastic encouragement of Mayor Lindsay. More than a hundred civic and environmental groups mounted informational displays along 14th Street, which was closed to traffic between Second and Seventh Avenue from noon to midnight. Swarms of people strolled through a block-long polyethylene bubble to breathe pure, filtered air which was eventually augmented by the sweet fragrance of marijuana.

When Fifth Avenue closed to traffic between noon and 2:00 p.m., more than 100,000 New Yorkers filled the street, walking in unusual silence, except for a group of demonstrators who dragged a net filled with dead fish down the thoroughfare, shouting, "This could be you!" Thousands gathered in front of stages at the southern end of Union Square Park and on the steps of the New York Public Library on Fifth Avenue for three separate programs of speakers and

---

[31] From the Environmental Action Coalition archives in the New York Public Library.

entertainers. Late in the day, they were still there, cheering and dancing, happy to be part of it all.

One of the happiest was Marilyn, who stood on the stage in Union Square Park with "universes of people in every direction, in the trees, hanging from lampposts." She recalled that Paul Newman was on her left and John Lindsay was on her right. "A pair of very blue eyes on either side of me," she said. "I remember thinking it was probably the most glamorous moment I would ever experience."[32] It would remain the highlight of her life, and even after three decades in corporate public relations, she would always first describe herself as "an environmentalist."

Time magazine devoted a full page to its description of the day across the nation: "It has aspects of a secular, almost pagan holiday.... In vacant lots from Boston to Sacramento, schoolchildren gathered up beer cans, soda bottles, and old tires, as if picking up after a violent party.... At 1,500 campuses and 10,000 schools, students, teachers—and sometimes parents—observed Earth Day by studying previously recondite subjects as hydrocarbons and acid drainage from coal mines.... Car wreckings—followed by internments—were a common protest against the internal combustion engine.... Dozens of politicians seized upon Earth Day as a new—and safe—issue."[33]

It was a nationwide happening that brought much of the countercultural energy of the 1960s into the mainstream of American life. An estimated 20 million people participated across the country. And in New York, as in almost every other city, they were a self-policing group that cleaned up after themselves and

---

[32] Quoted by Adam Rome, *The Genius of Earth Day* (New York: Hill and Wang, 2013), pp. 122–123.

[33] "A Memento Mori to the Earth," *Time*, May 4, 1970.

produced very little litter. But the first Earth Day had a lasting impact on the country, as well as on the people who staged it.

Over the next decade, Congress passed 28 major initiatives that became the foundation of the nation's environmental laws.[34] It was probably not coincidental that the public's priorities changed in the same direction. When polled in 1969, less than one percent of the U.S. public said protecting the environment was an important goal; in 1971, more than 25 percent did.

"Over two decades, the environmental movement became less of a headline grabber and many people assumed it had weakened," Marilyn said later. "But I would suggest rather that it had become institutionalized. What began as a fringe movement often reported as carried by hippies, Luddites, and middle-class preppies who preferred not to face the tougher issues of poverty and urban decay, is now a centrist global concern, discussed in Congress and in boardrooms as freely as at a Colorado folk festival."

And what of the people who made Earth Day happen? Denis Hayes dedicated the rest of his life to environmental causes, expanding Earth Day to 180 nations. Fred Kent became the leading authority on revitalizing city spaces and founded the Project for Public Spaces. William Hubbard practiced law and founded a company dedicated to developing socially responsible and environmentally sensitive affordable housing. Pete Grannis ran for political office, becoming a member of the New York State Assembly representing the Upper East Side of Manhattan and ultimately serving as the state's commissioner of environmental conservation.

---

[34] Among laws passed were the Clean Air Act, the Clean Water Act, the Endangered Species Act, the Safe Drinking Water Act, the Toxic Substances Control Act, Occupational Health and Safety Act, and amendments strengthening the National Environmental Policy Act.

Kristin Hubbard Alexandre went on to become a journalist, screenwriter, and producer.

After Earth Day, Marilyn accepted an offer to join the New York City Council on the Environment, which was a public and private group co-led by the Mayor and philanthropist Marion S. Heiskell. The "S," as Marilyn would soon learn, stood for "Sulzberger" because the affable if courtly woman who chaired the Council's meetings was a member of the family that still controls the *New York Times*. She was also married to Andrew Heiskell, the chairman of Time, Inc., but she was one of the most approachable socialites in New York City. She and Marilyn hit it off immediately because they were among the few women among the council's 70 members.

The Council's official role was to provide input to city policy on environmental and consumer issues, such as how supermarkets could be more environmentally friendly. But about eight weeks before the first anniversary of Earth Day, Mrs. Heiskell called Marilyn and asked, "Could you write a supplement for the *New York Times* to celebrate the first anniversary of Earth Day?" Not knowing any better—and hoping her husband Bob could fit it into his schedule—Marilyn said, "Sure."

"Again, you can't appreciate how young and dumb I was," she later said. Nevertheless, on April 18, 1971, the Sunday *New York Times* included a 24-page supplement describing what ordinary New Yorkers could do individually and together to "end New York's environmental crisis."

It featured famous New Yorkers from actors Pearl Bailey and Dustin Hoffman to journalist Jimmy Breslin and basketball player Willis Reed. The CEO of the Con Ed electric utility, was shown saying, "I turn out the lights when I leave a room." On the next page, quarterback Joe Namath, with a young lady on his arm, said, "I turn out the lights when I enter a room." It was printed on recycled paper, the largest such print run of its kind at the time. And there were only two names on the masthead, because Marilyn had written and edited the supplement; husband Bob had done the graphics.

Marilyn didn't know it, but among the supplement's readers was Robert Lilley, an executive vice president of AT&T who lived in Short Hills, New Jersey. Lilley was regarded by many as the embodiment of the new corporate executive for whom social responsibility was as great a requirement as business acumen.[35] And on that Sunday morning, having read the *Times*, he thought AT&T should be doing more about the environment.

---

[35] When Lilley was president of New Jersey Bell, he served as chairman of the governor's commission to study the rioting that followed the assassination of Dr. Martin Luther King, Jr. in 1967. The commission's report led to changes in minority hiring among businesses and government, as well as to the conviction of local government officials for bribery and extortion. Lilley later co-chaired a similar select committee at Columbia University to help resolve the conflicts resulting from the campus demonstrations of the times.

CHAPTER THREE

JOINING AT&T

Sometime between the first and second Earth Day celebrations, after the homeless man who lived on West 58th Street began using their building vestibule as a toilet, Marilyn and Bob moved their young family to the suburbs. Their new home in Edgemont, New York, had more space, a yard for their girls to play in, and an excellent school system. Its proximity to the Scarsdale and Hartsdale train stations made it a 30-minute commute into the City, as they would forever refer to Manhattan.

Marilyn was thumbing through the environmental supplement she and Bob had produced, probably thinking about improvements she should have made, when the kitchen phone rang. She lifted the receiver with one hand as she refolded the supplement with the other and said, "Hello?" It wasn't her mother or father, as she had expected, but a voice she didn't recognize—someone who said his name was Bill Horton with AT&T.

Marilyn knew very little about AT&T except that it was a stock for widows and orphans and had something to do with telephone service. That was not surprising—according to AT&T's own surveys back then, only about 10% of the general public had what's called "unaided awareness" of the company. Yet, it was the biggest company in the country with a giant manufacturing unit, the world's leading research and development labs, and about two dozen telephone company subsidiaries constituting what was called the "Bell System," but known simply as "the phone company" or "Ma Bell."

Still, this was interesting. Horton congratulated Marilyn on the supplement, told her he found it very instructive, and wondered if she might be available to have lunch to discuss it. Probably thinking it could lead to a freelance writing assignment, she agreed to meet for lunch at a small French restaurant on 57th Street in Manhattan, where she soon discovered that Horton was in charge of the company's exhibits. In a 27-year career, she never figured out how it fell to him to interview her, but that's just what he did.

"How would you like to start an environmental program at AT&T?" he eventually asked.

"You mean as a freelancer?" she said.

"No, no. As a full-time employee, working out of our New York City headquarters."

"Well, how many employees does AT&T have?"

"More than a million."

Now, this was more than interesting. "Here's an opportunity to make a million people environmentally conscious," she thought to herself. "What more exciting opportunity could anybody ever want?" So she said, "Yes. I'd be interested in that."

The next step was to be interviewed by the boss of her potentially immediate boss to discuss things like salary and office arrangements. He told her she would be making $12,000 a year and be a third-level district manager or, in telephone company parlance, a C level. "I had never worked at a big company, so I didn't pay any attention to the title or salary grade," she later confessed. In fact, the idea of working for a large corporation had never entered her mind. "I wasn't cut out for it, as far as I knew," she later remembered. "I was a typical young person who ricocheted from project to project. But I had no idea of a career. Business careers for young women with my kind of background were unusual. I just had no framework to do anything like that." But the prospect of raising the environmental conscience of more than a million people was intoxicating. She took the job.

The night before she was scheduled to start, her boss's boss called her at home.

"There's been a change," he said.

"Change? What kind of change?"

"Well, remember I said you'd be at level C?"

She really didn't remember what the level was, but said, "Yeah."

Well, it's not going to be C, it's going to be B."

"Is the salary the same?" she asked.

"Yes, same salary," he said.

"OK then. Fine. Thanks for telling me. See you tomorrow."

Getting to work from Edgemont required waiting for a nanny, driving 10 minutes to the Scarsdale or Hartsdale train stations, boarding a train of the New York Central railroad for the (hopefully) 30-minute ride to Grand Central Station, then joining the crush of commuters hurrying across the terminal's main vault to descend into the IRT subway platform for a (probably) 20-minute standing ride downtown to the Fulton Street station, where she would let the crowd leaving the subway carry her up the stairs to street level. Then she would walk two blocks, right by the revolving doors of the AT&T headquarters building at 195 Broadway to a slightly dingy office building on Cortlandt Street. There, she took an elevator up to her six-by-seven-foot cubicle on the fourth floor.

Marilyn was not working in the headquarters of AT&T, but in the headquarters of the Telephone Pioneers of America, an employee club begun in the company's earliest years, that had transformed itself into one of the largest volunteer service organizations in the country.

As Marilyn later put it, if AT&T and its subsidiaries were the solar system, she had been hired to work on Pluto. On the other hand, there were more than 500,000 Pioneers, retired and still working. They ran service projects in communities across the country. "I was a million miles from the center of power, and not expected to do anything of any significance," Marilyn said. "But it turned out to be a great playground for someone who wants to get something done."

One of her first assignments, given her by Bill Horton, who wasn't even in her chain of command but seemed to have a direct line to Bob Lilley, was to write an environmental policy for AT&T. "That seems like an awesome task," she said. But he insisted, "Do it before you get absorbed here and lose the perspective on what our environmental policy ought to be." She sat at her typewriter and wrote a policy that would make environmental considerations an explicit factor in the company's decision-making. It took six months of review and wordsmithing by people higher in the food chain, but much of what she wrote became Bell System policy.

Other than that, she said, "no one gave a damn about who I was, what I did, or where I fit into the organization chart." She was told right from the beginning, "You probably know what to do better than we do, so create your own job."

So she did.

She started an environmental community service program for the Pioneers that is still active today. Practically every chapter participated—planting trees, cleaning beaches and streambeds, promoting recycling. She gave speeches, started a newsletter, and produced brochures. "Again, I had no idea these things were specialized," she said. "So I did the whole gamut, stumbled against a number of walls in the process, but I didn't know they were walls. Just picked myself up and went on." She didn't know it at the time, but those "walls" were people who considered themselves speech, newsletter, and film specialists and jealously guarded their turf.

"The Bell System ran like a Swiss clock. Everyone had a well-defined job. Except they didn't have an environmentalist, and I came in as the one and only environmentalist," she later said. "And so I never learned to obey the rules. I never learned to sit in a box on an

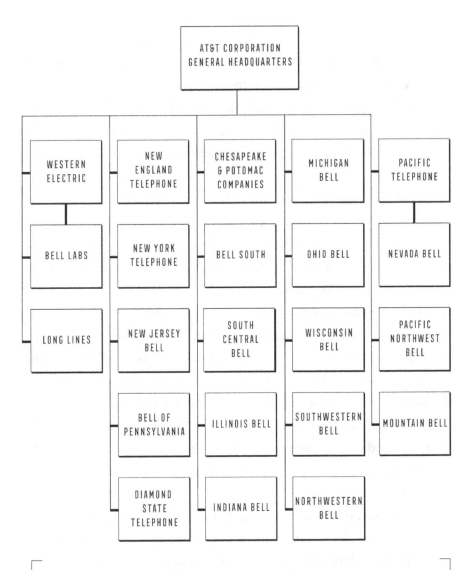

THE BELL SYSTEM IN 1971

Not including AT&T's minority holdings in companies like Southern
New England Telephone and Cincinnati Bell.

organization chart. And I never learned how the hierarchy determines what you're supposed to do and how you're not supposed to make waves. I was brought in to make waves."

Looking back on those early days decades later, she recognized that she was, in her words, "a tank in combat." She certainly was the target of more than her share of friendly fire. Not that she hadn't been warned.

Not too long after she started, a bright young woman named Mary Ardito, stuck her head into Marilyn's cubicle and asked if she had a minute. Normally impatient when interrupted, but eager to meet her new colleagues, she pushed away from her desk and invited Mary to have a seat in her visitor chair—a straight-backed, steel armchair in Army gray that didn't invite lingering.

Mary started with the usual niceties—do you live far from the office, how's your commute, have you found your way to the company cafeteria yet? Then she slid into the real purpose of her visit. "Listen," she said. "I was new once, and I would have liked to hear what I'm about to tell you." Long pause. "You're about to crash and burn. You've pissed off everyone around here. You can't just tell people to do something for you. You have to ask. And it helps if you start by doing them a favor first."

Mary essentially told Marilyn that she would not last long unless she adapted to the organization's way of doing things and became much more deferential. Just because people had job titles that explained what they did, didn't mean they would do it for just anyone who asked. That's not how things work. Marilyn said she appreciated the advice, but as she later admitted, "I just didn't get it."

Time passed and Marilyn had what she thought was a great idea—a film starring some of the telephone company presidents and showing what they were doing to be environmentally progressive. She sold it to the powers that be in her reporting line as a great promotional piece with multiple applications.

Then she went to the film group and got what she later described as "sleazy backing" and a reminder that *they* controlled the film budget, not her. They promised to think about it. Time passed.

Tired of waiting, Marilyn hired her own crew to shoot and edit the film in just a few weeks. "It's funded. It's done. It's good," she remembered. But the film group wouldn't release it. "The goddamn film—starring five Bell System presidents—never sees the light of day," she said. "Not one finished, paid-for scene ever gets any use whatsoever." There's never a harsh word spoken by the film group, never an acknowledgement that the film had even been discussed. Marilyn had just lost her first turf battle, and she didn't even know shots had been fired.

"That generous woman Mary Ardito tried to save me from getting whacked," Marilyn later said. "But it took a miserable, rotten lesson in humiliation before I graduated to being effective."

If Marilyn's colleagues initially treated her like an infection in the AT&T bloodstream, people at higher levels considered her a shot of B-12. She spent a lot of her time traveling to local Pioneer chapter meetings. The chapters were organized by telephone company. There were New York Telephone Pioneers, New Jersey Bell Pioneers, and so forth for each of the 24 telephone companies that were part of the Bell System. The telephone company CEOs all took a lively interest in their Pioneer chapters, and Marilyn often found herself in their company when she attended chapter meetings.

To her, they were each just another telephone company guy in a pin-striped suit. To them, she was a good-looking, plain-talking young woman from New York who knew a lot about a topic that was still a little unfamiliar to them, but clearly important because headquarters was making a big deal about it. They got along great. So as Marilyn put it, she was "never taught proper hierarchical respect and thinking."

Only the Vatican had a more intricate and deferential hierarchy. AT&T had seven management levels, in a pyramid that got narrower, more masculine, and heavier with perquisites as it rose from first level to seventh. As a third-level manager, Marilyn would have had a private office; as a second level, she worked in a cubicle with walls two inches shorter than she was. Her $12,000 annual salary was low for a third level, but high for a second level, reducing what the human resources people called "headroom" for salary growth.

The reason Marilyn's job was changed from third level to second at the last minute, was because AT&T didn't hire women at third level. In fact, of the 9,363 third-level managers in the Bell System at that time, only 120 were women.[36]

And Marilyn only learned that because, in December 1971, shortly after she started at AT&T, the U.S. Equal Employment Opportunity Commission asked the Federal Communications Commission (FCC) to deny the company's request to raise long distance rates because of its "discriminatory policies." Their argument was that the company wouldn't have to raise rates if it treated women and minority employees fairly. The National Organization for Women celebrated the holidays that year by sending a lump of coal to each of the Bell System presidents.[37]

This is not to condemn AT&T. Rather it highlights how oppressive behavior can exist, even flourish, in the most well-intentioned organizations. AT&T truly cared about its employees. But many of its policies—written and cultural—were the product of

---

[36] Lois Katheryn Herr, *Women, Power, and AT&T* (Boston: Northeastern University Press, 2003), p. 29.

[37] Herr, *Women, Power, and AT&T*, p. 29.

a different era. Some were silly. It was just as ridiculous to forbid women to wear pantsuits to work as it was to require men to wear hats. But in the late 1960s and early 1970s, that's the way it was in much of AT&T and its subsidiaries.

Other policies were unfathomable. If a male employee died while on company business—say, in a plane crash—his family would receive a death benefit. But the family of a female employee wouldn't. Even if she was on the same cursed airplane.

As a result of the government's suit, AT&T struggled to define what was just in a rapidly changing society. It was *forced* to build equal opportunity into the structure of its business. And because it was AT&T, other companies followed. As one feminist put it, "Government had challenged the best, not the worst, and raised expectations for all businesses."[38]

AT&T reached an agreement with the government in 1973 to make it easier for women to move into better jobs. And it made a compensatory one-time payment of about $15 million to some 15,000 management employees, most of them women.

But laws, regulations, and even company policies change more quickly than culture. This has been especially true for women. "Unlike gays and minorities, women have been cherished by their oppressors," law professor Kenji Yoshino points out. "Men have long valued the 'feminine' traits women are supposed to uphold, such as warmth, empathy, and nurture."[39] And they somehow convinced themselves that "feminine" traits best dispose women for the "private sphere" of home and hearth, while "masculine" traits of confidence, competitiveness, and aggressiveness make men better suited to the

---

[38] Marjorie A. Stockford, *The Bellwomen: The Story of the Landmark AT&T Sex Discrimination Case*, (Rutgers: Rutgers University Press, 2004), p. 92.

[39] Kenji Yoshino, "Sex-based Covering," *Covering: The Hidden Assault on Our Civil Liberties*, (New York: Random House, 2007), Kindle edition, location 2048.

"private sphere" of work and politics. So men could cherish and confine women at the same time. But 1973 was also when the Supreme Court ruled that cherishing women so long as they stay at home puts them "not on a pedestal, but in a cage."[40]

Meanwhile, thanks at least in part to the company's agreement with the government, Marilyn was moved to a higher-level job within the company's human resources department to handle environmental education and communications. Initially, her new sandbox was actually smaller than the first had been, focused largely on internal communications. But when the energy crisis hit in 1973, she found herself back in the center of the action. "My group became the center of knowledge and leadership for energy conservation, recycling, and a whole new way of thinking about how AT&T used energy" she said.

It also became clear to her that to really have an impact, she had to work herself out of her job. "I became absolutely convinced this responsibility did not belong in a staff organization that was never going to make something really happen, which is what I've always been obsessed with," she said. She decided the work belonged in the corporate engineering department, which had operating responsibility. After a period of what she described as begging, pleading, and cajoling, she succeeded in having the work formally transferred to engineering. "I celebrated on the day it happened because that was the day I knew that what I wanted to accomplish when I joined AT&T was most likely to happen," she said. "Engineering was where all the power was, and they would now be accountable for fulfilling all our environmental responsibilities in recycling and energy conservation. And it was wonderful."

---

[40] United States Supreme Court, FRONTIERO v. RICHARDSON (U.S. Supreme Court, May 14, 1973), No. 71-1694.

Marilyn had no interest in following her work to engineering, nor in staying in HR. So she was moved to PR. But although her interest in the business of the Bell System had grown over the past three years, she knew she wasn't a particularly valuable commodity. "I was a woman from New York with no particular background that anybody admired. And no mentor and no sponsor," she said. "This was a company that didn't particularly value people from New York and didn't have a lot of women running around in public relations. And I didn't have a journalism background."

Given all that, Marilyn assumed her days were numbered. And when the company announced that most of the jobs in public relations would be moving to a new corporate center in New Jersey, she decided to declare herself uninterested and unable to move to the Garden State. Her theory was that it would force someone to deal with her, even if it only resulted in a financial incentive to leave.

To her surprise, it got her an interview with Jim Brunson, an urbane vice president of public relations who loved New York City so much, he moved into Manhattan from New Jersey as soon as his last kid was out of the house. Before she knew what happened, Marilyn found herself in one of the few PR departments scheduled to stay in New York—media relations. She would be reporting to someone who had been a newspaper editor and still thought of himself as a journalist embedded in AT&T.

"I knew nothing about media relations," she remembered. "I mean, my Earth Day experience had been kind of a miracle, but I hadn't followed it up with any kind of media relations training. And I certainly didn't have a deep knowledge of the business, coming out of the Pioneers and the environmental end of things." She later admitted that she was terrified. "I really thought I would fail," she remembered, "and my boss really started to worry about me. He said much later that I was paralyzed."

Unequipped to follow the well-beaten path through media relations, Marilyn made a discovery that would eventually characterize her career. "I found that one of the ways to make a real difference in a large organization is to embrace change and create a new path. Anyone who wasn't complaining about change, but was ready to say, 'Whoa, there's an opportunity here to do something new' could be very valuable."[41]

Marilyn might not have known how a newsroom worked, but she had a pretty good idea how most people got their news, and she saw a big hole in the company's approach to media relations. In a time when most people were getting most of their news from television, no one in the department had ever worked in broadcast news. And none of the company's executives knew how to handle a television interview. She sold her new boss on the idea of giving the company's top executives media training. She not only got his approval, but he also recommended someone to help with training.

Chet Burger had been one of the first employees of CBS Television News, back when Douglas Edwards anchored the 15-minute broadcast from a studio on the mezzanine of Grand Central Station. Eventually, Burger became the first national manager of CBS Television News.

Somehow, he uncharacteristically got on the wrong side of an insecure boss who let him go. But he had no trouble getting hired to help a succession of advertising and public relations companies drum up new business. He was good at it. A sharp dresser with an ever-present pipe, he *looked* like a senior executive. He spoke in a quiet gravelly voice, making people lean in to hear him. He was smart, especially at reading people. And he had a way of piercing through complexities to the heart of an issue, telling people what they didn't

---

[41] Arthur W. Page Center oral history.

know they wanted to hear. He defined avuncular—a friendly uncle who has seen it all, can explain what it means, and what you should do about it.

In 1963, he decided to go into business for himself, opening a firm specializing in communications management consulting, a field he essentially made up. Among his services was media training. Today, there are dozens of media training companies across the country. But back then Burger was essentially inventing the practice. Unlike many of today's media trainers, his goal was not to avoid answering difficult questions by "pivoting" to another subject. His philosophy was that reporters have only one objective—to get a story. The executives' job is to do their best to ensure the story is accurate and complete. Among other things, that means getting comfortable with interruptions, dumb questions, and inflammatory language. It means speaking like a normal human being, even under bright lights and with a microphone under your nose. And never losing your cool.

The training design was straightforward. Marilyn and Burger would sit around a coffee table with three or four senior executives and briefly explain what was about to happen. The company had hired two reporters on their day off and, one by one, each executive would take a turn in front of a TV camera as one of the reporters interviewed him. (They were all men, save the company's treasurer.) Then a videotape of the interview would be played back for critique and suggestions.

What the executives didn't know is that the "reporters" were AT&T public relations employees who had spent the past week grilling people in each executive's organization to devise "the most difficult questions—the very last questions—they would want to be asked." It was a bonding experience for Marilyn and the executives, all of whom were sworn to secrecy about the "reporters." Conducting one or two sessions a week for nearly two years, Marilyn got to know every senior executive of AT&T and many from the operating companies. And they, her.

Unfortunately, many of her colleagues in the media relations department resented the fact that she was "doing her own thing"— and with the company's top executives at that! Meanwhile, they were back in their cubicles writing news releases and fielding reporters' calls. One media relations staffer at the time called Marilyn "political and calculating." Some of her colleagues simply didn't trust her.

When she left media relations, she was given an award that noted she was probably the only person to have a successful career in media relations without ever writing a news release. As Marilyn put it, "It was not a conventional stint in media relations, but it was useful." It was also flexible enough to allow time for her to supplement her English degree with a graduate business degree. The company sent her to the Executive MBA program at Pace University in Pleasantville, New York. Only 20 minutes from her home in Edgemont, classes met from 8:00 a.m. to 6:00 p.m. on alternate Fridays and Saturdays.

CHAPTER FOUR

BECOMING A PUBLIC RELATIONS WOMAN

Marilyn was one of only a handful of women among the 70 or so students in Pace's Executive MBA Program, which the college said reflected "the realities of mid-level corporate management"[42] at the time. Students worked at companies like IBM, General Foods, Ciba-Geigy, GTE, and other Westchester-based companies, as well as from New York City and as far away as Albany.

Whereas in most MBA programs students specialize in such narrow fields as accounting, marketing, taxation, or management science, Pace's program assumed most of its students had already developed on-the-job specializations. As a result, the curriculum was relatively broad and based on business cases. Students were expected to bring their work experience into the classroom in those discussions. And those who had never taken basic accounting—like Marilyn—were expected to make it up on their own time by studying a textbook on accounting for liberal arts majors.

In addition to Pace's own business school faculty, a catered buffet lunch every day featured guest speakers, such as the leading thinkers in economics, marketing, regulation, and management theory who normally taught at schools like Harvard, Princeton, Yale, or the London School of Economics. "Stimulating wasn't the word for it," Marilyn remembered. "It was a privilege beyond compare."

What she picked up in the MBA program would not have qualified her to work in any part of the business that depended on heavy quantitative analysis. At best, she had exposure to basic accounting principles. But the program went deeper into business

---

[42] Josh Barbanel, "The Executive Suite Moves Into The Classroom," Business Section, Sunday *New York Times*, April 2, 1978, p. 10.

strategy and the finer points of marketing. And that, along with her natural curiosity and voracious reading, would eventually equip her to hold her own in discussions at the company's highest levels.

At the end of the program, Marilyn was asked to say a few words on behalf of her class at the graduation ceremony. She delivered a few compact paragraphs and, after the ceremony, an unassuming fellow in a blue serge suit flecked with dandruff shambled up to her and, in a rather hoarse voice asked if she had ever written speeches for anyone. She said she hadn't, and he said, "Well, if you can write for yourself, you can do it for others."

Marilyn didn't know it until later, but she had just met Alvin von Auw. He had once led the PR department at AT&T's manufacturing subsidiary Western Electric. But when the president of Western was made chairman of AT&T, he followed him there. To give him the time to do what made him so valuable—which was to think—the company created a new title for him, "special assistant to the chairman." And because he believed writing made thinking easier, he also became the chairman's chief speechwriter. The rest of public relations reported to someone else.

Most people within AT&T thought of von Auw as the intellectual nerve center of the whole sprawling enterprise. "He pondered what we were about and where we were going and turned that into speeches that were firmly footed in the Victorian era of dense sentences and complicated phrasing," Marilyn said. "His talks had no lilt or cadence . . . they bent under the weight of content. I loved reading them because they were stuffed with meaning . . . and it was almost like being back at Barnard doing an English assignment to think about what he wrote."

Within a matter of weeks, von Auw had Marilyn transferred to the chairman's speech group. She was suitably terrified. "There were three of us. I was the lowest level, of course. And it seemed the two mavens would barely put the paper in their typewriters before it was rolling out the other side filled with words, while I coped with the panic of blank page syndrome." She felt as if the whole weight of the Bell System was pressing on her typewriter keys.

It didn't help that—through a combination of a change in dates and her own inattention—she missed the deadline for one of the first speeches assigned to her. When the officer who was giving the speech called to ask where it was, Marilyn was out of the office, and rather than calling her at home that night, her boss spent the weekend writing the speech himself. Word spread, and it was one more reason for some to dislike her.

Marilyn later confessed she both loved and hated speechwriting. Hated it because she always felt she could never do it as well as von Auw or even the other speechwriters in the group. Loved it because it represented an opportunity to make the company "hostage to its rhetoric," as von Auw put it. When she was writing for the chairman, if she was clever enough, she could use the speech as a vehicle to bring issues to his attention, emphasize one thing rather than another, and even suggest what one of the most powerful corporations in the world ought to say and do. "I thought it was as close to making policy as I'd ever get," she later confessed.

Early in her time as a speechwriter, the company had a change in leadership. AT&T's courtly Chairman John deButts decided to retire a year early in 1979, partly for health reasons, partly because the government had filed an antitrust suit to break up the company four years earlier, and he felt he had fought it off as long as he could. It was time to give someone else a shot.

His successor Charlie Brown was a more cerebral and measured executive, as quiet as deButts was gregarious. And in Marilyn's opinion, not a very good public speaker. She went to von Auw and suggested that they bring in an outside coach for the chairman. Von

Auw was not as appalled as her colleagues that she'd suggest such a thing. But he explained that "Charlie is not that kind of guy." Not that he couldn't improve, but he'd bristle at being "handled" like a politician or beauty contestant. On the other hand, Charlie had taken media training without any fuss.

"Why don't I suggest you will give him a little feedback on how he did after his speeches," von Auw said. Charlie agreed, and Marilyn slipped into the role of speech coach. "If you've ever had Charlie Brown's steely-blue eyes trained on you," she once said, "You know it takes a certain amount of courage to say, 'Not so good, chief.' But it was a time of enormous growth, and very exciting. I loved it."

It was also a period when Marilyn realized the company was sliding into two camps—those who wanted to protect the system they knew and those who wanted to change it. Marilyn was clearly in the latter camp, and it sometimes made her feel uncharacteristically lacking. "I didn't have this embedded, inspired commitment to the past," she said. "So I was a less passionate defender of the past, and much more optimistic about what a different future could be like." To her, the issue was figuring out what business strategy was in the best interests of the company's employees, customers, and owners. "This was a time when I was intensely aware of being pragmatic by nature rather than ideological," she later remembered.

She also began to realize that her top client was in the same camp. Brown was a product of the Bell System monopoly, but he realized competition was inevitable. People had accepted the Bell System as an exception to the normal way markets are supposed to work for nearly 70 years, but new technology and the emergence of new competitors had changed that. Plus, AT&T's top management was distracted from the complex job of running one of the world's largest companies by endless legal, legislative, and regulatory battles.

In his typically understated way, Brown later confessed, "My first years at the head of the Bell System presented a difficult managerial challenge."[43] It was becoming increasingly clear to him that unless something was done quickly, AT&T would miss the business opportunities spawned from its own invention of the transistor. And pricing long distance calls high to keep local calls low made it simple for competitors to undercut AT&T's rates. Charlie knew he couldn't preserve the past, but he vowed to find a way to protect as much of the future as he could.

John deButts might have been a stiff-necked opponent to competition, but even he had hedged his bets. In 1973, he hired Arch McGill, who at 33 had been the youngest vice president in IBM's history, to shake up AT&T's sales and marketing in preparation for whatever competition developed. By 1979, McGill had attracted a capable staff, many from IBM, to join him in transforming AT&T into a customer- rather than product-driven organization. In the process, he had become somewhat of an irritant, like the sand in an oyster trying to produce a pearl. It didn't help that he considered "corporate staff" a type of disease that afflicted companies by slowing everything down and consuming large quantities of resources. He was particularly skeptical about AT&T's 4,000-person public relations department and its multi-million-dollar corporate advertising budget.

That department was led by Ed Block, a 52-year-old former reporter who had reluctantly joined Southwestern Bell 27 years earlier when its offer to double his salary to $475 a month coincided with the birth of his first son. In the years since, he had shuttled back and forth between local Bell companies and AT&T corporate

---

[43] Charles L. Brown, "The Bell System," *Encyclopedia of Telecommunications*, (New York: Marcel Dekker, Inc., 1991).

headquarters, often trailing a boss who had come to depend on him. That included his current boss, AT&T Chairman Charlie Brown.

Not much taller than Marilyn and soft-spoken, Block was easy to underestimate. But his instincts were finely tuned, and he could feel McGill's crosshairs settling on the corporate ad budget. So he decided to move pre-emptively. He promoted Marilyn from the speechwriting group to corporate advertising to oversee the creation of an ad campaign that would keep McGill happy.

She had heard McGill speak when she attended the executive MBA program at Pace University and still remembered one line from his speech: "The Bell System will bleed from the ears before it does what it has to do." From what she could tell, since coming to AT&T, McGill had run his organization as if he was intent on hastening the flow of the System's blood. But she had to admit that, although he was megalomaniacal and insufferable, he was right.

Like McGill, Marilyn considered herself a change agent but she didn't waste time trying to find a new ad agency. She quickly involved N. W. Ayer, which had been doing most of AT&T's advertising for more than 70 years at that point. The AT&T campaign for which it was most famous—"Reach Out and Touch Someone"—promoted long distance service to consumers by turning it from an expensive luxury into an emotional connection with family and friends.

McGill's challenge to them was even more difficult—in the face of the $40 million the company was spending every year to convince consumers to call grandma, they were to redefine AT&T as an information management company that solves business problems.

Marilyn attacked the challenge in her typical fashion in those early days, focusing on the right thing to do with little regard for the right way to do it. She ran roughshod over her staff and agency, dragging them into one brainstorming session after another, pushing them into focus groups with business customers, having them interview and re-interview McGill and his top lieutenants, testing campaign ideas, and ordering up execution after execution. Even when she had settled on a campaign, it wasn't unusual for her to rewrite agency copy her staff had already approved without telling anyone. Marilyn knew what she wanted; she just didn't know how to get it out of the people who worked for her. She got results, but at the high cost of staff resentment.

At one point, the advertising staff was sent to an off-site management training course. One exercise called for them to provide feedback to their boss. Marilyn's direct reports huddled together and debated what they should do. They were afraid to tell her the truth, so they all agreed to say only nice things. Marilyn was denied the kind of honest feedback Mary Ardito had once tried to give her more than a decade before. She hadn't listened then. Maybe she would have listened this time. We'll never know, just as we'll never know whether her staff's criticism would have been as cutting had Marilyn been a man, rather than a young blonde who had not gone through the same corporate traps they had, cycling in and out from one of the local telephone companies.

In any case, Marilyn's team and the agency ultimately delivered advertising she would later characterize as "a wonderful campaign that was totally irrelevant to the company." It was called "The Knowledge Business" and claimed AT&T was all about helping business customers turn data into knowledge they could use to serve their customers. It was clever and properly defined the benefits of mining and managing information, but it was about ten years ahead of AT&T's actual capabilities. At that point, the most intelligent product the company's salespeople could sell was a private branch exchange (PBX) which routed phone calls around the office. "It taught me the difference between positioning a company on the leading edge of where you're going," she said, "and so far out that it's meaningless." It would be her first effort to position AT&T for the future. And by far, not her best. But McGill was relatively happy.

While all this was going on, Ed Block was negotiating with the Walt Disney Company to sponsor the most prominent ride at EPCOT, the second major attraction being built at Disney World in Orlando, Florida. The ride would take guests on a slow-moving trip through the history of communication from stone age to present, within a gigantic silver sphere at the very entrance of the park. Disney's Imagineers would handle designing and building the ride, and AT&T would have control of a large area where guests disembarked at the base of the sphere. As it happened, Bell Labs public relations had built an impressive exhibit about its many innovations in the lobby of its Murray Hill, New Jersey, headquarters. Block tapped the head of Bell Labs public relations to move to Orlando and take charge of the EPCOT project.

That left a big hole in the organization chart. In its heyday, Bell Labs was the most prominent R&D organization in the world. Members of its staff had invented the transistor, solar cell, and laser, discovered the Big Bang, and won seven Nobel prizes. Block offered the job of leading Bell Labs PR to four fifth-level men, who all passed on the job. They considered it like doing factory PR, far from the corridors of power. Plus, the president of Bell Labs was known to be a skeptic of public relations' "smoke and mirrors."

Block was expressing his frustration at lunch in the executive dining room when Charlie Brown—perhaps remembering his media and speech training—said, "Why don't you give the job to Marilyn? She's not afraid of anything." So Block asked Marilyn if she would at least interview for the job. Since it meant a promotion, and she felt she had nothing to lose, she agreed. "It was a devil-may-care kind of situation," she later said.

Ian Ross, Bell Labs' president, was a flinty Englishman who joined the company in 1952 when just about all the world's knowledge of semiconductors resided at the intersection of two aisles in the Labs' Murray Hill, New Jersey, building. Ross had a PhD in engineering from Cambridge University and by the time he was appointed president of the Labs in 1979, he had already invented new semiconductor technologies, provided technical support to the Apollo Moon mission (including calculating whether the Moon's surface could support the Lunar Landing Vehicle's weight), helped launch the first communication satellites, and overseen planning for the transition from an analog to an all-digital telephone network. In other words, he was whip smart. "I felt that, in a sense, [as president of Bell Labs], I was the technical conscience of AT&T," he once said. "I had to make sure that they didn't try and violate the laws of physics, which they frequently, particularly the marketing people, wanted to do."[44]

In that regard, Arch McGill was Ross's nemesis. It wasn't long into Marilyn's interview with him before McGill's name came up. Ross thought McGill was immoral, close to illegal, and was destroying the place. Marilyn defended him and, as she later described it, they had a "spirited debate." Ross pushed back and Marilyn stood her ground. "I took the position that I knew all these things were wrong with McGill," she later said. "But if this company didn't change soon, it was absolutely going to be destroyed because it was out of sync with what it needed to be to be successful in the future."

She left the interview without giving it a second thought and drove home to Edgemont. It turned out Ross loved the exchange and almost immediately called Ed Block to tell him he wanted to hire her.

---

[44] Ian Ross, Oral History (Piscataway, NJ: Computer History Museum, Aug. 19, 2009). See: http://bit.ly/31By4YK.

Two things were at work here. First, Marilyn had never developed a sense of hierarchy. In the Pioneers, she had not learned to be afraid of telephone company presidents because she flew around with them on their corporate jets; in media relations, her job was to put senior executives in uncomfortable situations and then guide them out of it; and in speechwriting, she had to tell the company's CEO how he did delivering a speech. To her, Ross was just another guy with a big office who happened to have a British accent.

For his part, what Marilyn didn't know is that Ross was one of very few people in the company's top ranks who had become convinced AT&T was likely to lose the antitrust suit it had been litigating for the past six years. Ross was the lead witness in AT&T's defense, and the response to his testimony had convinced Charlie Brown and his chief legal advisor that the judge would eventually rule against the company. He asked Ross and a very few other people to privately consider what a reasonable settlement might look like. Ross believed the best approach would be to separate the regulated businesses from those that had competition. In competitive markets, AT&T would have to have a very different set of skills to be successful, just as Marilyn had observed.

Ross wanted to see if she could infuse that attitude into the Labs. He wanted to see if she could help change the culture.

CHAPTER FIVE

IN THE LABS

Marilyn started at Bell Labs in 1980. Her daughters—who were then 16 and 13 years old—had no interest in moving. Nor did her husband Bob, unless it was back into Manhattan. So Marilyn decided to drive to Murray Hill, New Jersey, from Edgemont, New York, five days a week. She rationalized that the length of her commute wouldn't change that much. It was only 50 miles. She should be able to travel that far in about an hour. Door to door, that was less than driving to the train station and then taking a train and the subway to 195 Broadway.

But she had not taken into account the vagaries of traffic jams on the George Washington Bridge, the rain that fell in sheets faster than her wipers could swing, the ten-wheel trucks that only grudgingly shared the road, and the winter storms that coated her Chevy's windshield in frozen slush no defroster could melt. After a year of getting home long after her girls had gone to bed, with knuckles white from her iron grip on the steering wheel, she threw in the towel and convinced Bob they had to move to New Jersey. For Bob, it meant a train commute from a different direction. The girls, of course, hated moving even though their new house in a tony section of Westfield was grander than the home they left behind.

As for the job itself, Marilyn said, "I loved it. If they hadn't paid me, I would've paid them." She was in her element; she was home. "Bell Labs was just a cauldron of ideas, and your value as a person is based on what ideas you bring to the table," she later said. "They don't care if you're black or white, Jewish or not Jewish. They don't care if you're from New York or from Indiana. All they care about is what kind of ideas you have." And Marilyn had lots of ideas.

The brew in which she floated those ideas, however, was even higher in testosterone than at AT&T headquarters. Marilyn was the only woman at her level in all of Bell Labs. And even in her own public relations organization, there was only one other woman amongst the top 15 managers. None of this particularly bothered Marilyn at the time. She simply didn't think in terms of gender. And, even if she did, as Bill Weiss, a Bell Labs PR veteran, put it, "Every one of her male colleagues would be looking for her to be a 'women's libber' or to favor women—and she was way too smart not to know it." So even when she had the opportunity to hire from outside, she chose the best talent she could find without regard to gender.

Otherwise, "Marilyn was a tornado of fresh air in her first months at Bell Labs, meeting with individuals and groups, listening intently, and making fundamental observations that none of us would ever have thought of," according to Weiss. "For example, the editor of the *Bell Labs News* said his objective was to publish 50 issues a year; the media relations manager said his goal was to issue more news releases this year than last. 'You're too task-oriented, guys,' she said. 'You need to be more audience- or market-oriented'." So she set in place a lengthy, careful, and participatory process to restructure the PR department.

In fact, "participatory" was one of Marilyn's favorite tools whenever she had a big, complicated issue to address. She was, as she put it, "communicative to the core." She loved bringing people together to find a big idea, solve a big problem, or figure out how to do things better. She once said, "The most important thing to me is to make that bridge from my brain to yours." And she didn't think that should be a one-way street. "I really think people have tremendous potential that they want to give. I want them to contribute their best—for themselves and for me."[45] But not everyone who reported to her enjoyed diving into an intellectual mosh pit as much as she did. Some considered it an unnecessary distraction from their "real job;" some simply didn't see the point. And some secretly thought the point was to make *her* look good. But it never discouraged her from throwing piles of people against a problem; it just made her more selective about the people she threw. But reorganizing the Bell Labs public relations staff was only part of the task ahead of her.

She also needed to ensure that her organization was firing on all cylinders. "I spent a lot of time trying to make the professional staff in Bell Labs PR really functionally excellent so they could do well what needed to be done," she recalled. In one special case, that meant bringing in new, proven talent. Ross called the speechwriters assigned to him "scribes," as if their primary function was to commit his thoughts to paper in a narrow column of 14-point Helvetica he could read from a podium. He didn't expect them to have an original thought, and if anything like that showed up in an early draft, he invariably scratched it out. So Marilyn reached all the way into the White House for an experienced speechwriter who had written for Ross-sized egos. Stan Schneider had been a speechwriter for the science advisers to four presidents: Nixon, Ford, Carter, and Reagan, as well as assistant to the chairman of the Atomic Energy Commission. Now she wouldn't have to listen to Ross's complaints about the speeches given him. And Ross could brag, with only a little exaggeration, that he had Reagan's speechwriter.

But if Ross had few qualms about Marilyn's role at the Labs, his top officers—all men—were more skeptical. She asked to attend their

---

[45] Lynne Joy McFarland, Larry E. Senn, John R. Childress, *21st Century Leadership: Dialogues With 100 Top Leaders* (New York: Executive Excellence Publishing, 1994), p. 135.

staff meetings so she could get up to speed on the technical and business issues they faced. But they either didn't take the requests seriously or couldn't fathom why a "PR gal" should be admitted into the inner sanctum of their deliberations. They didn't want any of what went on in there *written* about.

After a few months of feeling like the kid who never gets picked to be on the team, Marilyn took matters into her own hands and simply showed up at a vice president's staff meeting. They all knew who she was of course, but the only woman who had ever wandered into the room before was carrying a pink message slip for someone. And then this short, blonde woman pulled up a chair and sat down! She knew they would be too polite to ask her to leave. And she was right. She stayed for the whole meeting, taking notes so she could ask one of her contacts in the technical ranks to explain the issues to her. She kept showing up and, in time, she asked questions. On occasion, she offered some thoughts of her own on the matters at hand. Over time, her curiosity and insatiable desire to learn, matched with the insight of her questions, won them over.

And that gave her the confidence to crash a meeting of Western Electric officers who she heard were gathered at the Labs to discuss a response to some competitive issues. The Western Electric officers were unfailingly polite, but they were also notoriously direct and asked her why she was there. "Well, since you're funding Bell Labs," she said, "I thought Labs PR should help address these issues." To his credit, the Western Electric vice president running the meeting said, "We need all the help we can get." And she stayed.

Word of incidents like these spread rapidly through the prison-quality rumor mill of AT&T. And by her example, Marilyn advised other PR people how to be successful. As Burt Wolder, AT&T's PR director in Europe put it, "The obvious and memorable message to me was to think about what's going on, about the big challenges, and insert yourself into the conversation where you think PR can help—not wait for the call that never comes."

She was also not bashful about forming alliances that could be helpful to her and to her clients. When Ed Block hired Reynold Levy to lead the newly formed AT&T Foundation in the summer of 1983, Marilyn held a party at her home in Westfield to introduce him to the Labs' senior leaders. Levy came to AT&T from New York's 92nd Street Y, then and still one of the leading cultural centers in the cultural epicenter of the nation. Holding both a law degree and a PhD, Levy is a bona fide intellectual. But he had never been in a home with so many other PhDs. And having just left his cramped two-bedroom apartment on the Upper East Side of New York, he was suitably impressed by the size of her home, from the wrap-around porch to the expansive living area. Her weekend farm, he later learned, was practically the size of Central Park!

As he made the rounds through AT&T's divisions and businesses, educating himself on the company, he discovered Marilyn herself could be just as expansive. "She introduced me to the top leaders of Bell Labs, real rock stars like Arno Penzias, Sol Buchsbaum, and Kumar Patel,"[46] he remembers. "And she was completely hands-off, even when I met with her boss Ian Ross." Levy considered public relations the pathway to the leaders of the company's businesses, but it was almost always a path with traffic cops in the form of minders who quietly took notes of the conversations.

Levy stayed at AT&T for 12 years, ultimately reporting to Marilyn as vice president of international public affairs and one of her

---

[46] Arno Penzias shared the Nobel Prize in physics with his colleague Robert Wilson for discovering evidence of the Big Bang. Sol Buchsbaum was science advisor to Presidents Ronald Reagan and George H. W. Bush and recipient of the National Medal of Science. Kumar Patel invented the carbon dioxide laser, among other devices, and also won the National Medal of Science.

closest advisors. Following his stint at AT&T, he served as chief executive of such prestigious institutions as the International Rescue Committee, Lincoln Center, and the Robin Hood Foundation—all of which gave him a unique perch from which to assess her as a leader. "Many leaders have two things in common," he has concluded. "They avoid conflict and they're deeply insecure." Marilyn, he concluded was one of the most courageous and secure people he'd ever observed. "Others dodge, weave, and hide to avoid conflict," he said. "She ran towards problems and made it her responsibility to help others out of trouble, even at the risk of becoming associated with it."

Indeed, whenever Marilyn had an opportunity to explain public relations' role to other executives, she tried to persuade them to think of PR as less like a pharmacy, where you get a prescription for a speech or a news release filled, and more like a clinic you visit to find out what ails you or how you can get even healthier.

In that sense, Marilyn knew that one of the Labs' most serious vulnerabilities was that the senior executives at AT&T headquarters didn't know what was going on in the Labs' ivory tower. So she arranged for Ross to conduct quarterly "strategic briefings" for the office of the chairman. She assigned a member of her staff to generate ideas for the briefings by using Ross's name to get face time with senior Bell Labs executives, delve into their secrets, ask for detailed explanations, and have them review and correct the resulting abstracts before sending them to Ross for consideration. "Techie execs often had difficulty in distinguishing PR professionals from the people who put the disinfectant pucks in the urinals," Bill Weiss said. "They were wary of us at first. But soon, the more alert among them welcomed us—our abstracts became a direct conduit to put their pet ideas and projects in front of Ross and AT&T's top officers—and to get funding for them."

Meanwhile, with Ross's enthusiastic urging, Marilyn made understanding, and perhaps reshaping, Bell Labs' culture her personal project. "My own introduction to the uniqueness of the Bell Labs culture came at my first Skytop[47] meeting in 1980," she later remembered. "I was the new kid on the block, the first woman in the 'Cabinet,' and for several days I was looked at rather closely. And then, on one of the last nights, when wives were invited to the dinner, Tina Ross met me and said, 'Thank God, we finally have an English major in the Cabinet.'" It was a warm welcome, but in reality, for her first two years at the Labs, Marilyn would spend less time translating the Labs' research into English than plumbing its culture. Some aspects of the culture were easily observable in the meetings she attended. Senior managers did not handle conflict well, big decisions were made by consensus, the process by which something was done was often considered more important than the result, and a big part of that process meant kicking the biggest problems up a level to minimize the risk of surprises. "It's ironic that we hire the best, brightest people we can find," she once said, "and then tell them we have a rule for everything."

"What we have is a university culture," she said. "What we want is a culture that is more entrepreneurial, easier to manage, more flexible; a culture focused on competitiveness, customer needs, and being early because we don't have time to waste."

The fundamental values underlying the behavior of the Labs' senior officers were not hard to articulate. Bell Labs' people valued intelligence, innovation, precise thinking, excellence, and collegiality. "That's a value system any company would be proud to have," she said. "The uniqueness of any company's culture—the particular way

---

[47] Skytop Lodge is a resort and conference center in the Poconos where Bell Labs' senior leaders, or Cabinet, met every year to discuss current issues, do long-range planning, and play a little golf.

we carry out our mission—is shaped by those underlying values. They're the bedrock of any company, the part of culture that changes slowly, if at all." But she had no doubt the Bell Labs culture needed more than fine-tuning. She hadn't been on the job for more than a year when she was presented with a survey documenting how difficult Western Electric executives thought it was to work with the Labs. They considered most Labs people arrogant, risk-averse, and suspicious of anything not invented within their own walls. The other senior Labs executive in the meeting angrily demanded the names of the people who completed the survey. She, for her part, accepted it as useful information. The big question, in her mind, was what kind of cataclysmic event it would take to change it.

*   *   *

Marilyn was on vacation in Bermuda with her husband Bob on January 8, 1982, when Charlie Brown and Assistant Attorney General William Baxter stepped to the podium of the National Press Club in Washington, D.C., to announce that AT&T would relinquish ownership of the local Bell telephone companies, retaining control only of its long distance division, Western Electric, and Bell Labs. In return it would be freed from an earlier agreement that restricted it to the telecommunications business.

The company was silent about what new businesses it might enter, but since the government had dropped a separate antitrust suit against IBM on the same day, speculation centered on the computer business. Since the switching systems in telephone networks are essentially special purpose computers, that made sense. Some even speculated that settling both antitrust suits on the same day was more than coincidental. Ensuring IBM would have a competitor of roughly equal size would solve a lot of problems.

Brown had quietly taken AT&T's future out of the hands of the judge presiding over the antitrust suit, a Congress that had been debating new telecommunications regulation for several years, and a Federal Communications Commission that was still trying to define the difference between a phone and a computer. And in a clever Jiu Jitsu move, he had flipped the government's argument. The Justice Department had originally wanted AT&T to spin off Western Electric. Instead, he offered to spin off the local phone companies.

Marilyn was shocked. No one had let her in on the plan or she wouldn't have decamped to Bermuda. And in a demonstration that where you stand is often a function of where you sit, Marilyn saw the whole series of events as a threat to Bell Labs. In the whirlwind of publicity about the breakup of the Bell System, she could hear the public asking, "What will happen to Bell Labs? Will the nation suffer? Will the AT&T company suffer?" And she could hear Labs employees wondering, "Will we still be able to get and attract the talent [we need]? Will we be able to contribute to the national good?"

It was largely a case of selective hearing. Save for some national security officials, most of the befuddled public was not concerned about Bell Labs, but about who they should now call for phone service. And even within the Labs, most employees were worried about their own job security, not about the quality of the next generation of technical staff. The immediate reaction was abject confusion. As one of the leading investment analysts put it, "Everybody is confused. Customers are thoroughly confused. Employees are confused. The companies are confused. So are the regulatory commissions, unions, and stockholders. And so am I."[48]

---

[48] William McKeever, telecom analyst at Dean Witter Reynolds, quoted in *Time*, Jan. 16, 1984.

Marilyn was anything but confused. She heard the urgent call of battle. "Suddenly, the public relations department is not to just polish what was," she remembered feeling, "but it becomes a place to get a really big job done—to convince the public that the Labs will continue to contribute to the national good." And to ensure the Labs could deliver on that promise, she saw an even more important task, "To make sure the people at Bell Labs understand they're still valued, but that they must change. Because if they don't change, in this new world we're going to, we're going to have major problems."

She took that message to a meeting of Bell Labs' senior management at the Skytop Conference Center in the Poconos. Coming so soon after the announcement of the Bell System breakup, it was a more intense and subdued conference than usual. These guys *were* concerned about the Labs' future. Many of them had spent their entire careers at Bell Labs. Their very identities were tied to it. They had worked in a relatively academic environment, largely free to pursue whatever scientific question intrigued them, funded by a benevolent monopoly and its captive manufacturing subsidiary.

Marilyn was last on an agenda that had already gone way overtime. It was late and the person who introduced her warned that time was short. "Well then, it's a good thing you've got a short speaker," she said. "But I'm not going to shorten what I have to say." Then she dived into an impassioned talk about Bell Labs. It had invented the Information Age and it was the Labs' job to lead the nation into it. Who had a greater capability to do so? Who had a greater right? And why should Bell Labs' future be less than its past? She spoke to "the aching need for greatness that drew people to Bell Labs in the first place."

She got a standing ovation.

Returning to her office the next day, she vowed to do her part to satisfy that aching need for greatness. "We dramatically increased and improved the amount of communication that was sent out to the public." As in a university, the Labs technical staff felt an obligation—and internally, some pressure—to publish the results of their work. The *Bell Labs Technical Journal*, then published ten times a year in issues that ran to 400 or 500 pages each, had been the Labs' premiere external publication since 1922. Although a prestigious journal, prized in technical circles, it was tough slogging for anyone who didn't enjoy critiquing the whiteboard notations in the background of science fiction movies. Marilyn had her staff create a publication for the non-technical readers among its telephone company customers. Where the *Technical Journal* was dry, the new publication, called *Proto,* was glossy. It covered many of the same technical innovations as the *Journal*, albeit a few months or even years later, but it was approachable, interesting, and expertly crafted, closer to *Time* magazine than to the *Scientific American*.

Marilyn also promoted a lot of opportunities for two-way dialogue within the Labs. "It was our way of encouraging change," she said. "We set up a lot of town meetings, small breakfasts, and lunches with Ian and his people, as well as with the executive directors and their organizations." She also brought in people from the telephone companies and Western Electric to discuss technical issues with Bell Labs people, so the latter would get first-hand exposure to the customers' needs. "We were just constantly rubbing people up against each other to talk about technology issues, customer issues, even social/political issues of where did Bell Labs need to go? And what did it need to do to be in a competitive position?"

All this two-way communication was not comfortable for everyone. The Western Electric, now AT&T Network Systems, people were uneasy about letting the Labs meet with "their" customers. The Bell Labs leadership itself didn't find candor always appropriate. And while all this was going on, Marilyn knew that Arch

McGill, over in business marketing, was trying to bring Bell Labs to its knees. "What McGill didn't know," she liked to say, "is that Bell Labs didn't have knees. It never bent."

Not that it was inflexible. In October 1983, Ian Ross, the Bell Labs president who was so skeptical about public relations "smoke and mirrors," made Marilyn a sixth-level officer, its only vice president with a liberal arts degree, the highest-ranking woman at the Labs, and one of only six women at that level in the entire million-person company.

CHAPTER SIX

STRIKING OPPORTUNITY

Within 12 years, Marilyn had been promoted four times, which at AT&T was a pretty fast track.

But if she felt ambivalent about the impact of the company's breakup on the public, or even on Bell Labs, she realized it was a good career move. "In one fell swoop, suddenly I was part of a much smaller group of senior public relations people," she recalled thinking. "Most of the guys who were candidates for Ed Block's job had just been divested. So for years people had been telling me, if you want to get ahead, you need to work for a telephone company, and all of a sudden I didn't have to do that." Plus, of all the potential candidates to succeed Ed Block, she was the only woman.

Some believed Marilyn owed her success to the fact that she was a woman. Others said she got ahead *despite* being a woman. As to the first theory, if a woman made it to a certain level, some men—and even some women—thought it was because the company had a quota to fill or, worse, because she had used her "feminine charms" to get ahead. Well, AT&T was under pressure to promote women, and Marilyn was not without feminine charms, but she was also so tough-minded, so creative, and so hardworking, it was obvious why she was getting ahead. On the other hand, the people who thought she advanced despite being a woman pointed out—correctly—that she was ambitious. Just like a man. And when she saw an opportunity, she took it. Just like a man.

In 1983, in anticipation of spinning off its local telephone companies, AT&T divided itself into three groups—AT&T Communications, AT&T Technologies, and AT&T Information

Systems,[49] each led by a vice chairman. Bell Labs was in Technologies, along with most of Western Electric manufacturing. Sensing a need, or perhaps an opportunity, with less than two months under her belt as a bona fide AT&T vice president, Marilyn wrote a memo to Jim Olson, the CEO of the Technologies sector, suggesting how he should organize his public relations department.

Olson forwarded the memo to his right-hand man, Vic Pelson. Pelson was a prime example of how opposites attract. Both men were smart, shrewd, and tough. But while Olson was short and husky, Pelson was tall and thin. Whereas Olson was impatient and impulsive, Pelson was thoughtful and deliberate. Olson had spent most of his career in local phone companies. He literally started in a manhole at the age of 17 and, after getting a business degree from the University of North Dakota, worked his way up to the top levels of AT&T. Pelson joined Western Electric as an engineer straight out of the Newark College of Engineering (now the New Jersey Institute of Technology). He spent most of his career in manufacturing and, after getting an MBA from New York University, took on jobs of increasing responsibility as Western Electric tried to deal with changes in technology and regulation.

Pelson had been on a Western Electric task force that hired McKinsey & Company to help it design and launch a marketing and sales organization in case the company were ever spun off from

---

[49] AT&T Information Systems was originally called American Bell until the judge overseeing the antitrust settlement forbade AT&T from using the "Bell" name for any unit except Bell Labs to avoid suggesting that AT&T and the Regional Bell Operating Companies were related. Ironically, all but one Bell company changed their names shortly after leaving AT&T. In 1985, AT&T Information Systems was folded into AT&T Technologies, when the FCC reversed a requirement that it be in a "fully separated subsidiary" to keep regulated and unregulated businesses from subsidizing each other. In 1986, when Jim Olson succeeded Charlie Brown as AT&T chairman and CEO, AT&T Information Systems became part of AT&T Communications.

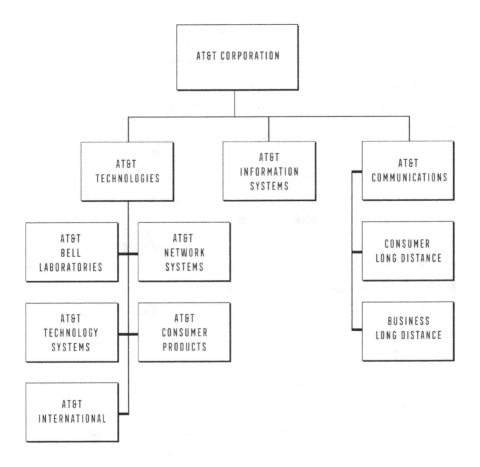

AT&T IN 1984

AT&T emerged from divestiture as a communication services and products company. The FCC required it to put its business products division, called AT&T Information Systems, in a separate subsidiary to avoid cross subsidies between regulated and unregulated businesses.

AT&T. Pelson had the institutional memory and native guidance Olson needed to forge AT&T Technologies out of Bell Labs and Western Electric. Pelson also understood how important marketing and public relations would be to Technologies as it tried to enter new markets and, even more of a challenge, to sell to the former Bell telephone companies. Those companies, which had once been *required* to buy all their equipment from Western Electric, were already being wooed by equipment manufacturers from around the world. And they were already pedaling away from a parent who they knew would be an opponent before state regulatory commissions as they tried to sort out how much AT&T should pay local companies for handling the first and last mile of a long distance call.

Marilyn's memo wasn't particularly erudite. She knew her audience, and she described "PR's job" in down-to-earth terms a CEO could relate to:

Tell employees what management wants from them (and vice-versa).

Explain to everybody why the company is doing all the strange things it's doing.

Shape public opinion to welcome policies driven by business needs.

Persuasively present stakeholders' needs to management -- before business decisions affecting them are made.

Protect the company's image, so the CEO enjoys reading the Wall Street Journal.

Make every line of business head a hero, but clearly subordinate to the business interests as a whole.

Manage the company's mass communications to zillions of customers, opinion leaders,

```
students, employees, and retirees -- achieving
several conflicting corporate goals -- at minimum
cost.

Get the government to love us.
```

Not exactly Peter Drucker, but it got Pelson's attention, and he invited Marilyn in for coffee and a chat. He didn't quiz her on her memo to Olson as much as about her impressions of Bell Labs. Pelson had never worked at the Labs, but he had a kind of schizophrenic attitude towards the organization. On the one hand, he was tremendously proud of its reputation—3,000 PhDs, seven Nobel prizes, inventions like the transistor, solar cell, and lasers. But he had the impression that its success engendered a fair amount of arrogance and that Labs people thought they should be running the company, not the other way around.

As it happens, Marilyn was in the middle of preparing a presentation to the Labs' senior executives on the topic of its culture and the need to adapt to changed circumstances. "Everybody says culture is 'the way we do things around here,'" she said. "But I think that oversimplifies the issue. Sure, culture is the way we do things, but that's shaped by what it is we want to do—our mission—and by our fundamental shared values. Not to mention the particular business environment we operate in.

"Now, Bell Labs' mission and business environment have changed dramatically. It's no longer part of a monopoly with the mission to furnish 'the best possible telephone service at the lowest cost consistent with financial safety.'[50] The monopoly has been blown up," she said. "And the Labs' mission is to give AT&T's businesses the technology they need to be competitively successful."

---

[50] This is how AT&T Chairman Walter Gifford described the company's mission of "universal service" in a 1927 speech to regulators. See: http://bit.ly/378IKR1.

"In a monopoly environment, we controlled the timing of technology . . . we could polish the details, seek the perfect product, set the price. Now competition controls the introduction of technology into the market, there's less time to polish details. . . . And the marketplace decides the price. In a monopoly, everything was ordered and smooth, but the competitive environment is characterized by uncertainty."

"Changing the culture doesn't mean abandoning our fundamental values. Excellence doesn't have to be expressed in ways that slow us down—like an intolerance for risk that leads to decisions by committee. A drive to innovate is what led to some of our greatest discoveries, but it doesn't have to lead to a not-invented-here syndrome. We can value rational decision-making without being paralyzed by ambiguity. And we can be collegial without avoiding constructive conflict."[51]

Pelson must have been impressed. She got the job, leap-frogging whatever competition she had for a position no one knew was open. Marilyn became vice president of PR for AT&T Technologies.

It would prove an even more challenging job than doing public relations for Bell Labs. AT&T Technologies consisted of two organizations with completely different cultures—Bell Labs and Western Electric. The Labs people didn't trust anything that worked in practice until they could prove it would work in theory. Western Electric managers, who constituted the largest block within the new enterprise, didn't trust theories until they could see them work in practice. It was the difference between academia and factory. One measured its success in patents and published papers; the other, in production flowing to spec. But it would be a mistake to think factory

---

[51] There is no written record of her discussion with Pelson who passed away in 2012. These quotes are from the speech she gave to Bell Labs management at around the same time.

hands were intellectually inferior. They might not match the Labs' best people in raw IQ. But they put an even higher premium on mental toughness and getting things done.

The dilemma Marilyn faced was where to put her public relations resources—at Technologies' headquarters or in the operating lines of business (LOBs). She outlined the trade-offs for herself on a three by five sheet of her personal Bell Labs stationery:

Trade Offs

Load LOB -- can't shrink, tend to grow even larger.

Large groups tend to do less important things because they can.

Sector support too far away to be relevant.

Sector people always too busy to help.

LOBs build secret PR groups to cope.

In the end, she realized the lines of business operated in such specialized areas, from microelectronics and software development to manufacturing switching systems and fiber optic cable, their PR support had to be tech-savvy and close. So she built a relatively small sector staff focused on issues and functions that crossed all the lines of business. She staffed the lines of business with dedicated account teams. And she promoted a lot of women who she thought had been underutilized in first- or second-level PR jobs at Bell Labs and Western Electric.

Marilyn described her new client, Jim Olson, as "a bundle of energy, bound under a very thin skin." He was a hard-charging, no-nonsense executive, famous for wearing short-sleeved white shirts that made rolling up his sleeves unnecessary and signaled that he didn't want to waste any time. When one of his meetings ended early, Olson famously asked his lieutenants who among them had conflicts he could resolve in the time left. Outgoing and energetic to the point of being forceful, he was known to slam his fist on the table to emphasize a point. He was also known to occasionally open senior officer meetings by leading a rousing chorus of the chart-topping country song "Oh Lord It's Hard To Be Humble."

Olson established the headquarters of AT&T Technologies in a nondescript office park just off Route 78 in Berkeley Heights, New Jersey. Except for some exhibits in the lobby showing how many components could be stuffed on a microelectronic chip, it could have been the regional office of an insurance company, just like the identical building next door.

He allowed an open house for employees' families when everyone first moved in, but then just before the doors opened, he personally took down lights the decorating committee had strung on the lobby's potted plants. That was too much glitz for him. Referring to AT&T Communications' expansive offices in New Jersey horse country, he told the employees struggling to keep up with him, "If I wanted a headquarters like Basking Ridge, I would have built a building like Basking Ridge."

Watching all this from a corner of the lobby were a short, elderly gentleman in a suit and tie and his equally well-dressed wife. Marilyn's mother and father had flown up from Florida to see their little girl's new office. Irene and Abraham Gold were justifiably proud of their younger daughter and considered her proof that *their* parents had been right to immigrate to the United States.

For Marilyn, her new job was almost as audacious and challenging. Jack Shultz followed Marilyn to AT&T Technologies and put it this way, "She worked in some of the toughest, most technical, and most male-dominated parts of the business. But this little Jewish woman from New York held her own in debates with their hard-nosed leaders by her knowledge of the key technical and marketplace issues facing them, by the clarity of her arguments, and by the courage of her convictions."

On the other hand, one senior executive who sat beside her in Olson's staff meetings, suggests she may have over-compensated for being the only woman in the room. "Initially she tried to be more of a 'guy' than the 'guys'," he remembers. "She dropped more F-bombs than anyone and swore like a sailor." Someone must have spoken to her about it, because she quickly dropped her four-letter vocabulary. At least in meetings. But she never completely won over the crustiest Western Electric executives, who suffered the illusion they had been shanghaied by their former parent and couldn't understand why this little blonde was part of the deal.

For his part, Olson had run phone companies, but he had no experience in high-technology, manufacturing, or marketing. He also could have used a degree in psychotherapy. The executives who reported to him were less a team than combatants. The monopoly in which they had built their careers put a premium on internal competition. With customers a given and "a fair return" on its investments practically guaranteed, AT&T could focus on standardizing operations. It issued detailed instructions[52] on how to do everything from staffing operator services to wrapping a wire around a screw. It also gathered service metrics on everything from how long it took operators to answer calls to how many phone circuits were available during high-traffic periods. Managers who had above-average performance on these measures got promoted; those who didn't, didn't.

---

[52] AT&T began issuing Bell System Standard Practices (BSSPs) in 1930 to ensure standardized service quality throughout all the operating companies. Regularly updated, the BSSPs covered everything from accounting and human resources procedures to complete technical descriptions of every product the Bell System used.

It worked beautifully in a monopoly. But that focus on internal competition assumed a relatively stable and manageable environment. In a competitive world, there were few manuals to follow, lots of uncertainty, and customers were no longer a given. Organizations had to work together, even if it meant putting their traditional concerns aside.

To Marilyn's surprise, one of the most intractable executives was her old boss and patron Ian Ross. While Ross recognized the need for change in AT&T, as Marilyn later put it, he was doing his best to "protect every conceivable part of Bell Labs exactly as it was, like a fly preserved in resin." But what was needed, she believed, was "a re-invention, which is the hardest thing in the world to do."

"As Ian went into deep defense, he used a very potent tool," she said. "Everyone was afraid of being the one who destroyed Bell Labs. So if you wanted to take a million dollars out of the multi-billion-dollar budget, you couldn't get the [switching system] you wanted. If you wanted to change something about the way personnel was handled or even the way you put the food in the cafeteria, it would destroy the culture, and *you* would be the one held accountable for Bell Labs going down the toilet." According to Marilyn, Ross held everyone at bay until he retired. "By then, it was too late to make graceful changes," she said.

Further adding to the challenges Olson faced, the lines of business under him were overstaffed for the levels of revenue they could generate and, in at least one case, had more than a little market overlap with their sister group, AT&T Information Systems. The switching division of the old Western Electric company had come up with a line of computers built around UNIX, a popular operating system invented at Bell Labs. But AT&T Information Systems considered the businesses that would buy those computers *its* customers. Internecine warfare raged for months until Olson took the problem to Charlie Brown who issued the Solomonic decree that AT&T Technologies would introduce the new line of computers and AT&T Information Systems would sell them.

In early 1984, Olson gave Marilyn the assignment of planning and running the introduction. It wasn't exactly New Coke,[53] but it went about as badly. The techies dragged about two dozen of the new computers, some the size of refrigerators, into the marble-clad Sky Lobby of the new AT&T headquarters building on Madison Avenue and put them in front of large aluminum-skinned panels printed with text that could have been lifted directly from the *Bell Labs Technical Journal*. The people who staffed the exhibits were fully prepared to run through the machines' specs with fellow techies but left the average business reporter befuddled.

At the briefing scheduled for media and industry analysts, the AT&T Information Systems officer who followed Jim Olson to the podium suffered a full panic attack when his slides got jumbled, and he didn't recover until someone mercifully turned the projector off. Then, as Marilyn was being driven home, she got a call from Charlie Brown pointing out that the announcement ad run at the beginning of the day, headlined "Count Us In," appeared to have been lifted wholesale from an ad being run in Connecticut by Southern New England Telephone, one of the company's former holdings. To top it all off, the next day's media coverage was underwhelming. "The title bout has been postponed," read the lede in the *New York Times* story. "The challenger isn't ready yet. The computer industry has been bracing for a battle of the titans between newcomer AT&T and IBM.

---

[53] In a hasty reaction to Pepsi's blind taste test challenge that showed a preference for Pepsi over Coke, The Coca-Cola Company changed its 99-year-old formula, and staged an elaborate introduction for what it called New Coke. The new formula enraged loyal customers and sales of New Coke foundered. After three months the company relaunched the old formula under the name Coca-Cola Classic, eventually dropping the Classic name to just Coke.

But AT&T, which announced its entry . . . yesterday, showed itself to be merely an interesting challenger that still needs seasoning."[54]

That stung, but Marilyn was determined not to depend on the judgment of others for her next big challenge—layoffs. The only part of AT&T that was making money was AT&T Communications, the long distance service. The rest of the company was losing billions, largely because its businesses selling telephones and business communications equipment had been loaded with redundant staff as they moved from the divested telephone companies. Hal Burlingame, who handled public relations for AT&T Information Systems from the day it was organized, put it this way: "When we broke up the Bell System and the equipment business came over to AT&T, all the people the Bell companies could pile on the truck came with it. About 120,000 people came with the equipment business, which was a very small revenue line."

Olson was determined to size the workforce to the level of revenue the business could reasonably produce, which meant eliminating unnecessary jobs. Western Electric was used to managing layoffs. Manufacturing is seldom uniform. It is in the nature of the business to let people go when demand falls and rehire them when it returns. But it was always done quietly, factory by factory, without summing it all up for the national media.

But when Marilyn learned the first layoff would be for 13,000 positions, she was convinced the traditional way of handling it wouldn't fly. "We were under the most intense public scrutiny," she said. "And my position was that this was not something that could be handled in a way that was going to be subtle and escape being noticed." The rest of the leadership team thought there ought to be

---

[54] Andrew Pollack, "AT&T offers its computers," Section D, *New York Times*, Mar. 28, 1984, p. 1.

a way to dribble the news out and avoid drawing attention. It was a massive internal battle that Marilyn ultimately won. But it was one she would refight for the balance of her career whenever there was a major layoff, with one exception as we will see. Her colleagues on the executive team would argue that their competitors didn't announce how many people they were laying off and Marilyn would counter that AT&T was held to a different standard (without mentioning that she invented the standard).

It would not be the last time Marilyn argued for more transparency than her business colleagues felt necessary or raised issues they preferred to ignore. During the long distance price wars of the 1990s, the Consumer Services leadership questioned why they had to issue a news release every time they raised prices on long distance calls. After all, their competitors never did. Marilyn held her ground, but she did allow them to test whether expressing the increase as a percent or in pennies per minute would look like less.

And as early as 1992, Marilyn drew the management executive committee's attention to the need to re-examine the company's privacy policy, setting standards for what customer data the various AT&T businesses were collecting, how they were using it, how they were protecting it, and what options customers had regarding its collection and use. Her hope, expressed in a memo to the company's general counsel, was "to position AT&T as a company that meets its customers' expectations to protect their privacy rights." Like the questions about transparency regarding layoffs and price increases, the debate about privacy would long survive her tenure and that of her successors.

In that early round debate, the company announced the elimination not of 13,000 positions, but 24,000. And the reaction was pretty much what she expected. "We were swamped by all these huge negative currents surrounding the company and anger about what had been lost," she later remembered. "AT&T had been such a symbol of what was good about American business that the country went through the stages of loss, anger, denial, and so forth. And there was precious little we could do from a public relations point of view to either shape or get ahead of the tidal waves of emotion that surrounded the company in 1984." She could only take comfort from the knowledge that dribbling the news out would have eventually resulted in an even higher tidal wave of emotion because the company would have looked duplicitous. Two more waves of job eliminations would follow, reducing the company's ranks by 80,000 positions or 20 percent of what it was at divestiture.

CHAPTER SEVEN

CORPORATE POLITICS

Over the Christmas holidays at the end of 1985, Charlie Brown went to Florida, pen in hand and determined to reshuffle the top deck of the company in preparation for his retirement the following year. Olson retained the chairmanship of AT&T Technologies but added the title of president and chief operating officer of the whole company. The vice chairmen leading AT&T Communications and AT&T Information Systems moved to administrative positions in corporate headquarters, to be replaced by two younger executives.

The executive tagged to lead AT&T Communications was Randy Tobias, who had been a protégé of Olson's since their days together at Indiana Bell. One of the first things Tobias did after his new job was announced was to ask Marilyn to handle his group's public relations. He had never worked with her before, but he liked the idea that, as he put it, "She wasn't born in a manhole." At that time, "most of AT&T's top executives had joined the company in the 1960s and still had the functional mindset that matched the old Bell System structure," he explained. "Marilyn was a superb PR professional, but that didn't define her. She wasn't in any box and didn't come from a position she felt she had to protect."

Tobias also remembered something Brown's speechwriter Al von Auw had told him. "I don't write speeches," von Auw said. "I articulate policy. When the chairman gives a speech, he's really announcing policy." Tobias wanted someone who could help him shape and articulate policy. And from what he had seen of Marilyn in senior leadership meetings, she knew the business well and thought creatively with no Bell System baggage.

Since AT&T Communications was the only part of the company making money, it didn't take Marilyn long to accept. "That's when I really learned how the other side lived," she later said. "I was amazed." While AT&T Communications had lots of competition for its long distance service, it still had an overwhelming share of market. It was losing some customers and had to lower prices every year or so, but in those early days, it was at a predictable, steady rate.

Perhaps for that reason, Marilyn initially described 1985 as "more routine for me than almost any other period." She termed it "a pretty straightforward time of building." It also helped that Tobias operated at a conceptual level that appealed to Marilyn. Tobias says he still remembers "many door-closed, feet-on-the-desk" discussions with her about the company's structure. "Charlie [Brown] worked hard to preserve the assets that were historically important to AT&T," he says. "But as we got further from divestiture, it became apparent that assumption was flawed. Having Western Electric under the same roof as Communications while it designed and manufactured equipment for the Bell companies was problematic." Given her time in Bell Labs and AT&T Technologies, Tobias says Marilyn recognized the problem early on. "She was very insightful about the issue, without personalizing it," he says.

But Marilyn's work life wasn't all "blue-skies." When she moved to the communications sector, she inherited a bedeviling conflict. Prior to her arrival, public relations for communications services had reported to the senior vice president of external affairs, who was a lawyer primarily concerned with state regulatory and legislative matters. She and he shared the same client—Randy Tobias, the CEO of AT&T Communications—and they reported to the same executive vice president back at AT&T headquarters. But they each had separate field organizations reporting to them in the same major cities, from Boston to Los Angeles. She could have lived with that if the two field organizations' activities had not only overlapped but were often in conflict.

In January 1986, she wrote a memo to the senior vice president of external affairs, suggesting a joint task force to resolve the duplication and to construct a better working model. He asked two subordinates to consider her request. They had several concerns and drafted a reply for his signature, suggesting that "since AT&T Communications is the entity most impacted by the opinions of external stakeholders . . . , corporate management is not appropriate." Furthermore, they said it was unnecessary since they already had national and regional groups to oversee coordination. And finally, they pointed out a high-level committee had already been working on the issue, meeting every other week for a year.

She could have replied that the third point refuted the first two. She could have sent back a copy of the organizational notice announcing her appointment as vice president of public relations for AT&T Communications, not "corporate." Instead, she charged one of her highest-energy people to "review and assess the current relationship between public relations and external affairs," including between her own headquarters and field people.

After interviewing everybody involved, he discovered that some external affairs people were happy with the PR support they were receiving, and some were unhappy, none more so than the external affairs officers at headquarters. He also saw that because the regulatory burden on AT&T had lifted a bit in some places, external affairs people were looking for something to do and settling on initiatives that had traditionally been handled by public relations. Meanwhile, some field PR people had so many new clients in the regional business groups that they had less time for regulatory affairs.

In response, Marilyn charged the regional PR teams to treat the local regulatory people as "clients" and to work with them to develop joint plans that clarified their respective roles. She also created a new PR "regulatory team" charged with providing public relations support to the headquarters' external affairs department. She even volunteered to occasionally attend the senior vice president's bimonthly meetings. In just five months, she essentially did what the external affairs officers suggested had already been studied for more than a year. But she didn't rub it in. Her memo to the senior vice president of external affairs described all this, attached a summary of the interviews her team conducted, and ended with, "Can we get together to discuss?"

They did. And within days, they had co-signed a letter to their respective officers and field organizations, attaching the report Marilyn's people had written asking the external affairs and public relations people in each city to arrange meetings "to discuss and resolve these matters" as those in headquarters were doing. "Candid and open discussion is a critical first step to resolving issues that might prevent us from achieving our common goals," they wrote.

That didn't settle all the problems between the two organizations—many probably persist, even to this day—but it brought them out into the open where they could be addressed if they didn't fade away on their own in the disinfectant of bright sunlight.

But that organizational problem was no sooner resolved than an even bigger one raised its troublesome head. When Olson was made chairman and CEO of AT&T in May 1986, he tried to create a structure that would integrate all the units' strategies. AT&T Technologies would continue to sell equipment to telephone companies and electronic components to other manufacturers. But all the other AT&T organizations, which served households and businesses, would report to a single executive. It was something Olson had been aching to do since 1983 but couldn't because of government regulations that had only recently been changed. He promoted Bob Allen, the head of AT&T Information Systems to president of the entire company. The businesses Allen had led, now whipped into a more realistic cost structure, would report to Tobias, who adopted the business card-choking title of Vice Chair of AT&T, CEO of AT&T Communications, and CEO of AT&T Information Systems. Internally, he wanted to be known as CEO of AT&T's End-User Organization.

The rationale for this move was to force the sales teams selling business services and systems to work together, instead of arguing about who "owned" the customer relationship. As a consequence, Marilyn found herself working side-by-side with Hal Burlingame, the long-time vice president of public relations for Information Systems.

Burlingame was an amiable Midwesterner who had grown up on a dairy farm and still got up with the cows, even though the nearest one to his home in Chatham, New Jersey, was at least 50 miles away. Despite his small-town roots, he was socially progressive. At Ohio Bell, he had hired six female college graduates to be trained as managers, one of the first management development programs for women in the whole Bell System.

He had risen through the ranks in different phone company and AT&T management jobs, ending up as a vice president of public relations. He handled PR for Arch McGill and survived, which proved his political skills almost as much as his public relations savvy. He had helped plan the 1984 telephone company divestiture alongside Ed Block, drafting it all out on a large easel pad he still had in his office. He played a similar role in planning the announcement of Jim Olson's selection as chairman and CEO, an event of perhaps less importance to the general public but doubtless of at least equal interest to Olson.

Burlingame and Marilyn had never worked together before, but he had already felt the sharpness of her elbows. When AT&T formed a joint venture with Olivetti to sell their personal computers in the U.S., Ed Block arranged for a full briefing on their vaunted industrial design at Olivetti's offices in Milan and invited Burlingame to accompany him. When Marilyn heard about the trip, she wormed her way onto the plane, claiming she was in a better position to represent "the sector" and Bell Labs' interests in industrial design. Not wanting too many rangers at a fire, Block gently disinvited Burlingame.

As much as that stung, Burlingame determined to make their shotgun marriage work. To start, he and Marilyn developed and issued a joint public relations plan for 1986. "Our specific emphasis is to bring coherence and focus to the messages we deliver to the end-user marketplace," they vowed. At the top of their list of objectives for customers was "to clarify how to do business with us and reduce confusion." And their goal for employees was "to help build a common culture . . . dedicated to satisfying customers as one business." Unfortunately, those were, at best, aspirational goals. The actual sales organizations for Communications Services and Information Systems knew very little about each other's product line. And in many cases the decision makers on the purchasing end of their sales calls were different.

Meanwhile, the last two executives with primary offices in the company's New York City headquarters building on Madison Avenue—perhaps tired of rattling around the empty hallways on the 35th floor executive warren—decided it was time to retire. Ed Block, who led the company's public relations organization, had set Hal Burlingame up as his successor by putting him in charge of planning the announcement surrounding Jim Olson's ascension to the company's chairmanship. For weeks, Burlingame rode home in Block's limo for a rolling seminar in public relations counseling at the highest level. Shortly after Olson was named CEO, Block announced his retirement and Burlingame was appointed senior vice president of public relations in September 1986.

Wes Clarke, the company's powerful human resources chief, decided to move on in early 1987. All his obvious successors had left with the spun-off telephone companies, but Olson had been so impressed with Marilyn's thoughts on changing the company culture he decided to promote her to the human resources job. However, the company's chief financial officer, who personally liked and respected both Marilyn and Burlingame, suggested some senior officers might not be comfortable with a woman recommending their salaries.

So Hal Burlingame, who had been in the top PR job for only five months, moved to human resources. And Marilyn became the senior vice president of public relations, the highest-ranking woman in the company's 100-year history, a member of the company's highest policy-making committee, chair of the AT&T Foundation, and steward of a $120 million corporate advertising and PR budget.

Marilyn didn't know about her circuitous route to the top job in PR until long after she retired. She and her husband Bob were having dinner with some other retired AT&T executives and their wives, including the senior executive who had told Olson she would be more suited for public relations than human resources. He told her the story without a scintilla of embarrassment.

To this day, he's rather proud of the role he had played in her career. But in that moment, it dawned on Marilyn—her entire AT&T career had been bookended by systemic sexism. Indeed, as she later told an interviewer, "I was told later about various and sundry things that affected me because I was female, but I didn't get it. I was just an AT&T person. I didn't even think of myself as a PR person. I thought of myself as an AT&T person—with ideas that really could make a difference there."[55]

As far as Marilyn was concerned, if you could compete on ideas, the playing field was level. Still she realized that corporate politics was a contact sport and she was not averse to throwing an elbow or two when necessary, as she had when she nudged Burlingame off the trip to meet Olivetti's design team. And when Burlingame succeeded Block as senior vice president of public relations, she didn't hide her disappointment. In fact, she complained about it loudly enough in a tony Morristown, New Jersey, restaurant near the company's headquarters that she was overheard by several other AT&T PR people, one of whom warned Burlingame to "watch his back."

If all of that was a bit "unladylike," it didn't bother her. In fact, in a kind of perverse logic she claimed being a woman gave her an edge. She thought she was always able to speak her mind without fear and with less repercussion because, as a woman, she was less threatening. No one thought she was competing for the top line job.

So even though she was not in the HR job, she was able to get away with drawing Allen and Tobias's attention to "some interesting—and revealing—characteristics of the AT&T officer group." It's "overwhelmingly white male," she noted. Out of 132 officers, only five were white females, only three were black males, and only one was a Hispanic male. More than half were between 45 and 55 years old. And they had been with the company for an average of 25 years. She summed up what it all meant:

> At the risk of arm-chair psychologizing, the
> profile is not one that suggests making
> fundamental changes in behavior will be an easy
> task. It reflects a veteran, inbred group,

---

[55] Arthur W. Page Center oral history.

```
steeped in tradition. On the other hand, we have
ample evidence of discontent with the status quo
-- so they may be ripe for change (if not in
themselves, in others).
```

Then in the early 1990s, she was in an executive committee meeting to select new officers from a dozen or so candidates, male and female. When the meeting was over, she realized all the women candidates had been eliminated for one reason or another. "It was one of the few times I actually spoke up on the subject," she said. "I remember saying, 'Are we sure we're using the same standard here? Seems to me, it's much easier to give the men the benefit of the doubt when they are missing something. Whereas that didn't happen with the women'."

Marilyn said it didn't change any decisions in that meeting. But it did trigger a long discussion about women in the pipeline, and a commitment that more women would be selected in the next round. And indeed, that happened the very next year when a woman was named president of the business equipment unit. As the 1990s moved on, women assumed more senior leadership roles, including as president of its largest and most profitable business and, ultimately, as president of the whole company.

CHAPTER EIGHT

CORPORATE POETRY

For the balance of her career as one of AT&T's most senior executives, Marilyn was like Don Quixote, roaming the landscape of the company's empire, occasionally tilting at windmills, sometimes fighting off flesh and blood enemies, often averting crises, more often trying to dig out of crises unaverted, but always in search of the holy grail of a compelling mission that could tie the company's employees together with a sense of common purpose.

She had better modes of travel than the original Don Quixote. Where he had his trusty steed Rocinante, she had full use of chauffeur-driven limousines, a G5 jet, and a corporate helicopter. She also had the company of a succession of Sancho Panzas, some long-time employees who were unquestionably loyal, some who were perennially frustrated by her steady stream of ideas and meetings to flesh them out, and at least one outside hire who did his best to replace her and, failing that, to displace her.

Her first attempt to articulate the company's mission had been more of an aspiration than anything based on reality. She proposed presenting AT&T as "the most helpful company." It would provide the most helpful service and offer products and services that are easy to use. Kind of a combination of Nordstrom and Apple. Unfortunately, that had not been true of AT&T since operators were replaced by rotary dials. She had a brief round of meetings to sell the idea as at least a worthy aspiration. But then the company's chief counsel copied her on a memo he had sent to the chairman, complaining that every AT&T product in his home—from the multiline phone he had never learned to use to the alarm system that went off at odd hours—was not working, and he couldn't find anyone who could fix them.

"Helpful" and "easy" showed up in an occasional executive speech, but she decided redefining AT&T's mission—its purpose for being, its meaning—would be a heavier lift than she anticipated.

To paraphrase New York Governor Mario Cuomo, she knew the company did its day-to-day work in prose, but its higher purpose had to be expressed in something approaching poetry. The company's original mission was a mere two words—Universal Service—but it was the engine that drove the company for more than a century. Every employee knew their goal was to put a telephone within an arm's reach of everyone in the country. It drove personnel policies, capital spending, R&D, everything the company did.

AT&T divested the local telephone companies so it could move into other businesses at the intersection of communications and computing. But some of those businesses had not been defined in 1986 and, if they had, the company had taken only preliminary steps into them because it didn't have an overall plan to tie it all together. How do you write a mission for a company in that situation?

Many were willing to try. In 1984, the Network Systems business within AT&T Technologies had been hot for something it called Universal Information Services that would turn the plain old telephone network into a multimedia service carrying voice, video, and data on an "open" network with common standards to encourage third parties to develop end user applications. It sounded like the evolution of universal services into what we now know as the internet. Network Systems' plan was to sell equipment for the networks underlying these advanced services to all comers.

AT&T Information Systems—its sister end user equipment business on the other side of a regulatory divide created by the Federal Communications Commission—had a similar idea that would run on proprietary networks and devices. In a striking coincidence, both groups advertised their future service using an image of a tree branch bearing an apple, an orange, and a banana, standing for voice, video, and data from a single network.

However, in 1984, the tree to which that branch was attached wasn't rooted in anything. Both groups were years ahead of themselves. Not even Bell Labs knew how to actually do what they were advertising.

Jim Olson was tired of the internal bickering and impatient to implement what he called his "Single Enterprise Strategy." When he became captain of the whole ship in 1986, he wanted everyone rowing in the same direction. It frustrated him to no end that most of his top lieutenants seemed to have their bows heading towards different shores. So when he caught Marilyn in a hallway, moving from one meeting to another, he stopped her in her tracks.

"Look at this," he said, taking a three-by-five laminated card out of his shirt pocket. When she took it, she didn't know if he was giving her a photo of his grandkids or a recipe he liked. It had the Ford Motor Company's mission on one side and its values on the other. It read: "People working together as a lean, global enterprise to make people's lives better through automotive and mobility leadership."

"We need something like this," he said.

Marilyn suspected Olson got the card from Richard Pascale, a consultant he liked to keep around, but no matter, she was on board. Before she had a chance to say so, however, Olson—as usual—trotted off to another meeting or phone call.

Bob Allen, who was now president and chief operating officer of the company, got wind of Jim's request and sent Marilyn a brief, handwritten note:

```
11-07-87

Marilyn --

I realize the chairman asked you to write a
credo, or mission statement, or whatever,
but . . . I don't believe that's the way we
should arrive at one. If we just modify a
"strawman," it has no value. I will say so if
Jim gets ahead of the cart. But you have an
obligation to tell him how you feel it should be
developed.

-- Bob
```

Allen was cut from the same Midwestern cloth as Charlie Brown and shared many of the same values of modesty and composure. An only child, he was soft-spoken and a little stiff except on the golf course, where he truly relaxed. The game suited his personality—he was quiet, focused, and deliberate. He could spend long hours in his office, rolling an unlit cigar around in his mouth, just thinking.

So Marilyn knew that if Allen would take the time to send her a handwritten note, it wasn't the product of an impulsive man. He thought it was important. So she crafted a follow-up memo to Olson.

```
November 20, 1987
Mr. J. E. Olson

Jim --

I've been on the road for so many days in the
last two weeks, I haven't been able to catch up
with you since our brief hallway conversation
about Ford's mission and values statement and
its relevance to AT&T.

First, yes, we do need such a set of statements
for AT&T. The issue, of course, is not the words
used to express the corporate mission and value
```

system, it's the process by which the leadership arrives at agreement on what those values and statement of purpose should be.

You are surely aware that opinion among AT&T's senior management is coalescing around a reasonably common understanding of our mission. However, and this is a big However, there is frequent disagreement or great ambiguity about what commonly used terms mean when it comes time to "do business."

That leads me to suggest [that we] <u>launch a process by which senior management comes to a common understanding and agreement on our mission, values, and strategy.</u> The senior officer group needs to be of one mind. To get there requires enough time for an open discussion in an environment of trust to allow disagreements to surface and to consider how proposed values translate into practical action. We need to wring some of the ambiguity and vagueness out of the philosophy and goals of the corporation.

By the time we talk to employees, they must see their supervision and leadership acting out the words.

Interestingly, while Marilyn's memo was cast as a "suggestion," it noted that "I am already deeply involved in a project . . . to reshape our identity to all AT&T stakeholders."

"Articulating what we stand for," Marilyn told Olson, "falls in my bailiwick." And while one might think articulating the mission would follow defining it, she suggested they are really the same task and "the public relations department's *top* priority." She pointed out that she had already "done some work over the last several months in the areas of corporate values, AT&T attributes, potential differentiating characteristics, even a few shots at a mission statement," which she would be happy to share as "work in progress."

Meanwhile, she told Olson that she had already asked Alex Kroll, the CEO of the Y&R advertising agency, to help her distill the "essence" of the company's mission from the competing views of its senior leadership. It would not be an easy task.

"Although we've written many speeches and articles," she wrote, "we have not yet captured the benefits of the convergence of computing and communicating in a way that is understandable to our employees and compelling to our customers." That's a problem, she wrote, because computer companies like IBM, who are already identified with the "future" can more easily assimilate the past (i.e., voice communications) than AT&T can assimilate the "future" into its identity.

It had also become obvious to Marilyn that the company's leaders glibly used different words to say the same thing and the same words to say different things. Furthermore, she pointed out that AT&T was competing with itself for people's share of mind. While most of AT&T's talk of the future was in terms of big business customers, most of its communications spending was on consumer long distance service. As a result, regulators thought of the company as primarily a consumer company that deserved close watching, not as an engine of national competitiveness that should be unleashed.

Finally, she cautioned that AT&T had to differentiate itself from all the other companies chasing the same dream. Marilyn and Olson had spent a week together in Geneva, Switzerland, walking the halls of Telecom '87, the giant trade show and exhibit put on by the International Telecommunications Union every four years. They were both struck by the sameness of all the exhibits, whether from

Siemens, Alcatel, Northern Telecom, IBM, NEC, or even the Regional Bell Operating Companies which then went by names like NYNEX, Ameritech, and SBC.[56]

Marilyn was confident Kroll had just the right qualifications to be her partner. At six-feet-two inches, he had the kind of commanding presence you would expect in a former professional football player. But he was also highly creative and of sufficient business stature to deal with AT&T senior executives as a peer. At Y&R, he rose from cub copywriter to agency creative director in five years. He had only been CEO since 1985, but he had led the team that won a big share of the AT&T advertising account five years earlier. He knew the company but still had sufficient distance to inspect it with fresh eyes. It would take confidence and fresh eyes to cut through the semantic fog surrounding the whole topic of the company's mission.

The CEOs of ad agencies the size of Y&R don't normally take on side work, even for large clients. But not many clients are the size of AT&T and the project Marilyn laid before him was intriguing. "While many thousands of words have been used to describe AT&T," Kroll wrote, "none quite defined the 'whole' through the clear lens of a single idea." Finding that idea was a delicious challenge.

Kroll had already commissioned desk research into each business's market. He and Marilyn had conducted individual interviews of the leaders of the company's major businesses and functions. "We're asking how the different parts of our business

---

[56] Many of these equipment companies ultimately failed. Lucent Technologies, the successor company to Western Electric, merged with Alcatel in 2006 and the resulting company was subsequently bought by Nokia's network division in 2016. Northern Telecom filed for bankruptcy in 2009. The Regional Bell Operating Companies began merging in the late 1990s. NYNEX merged with Bell Atlantic to become Verizon and SBC bought Ameritech and other former Bell telephone companies. In 2005, it bought the AT&T Corporation and re-branded itself AT&T, Inc.

interrelate; why customers buy from us; what our strengths and weaknesses are; and what benefits networking delivers," she told Olson. "We're trying to see what 'promises' are real today; which will be real in two to five years; and where we're going in the long run." Now they were ready to review their work with a group of even more senior AT&T executives. "Our goal," she wrote, "is to avoid the worst mistake of the last three years—overpromising."

Marilyn was confident enough about the project's progress to end her memo to Olson with a relatively upbeat prediction. "Between 1984 and 1987, I believe all of our publics were at some level unwilling to believe new things about AT&T because they were still wishing we would be the old AT&T and deliver to them on the old promises," she wrote. "Recently the wind changed. Financial analysts have a more positive updated view. So do regulators. Perceptions are improving among customers, in the media, even among employees. Next year is a year of opportunity for shaping our identity, a kind of PR market window. We must take advantage of it."

Sadly, in less than five months, Jim Olson would be dead.

CHAPTER NINE

THE END OF THE BEGINNING

In early spring of 1988, Jim Olson took a two-week vacation, ending with a few rounds of golf at the Augusta National Golf Club in Georgia. On the way home, he had gastrointestinal problems and spent most of the flight in the corporate jet's bathroom. When he returned to the office on Monday, March 21, he had breakfast with Bob Allen to get caught up on what had happened while he was gone. "I asked him how he enjoyed his vacation," recalled Allen. "He said it was fine, but his stomach was bothering him."[57] After breakfast, Olson went home and called his doctor.

Olson didn't know it yet, but he had stage IV colon cancer. He underwent surgery on Friday, March 25. Over the weekend, Marilyn huddled with Bob Allen, the company's general counsel John Zeglis, and Hal Burlingame, head of human resources. All four were close to Olson and very concerned about him. Unknown to Marilyn, Zeglis and Allen had been in touch with Olson's wife Jeanne, who wanted as little said about her husband's condition as possible. Caught between Marilyn's insistence on transparency and Jeanne Olson's insistence on privacy, Zeglis looked into the relevant regulations of the Securities Exchange Commission and concluded there was no requirement to disclose Olson's illness yet. They all agreed to make his privacy the primary consideration in communication decisions.

The people who reported to them felt differently. Olson's illness had already forced the cancellation of an employee telecast. Senior management people were gossiping about Olson's absence, which at

---

[57] This and later quotes attributed to Bob Allen are from his oral history in the AT&T Archives and History Center, Warren, NJ.

this point had lasted almost a month. And the company's annual shareholder meeting was just a few weeks away.

Marilyn decided it would be better to get ahead of wild speculation and convinced Allen and Zeglis to notify the company's top 400 managers of Olson's condition. With Zeglis walking Marilyn back from any suggestion that Olson would soon return to the office, on Tuesday, March 29, she sent top managers this notice:

> AT&T Chairman Jim Olson underwent surgery this past weekend, following tests taken to diagnose persistent symptoms originally associated with the flu.
>
> He is recovering well from the surgery, which removed a tumor from his colon. Jim is already up and around and will probably leave the hospital by the end of this week for further recuperation at home. It's too early to tell how soon he will return to work.
>
> President Bob Allen is in charge, as is usual during the absence of the chairman.
>
> As you know, we consider information about any employee's health to be a personal matter. We are providing this information not to suggest that you initiate discussions, but so you can respond to questions from your people. Any media inquiries should be referred to media relations.
>
> -- Marilyn Laurie

Olson was released from the hospital on Friday, April 1, and the *Report On AT&T* newsletter reported that he was "recuperating at home from minor surgery." When that stimulated calls from the media, the company initially declined to reveal the nature of the surgery or the illness, following the lawyers' advice that they had no obligation to do so until it was clear it would be a "long-term incapacity." And no one was prepared to conclude that yet.

But Marilyn told her media relations people to say "yes" if someone directly asked whether Olson had undergone colon surgery. By Monday, April 7, Reuters asked the right question. The next day, a *Wall Street Journal* story said Olson was recuperating from surgery for colon cancer, and the company had only revealed it because it had been bombarded by reporters' questions. The *New York Times* story added that Bob Allen was Olson's likely successor, quoting a financial analyst saying, "He's been groomed to be the chairman."[58]

Very early on the morning of Monday, April 18, Olson's wife called Bob Allen and told him Jim had not made it through the night. He was 62.

"We knew Jim's illness was serious," Allen remembered, "But I don't think any of us contemplated Jim would die. I didn't want to believe that." The company's annual meeting was scheduled for Wednesday of that week so Allen had been preparing to run it in case Olson couldn't travel to the meeting site in Denver, Colorado. "But I never contemplated he would go so fast," Allen said. "And [running the meeting] on the heels of his death was quite a shock."

The board convened on Tuesday night to elect Allen chairman. He had been in every board meeting since mid-1983, so he knew the directors well. And he knew how Brown and Olson ran the meetings. "So, I was probably more prepared for that than one might have thought," he said. "But the job itself, the responsibilities of it, I think it took me some while to really understand that, think through it, observe others, and really understand what a CEO did, or should do."

---

[58] Calvin Sims, "AT&T Chief Steps Aside Temporarily," Section D, *New York Times*, Apr. 12, 1988, p. 4.

Marilyn had also been giving a lot of thought to the transition. She thought the company had found the right balance between the Olson family's right to privacy and the shareholders' right to know what was going on. She had sent employees a note about Olson's passing, this time over Allen's signature. It balanced sadness and shock with a promise of continuity. "I know you were as shocked as I am at the suddenness of Jim's illness and death. We will miss him," it read. "Our legacy to him will be the vigor with which we carry out the strategic course he laid out for us."

But Marilyn's immediate problem was working through her personal loss while simultaneously staging an annual meeting in less than two days. "We felt it was absolutely critical to demonstrate the stability of the AT&T company," she remembered. "Not to cancel the annual meeting, but to carry through so this massive investor base would know that this company was okay, and that it was going to be a smooth transition."

Indeed, in the end, the stock went down slightly when Olson's illness and death were announced but more than recovered after the annual meeting.[59]

Marilyn had not been involved in planning Olson's "coming-out party" when he became Chairman and CEO; that had been Burlingame's job in the months leading to his brief tenure as senior vice president of public relations. So, in a sense, Allen's coming-out party was hers too. And she didn't have months to plan it.

Olson and Allen could not have been more different, not only in physical stature, but also in style. Olson was very outgoing and would think out loud, welcoming challenge. He worked along with his staff as he was developing his thoughts. There was seldom a question about

---

[59] Adjusted for splits, AT&T's stock price dropped from $8.75 on April 4, before news of Olson's illness was widely known, to $8.72 on April 20, the day of the annual meeting. It ended the month at $8.81 on April 29.

what was on his mind. Allen was introverted and kept his own counsel. You didn't know what he was thinking or planning until he'd thought it through on his own. By the time he was ready to share it, it had been so far developed that it wasn't subject to much change.

As was her custom, Marilyn gathered her senior public relations people together and thrashed through different strategies. "We spent some time talking about whether—again, in the interest of stability—we should bring Bob right out and show how strong he is," she later remembered. "And we decided to take the opposite tack, which was to take advantage of the fact that he was known to be a serious, thoughtful, reflective kind of guy with a very stable history—operating company president, CFO, president, and all that stuff." So, they did not bring him in front of the media for six months.

As quiet and reflective as Allen was, it was difficult keeping him behind the scenes for that long. AT&T was still such a major player in the economy that most of the major print media, such as the *Wall Street Journal*, the *New York Times*, *Businessweek*, and *Fortune*, had reporters assigned to follow the company as their "beat." There were even two or three newsletters, like *Report On AT&T*, that were built around news, gossip, and rumors about the company. All those reporters were clamoring to interview the CEO.

Initially, Marilyn didn't have the same warm relationship with Allen that she had enjoyed with Olson. When she met with him in those early days, she felt he was tense and impatient. It bothered her so much that she asked Reynold Levy, who seemed to have an easy-going relationship with Allen, to accompany her to one her meetings with him. By the end of the meeting, Levy saw what she was talking about and thought he also saw the solution.

When they were back in her office, he gave her his diagnosis. "Marilyn, when you ask him a question, if he doesn't answer right away, you fill the silence by re-asking it in different words. But he doesn't respond like a New Yorker. He's thinking. Don't step into his space. Let him think." It was good advice. She followed it, and her meetings with Allen became less strained for both of them. He still didn't like to be "handled," was suspicious of the media, and didn't trust politicians. But he valued candor, and that was Marilyn's specialty. She majored in it.

In these early days, however, what he needed most was time to think. Olson had done a lot to move the company from dead in the water at divestiture to something approaching slow steaming. But Allen concluded that Olson's efforts to integrate the company's multifarious piece parts into a single enterprise made the company's problems appear to be so big they were insoluble—whether they were antiquated billing systems, market overlap, or even scheduling a meeting. Besides, even if that level of integration could be achieved, it was too internally focused. Allen thought the better approach was to build smaller, more manageable business units within AT&T and to give them extensive responsibility for virtually every aspect of their operations. He would turn AT&T from a giant steamship into a fleet of agile speedboats, each with its own captain.

He planned to announce this change in course to the company's top 400 managers when they met in early November 1988. But he didn't want them to see the new approach as just another reshuffling of the organization chart. Most importantly, to gain speed, he wanted them to change their operating style from one of command and control to one that gave employees more latitude in the way they did their jobs. He wanted them to think in terms of *supporting* their people, rather than directing and supervising them.

He asked Marilyn for help in driving that message home at the conference, and she assigned Reynold Levy to draw on his experience at the 92nd Street Y to plan it. He didn't disappoint. The agenda started with Bob Allen and his immediate reports serving dinner to the assembled officers in a real-time demonstration of the new operating style, and it moved on to candid, small group discussions about the implications and challenges of doing business in a decentralized structure.

When Allen rose to speak at the very end, his remarks were brief and pointed—AT&T, meaning the people in the room, had to change direction. "Business units of manageable size will become the building blocks of AT&T's success, with the rest of the company as a support structure," he said. "Integrated offers will continue to be important, but each product or service must stand successfully on its own, based on quality and customer satisfaction. Though each business unit will have its own style, shaped by the industry it is in, all must operate with a spirit of cooperation and within a framework of AT&T values."

To Levy's surprise, Allen finished by thanking him by name for organizing the meeting, which he interpreted as an example of the very support the meeting was about. As the room cleared, Levy went up to the podium to gather any papers left behind, and he saw Allen's speech. At the bottom of the last page, in Marilyn's flowing cursive, was written, "Don't forget to thank Reynold."

For her part, Marilyn ensured that Allen's remarks were sent to all employees as "A New Direction for AT&T" later that month. Perhaps reflecting the wisdom of hindsight when she recorded her oral history just before retiring, Marilyn said, "Large enterprises ebb and flow from centralization to decentralization. It was our turn to go in the opposite direction from where we had been." There may have been an element of pendulum-swinging in Allen's new initiative, but even Marilyn had to admit, "It did unleash an enormous amount of energy . . . with people saying, 'at last I can go off and get something done.' It was definitely the right thing to do in 1988." Giving each business a balance sheet and an income statement clarified accountability for serving customers and enabled the company to identify real costs and obsolete assets, as well as to compare its businesses with others in the marketplace.

Marilyn had her own organizational issues to resolve. She had already assigned public relations people to each business, but going forward, each unit would be able to control the cost of their PR support by contracting for it on an annual and ad hoc basis. A smaller public relations staff at corporate headquarters would provide company-wide services as directed by the chairman. But there would be only one professional public relations community, and she would retain control for its training, salaries, career pathing, promotions, and professional standards. And both the business and corporate groups would be united in pursuing three long-term, overarching goals: to make AT&T worthy of trust, to encourage competition across the telecom industry, and to build stronger public relations capabilities across the enterprise.

So when Allen finally began meeting with selected reporters in November of 1988, he could talk about the "redirection" he had set for the organization to get it closer to customers and to be more competitive. *Fortune*'s resulting story noted that Allen had maintained the momentum started by Olson and grown sales "by creating strategic business units for specific customer groups."[60]

That was just the first fruit of a 24-page, carefully constructed "platform" Marilyn and her people had prepared to present Bob Allen to the world, including "employees, customers, the media, shareowners, the investment community, opinion and government leaders—domestic and international." In format and purpose, the document would have been familiar to anyone who had run a high-

---

[60] "Was Breaking Up AT&T A Good Idea?" Kenneth Labich, *Fortune*, Jan. 2, 1989, http://bit.ly/3biKNUB.

stakes political campaign. There were key messages for every constituency. Talking points for every issue. Surrogates identified to deliver them. A calendar of carefully-considered internal and external events. And a rapid response team to squelch rumors and correct erroneous information. The plan also noted Allen's "strong distaste for hype, banners, and any cult of personality."

But Allen was not the intended audience for the platform. It was guidance for the people in Marilyn's organization who would support the chairman as he moved across the platform they had built, whether they wrote speeches, dealt with the media, handled employee communications, supported marketing, or managed community relations and philanthropy. "You can't be a visionary leader standing on a platform of cost reduction," she said. "People won't hear anything else." But a platform based on restructuring the company to get closer to customers was energizing.

Of course, it was still more "inside baseball" than she would have liked. But articulating the company's purpose, a project begun more than a year earlier at Olson's request, was proving more difficult. Working with some of the company's most senior officers and outside consultants she had crafted a somewhat aspirational draft mission statement that tracked with Ford's:

```
By applying the talents, knowledge, and skills
of our people, AT&T will become the global
leader in enabling customers -- individuals,
businesses, governments, and other institutions
-- to reap the benefits of information
technology.
```

A series of focus groups with employees at different levels had uncovered a few concerns. "Our focus groups are telling us they have trouble understanding it," she told Allen. And "employees' current view of reality is so distant from where the mission statement says we will go, the absence of any actions for getting there appears to be seriously undermining its credibility." Marilyn had discussed this with her counterpart at Ford who told her that it had taken them "between one and two years" before they had sufficient employee buy-in to publish their mission.

She cautioned that she was *not* suggesting a process of that length, and she acknowledged that the senior officers who had worked on this with her were impatient to move forward. "But until we have a clearer, committed agreement to where this business must go and what we must do to get there, we should beware of promoting new banners and potentially empty rhetoric."

In speaking to his own team, Allen would simply say "AT&T's mission is to be the global leader in enabling customers to reap the benefits of information technology." One could assume AT&T's officers would have a pretty good idea what "information technology" he was talking about and what its "customer benefits" were. What he didn't realize, however, was that they would all define it differently and in a way that favored their individual businesses more than the overall company.

When the mission statement was presented to the company's executive policy council, four of the nine members said they weren't comfortable with it. One wrote a long memo suggesting it was more important that each business unit have its *own* mission statement. A "corporate" mission could never be more than directional and would necessarily be too vague to be useful. Besides, AT&T might become "a" leader in bringing all these benefits to customers, but no company would become "the" leader. Marilyn would spend much of the balance of her career at AT&T trying to square that circle.

The articulation of AT&T's shared values went through a similar iterative process, spanning more than two years. Dividing the company into customer-focused business units and supporting divisions generated the expected amount of turmoil as they each tackled the painful task of adjusting costs to market realities. As Allen traveled the world, visiting employees in different units, he began to discern common questions: "What do we stand for? What's the glue that holds us together?"

One evening in October 1990, sitting at his kitchen table in Short Hills, New Jersey, Allen drafted an answer he called "Our Common Bond." He gave copies to Marilyn and to Burlingame. Their reactions were positive, but they worried about the perceived gap between the stated values and the way employees—especially in management—behaved. Marilyn remembered a story a senior executive had once told her. He had attended a dinner meeting at McCaw Cellular where the founder and CEO of the company interrupted an executive's presentation by yelling, "That's bullshit!" and threw a dinner roll at him. The executive promptly threw the roll back and explained why he thought he was right.

"They really got into it," he remembered. "They had the same professed value of respecting each other; except at McCaw, respect meant expressing your disagreement now, not later. They considered it good to work disagreements out, and for others to see them work them out." It demonstrated what radically different definitions people have for the same values. At AT&T, respect for others meant not showing disagreement, unless speaking about it to someone else. It convinced Marilyn that publishing a list of values wouldn't mean much unless it included a process for building a common understanding of what they meant in practical, day-to-day terms. Getting everyone on the same page would be a long difficult process.

She also harbored serious doubts that values can be taught to employees in any meaningful way. "I think you develop your moral compass earlier in life and then you have a variety of experiences that either teach you they're something that will help make you a more successful human being in whatever you're doing, or you don't," she said, looking back. "But you *can* teach employees what actions represent values that the company stands for and what actions are outside those boundaries." Unfortunately, she didn't think there was as much work done on describing those concrete actions as on articulating the high-flown values, which is why she thought most employees were somewhat cynical about them.

"We put the values on the walls, we tattoo them on our shoulder under the butterfly or whatever," she said. "And then employees look around and see how things really work around here. Maybe it's company politics. Maybe it's senior leaders taking their family on the company plane for vacation. All this stuff." She was determined to make the values real for employees, by making very clear to everybody "what the [business] strategy is, what the behaviors that support it are, and what values are represented by those behaviors."[61] Meanwhile, a telephone survey of 400 employees found gaps in behavior on almost every value.

Allen got the point and asked the company's 60 most senior officers to test the values with their employees and send their findings to Marilyn. Meanwhile, she scheduled more focus groups and another wave of telephone surveys, including with AT&T employees in other countries. Employees said two of the values—corporate citizenship and shareholder returns—were givens. If employees follow the other values, those will follow naturally. Using two years of employee and officer input, Marilyn refined the "Common Bond" Allen had written to five values: respect for individuals; dedication to helping customers; highest standards of integrity; innovation; and teamwork.

Allen unveiled "Our Common Bond" during the 1992 annual meeting, televised to employees at all major company locations.

---

[61] Arthur W. Page Center oral history.

Separately, he asked the 60 most senior executives to send him a memo describing how they would incorporate the values into their work. And he asked them to do the same with their direct reports, starting a cascade of discussions and commitments.

Despite applying her energy and talents over a period of better than four years—along with that of key senior officers, advertising gurus, and management consultants—Marilyn never really felt she had broken the code on a corporate mission that would mobilize employees in the service of customers. She was never able to produce a three-by-five-inch laminated card. All she had to show for all that effort was a shelf of binders that went nowhere.

But at least one C-suite colleague credits her with fighting the right battle. John Zeglis rose from general counsel to president of AT&T and ultimately to CEO of AT&T Wireless when it was spun off as a public company. With that experience and the benefit of hindsight, he credits Marilyn with pinpointing AT&T's fatal flaw and doing her best to fix it.

"Marilyn was way ahead of the rest of us in realizing AT&T post-divestiture was doomed to fail because it didn't stand for anything compelling," he said. "She tried to engage us in defining our new mission once we separated from the local Bell telephone companies, but too many of us just didn't get it. We went through the motions, but I wish we had helped more. If we had, we could have avoided a lot of expensive mistakes. When you know your mission, a problem is just a problem. When you don't, it's existential."

And as the final decade of the 20th century gathered momentum, Marilyn would have plenty of existential windmills to tilt against.

CHAPTER TEN

NETWORK DOWN

AT&T's 4,200 square foot Network Operations Center—built into a hillside in Bedminster, New Jersey—is normally as quiet as a college library. A two-story, curving wall of giant video screens display traffic coursing across the company's worldwide network. But the real action happens at three rows of consoles spread across the room in front of the screens where engineers monitor more discrete elements of the network, including the signaling system that finds the most efficient route for each call and data packet, the 114 electronic switches scattered across the country that put calls and data on those routes, and all the cables over which the calls and data flow, zigzagging across the country and under the seas. The lighting is low to make it easier to read the screens. Just about the only sound is the clicking of computer keys and hushed telephone conversations.

On Monday, January 15, 1990, the network was projected to handle 115 million calls, average for a business day back then. But at 2:25 p.m. the engineers in the center began to notice an alarming number of red warning signals from various parts of the network. Within seconds, the wall of video screens was crisscrossed with a tangle of red lines as a rapidly-spreading malfunction leapfrogged from one switching center to another. While his engineers tried to figure out what was going on, the network operations manager on duty grabbed a phone and started a cascade of notifications. The long distance network was down.

One of the people notified was Marilyn Laurie. She had a PR manager assigned to the Network Operations Center. He called and told her what he knew, basically that AT&T customers couldn't make long distance calls. At least, not on AT&T's network. It was so inconceivable that she had trouble understanding what he was saying. "You mean some farmer tried to bury a cow and cut a line somewhere?" she said. "No, it's not a cable cut. They don't know what it is. But the network—the whole network—is down." Then he excused himself to join an operations conference call to see what more he could learn. Marilyn rushed up the circular staircase in the executive offices to make sure Bob Allen knew.

When she got to his office, he was on a conference call with the senior officer responsible for the network and his counterpart at Bell Labs. She would spend the rest of the day shuttling between conference calls with the operations people, salespeople, and her own PR staff. In the process, she scrawled a long column of notes to herself on the pad of lined paper she carried with her everywhere.

```
Get this behind us.

Explain what happened (technical backgrounder).

Make clear problem fixed.

Give customers something.

Don't promise won't happen again.

Steps to minimize likelihood.

REA? News conference at NOC?⁶²

Customer, opinion leader contacts, consumer
leaders?

Employee letter, advertisement.

Strategy for all future communications
(customer seminars, technical papers, media
interviews).
```

---

62 REA is CEO Robert E. Allen; NOC is Network Operations Center.

The first media calls came within 35 minutes of the Network Operations Center's alert. Her public relations people already knew the drill—acknowledge the problem, assume responsibility, volunteer the facts, minimize speculation, and correct inaccurate information. Tell the media what the company is doing to fix the problem and keep them updated as the situation changes. If there's something you don't know, admit it; tell the reporters you'll try to find out; and as soon as you *do* know, fill them in. Don't speculate about anything but try to anticipate what speculation will bubble to the surface so you can correct it quickly. For example, AT&T's media relations people assumed someone would ask if the problem was the work of a hacker. An early call to Bell Labs quickly determined that wasn't the case, and the information was put into a Q&A distributed to AT&T PR people for use if asked. Within minutes, it was asked and answered.

AT&T had a long history of dealing with the media as transparently as humanly possible. Every reporter covering the company had the office, home, and cell phone number of at least one media relations person. And contact information appeared at the top of every news release. AT&T media relations people were expected to be available 24/7. They were forbidden to offer a curt "no comment;" every question was to be answered even if only to say, "As a matter of long-standing policy, we don't comment on rumors of material matters because if we do, we have an obligation to update you if the situation changes." And if a story included "the company did not immediately respond for comment," someone would have to explain why.

These policies dated back to the company's first vice president of public relations, Arthur W. Page, who was the son of one of the founders of Doubleday Page Publishing and, in his own right, editor-in-chief of *The World's Work*, one of the leading magazines covering business and public affairs in the 1920s. Thanks to Page, AT&T's

public relations people had an unusual degree of autonomy in responding to media inquiries. They were close enough to the business to know when they needed to check with the lawyers or engineers, but most of the time, they knew how to respond. Marilyn had structured her organization so public relations people were working shoulder to shoulder with the company's line managers to identify risks—even the "unimaginable" possibility that parts of the phone network would go down. So when the unimaginable happened, line management and PR staff knew what to do.

And Marilyn didn't need to immerse herself in the day-to-day give-and-take of media relations. She could concentrate on the bigger picture, which in this case meant figuring out what to do when the network was restored or if the problem lasted into the next day. But first she had to deal with some company executives who were more worried about their bottom line than their customers. Back then, AT&T handled about 70 percent of all long distance calls. Competitors like MCI and Sprint handled the rest. But if an AT&T customer wanted to use a competitor's network they couldn't just dial "1" before the number they were calling, they had to dial a ten-digit access code. Still, it was better than nothing and some customers were calling AT&T operators for the other companies' codes. Someone in the five-to-six-level hierarchy above the operators didn't want them to cough up the codes. While she was trying to think beyond the immediate crisis, Marilyn found herself in pitched battle with the businesspeople to reverse that decision so AT&T's customers could make calls on its competitors' networks until its own was restored.

Meanwhile, hundreds of engineers were frantically poring through the millions of lines of software code on which the giant switches run. In late evening, they found it—a single line of code in software installed a month earlier made the switches act as if they had reached the limit on the number of calls they could handle. Busy signals cascaded through each of the 114 switches, blocking more than 50 million calls in the nine hours the network was down. It was 10:30 p.m. before the company's network engineers could stabilize the network by shutting off the signaling network that was propagating the error.

Many would have put out a news release and called it a day. But Marilyn argued that more was called for. She had an unusual talent for pulling back and looking at issues from a much broader perspective than those around her. To her, the network outage didn't mean people couldn't make phone calls, it meant they had lost something they thought they could count on. "When people get a wrong number," she reminded everyone, "they assume they dialed wrong, not that the telephone network misdirected their call. That's how reliable they think it is. They assume it will always work. They don't understand the technology, but they assume we do. And we betrayed them. It was a betrayal. And an apology just won't cut it."

That's why she pressed Bob Allen to personally brief the media, rather than delegating it to some unknown engineer who probably had a better understanding of the technical problem. That's why she wanted the briefing at the company's Network Operations Center. All those video screens were impressive and a great photo opportunity, but the real point was the white shirted managers in front of them. There was lots of technology here, but there were people too, and the people were in charge.

And that's why she also pressed for something more—the company had inconvenienced its customers; it should give something back to make its apologies real. She knew it wouldn't change anyone's mind about AT&T all by itself but, combined with everything else, it would show that the company was at least trying to do the right thing. And that was one of her core beliefs—a belief handed down from the company's first PR officer, Arthur W. Page—public relations is 90 percent doing, only ten percent talking about it.

The next day, at 11:00 a.m., Allen held a news conference at the Network Operations Center and explained what he knew about the outage at that point—it was a software error that the company should have caught. Bell Labs was working on a permanent fix. And to underscore how much AT&T valued its relationship with its customers, the company would ask the FCC for approval to declare February 14, Valentine's Day, as an additional day of holiday calling, reducing normal rates by an average of 33 percent. It was a nice gesture, not entirely wasted on the cynical reporters, but they continued to pepper Allen with questions about the outage. His answer to one of those questions—totally unrehearsed—demonstrated what the man was made of. "Mr. Allen," one of the reporters asked, "exactly who was responsible for this?"

Without missing a beat, Allen looked the reporter in the eye. "As far as our customers are concerned," he said, "I'm responsible. And I'm going to make sure it never happens again."

"After that," Marilyn said. "AT&T employees were ready to carry him out of the room on their shoulders." Most customers were also in a forgiving mood. As the publicity died down, the company measured its quality and reliability ratings among customers with some trepidation. They were unchanged, holding firm at their historically high levels. And Marilyn admitted to some sense of pride when the *Wall Street Journal* quoted her on how to handle a crisis: "Tell the truth, tell it fast, take accountability," she said. "And give something back."

The first three precepts were standard PR advice—when you have a problem, get ahead of it by making yourself the most reliable source of information about it. Otherwise, someone else controls the conversation and you're always playing catch-up. But the fourth piece of advice was classic Marilyn. She knew that a company worthy of trust unlike a company that would settle for being *perceived* as trustworthy—would not be satisfied with simply making a heartfelt apology after letting its customers down. It would want to do something that demonstrated the sincerity of its regret.

Unfortunately, it did happen again, although not for the same reason and not on the same scale. On September 17, 1991, anticipating an unseasonably hot day, Con Edison asked AT&T to take one of its switching centers in lower Manhattan off the power grid. All the company's switching centers had redundant power sources, including back-up generators and battery plants in addition to commercial power. To help the electric utility avoid brownouts, AT&T had long-standing agreements with Con Ed to move its switching centers to diesel-generated power on high-usage days. Instead of cutting over to a generator, however, the switching system began to draw power from a last-resort battery system.

Ironically, the switching center power crew, who would normally do a walk-through of the power plant when commercial power was switched off, went straight to an alarm training session when they reported to work that morning. Audible alarms, which should have sounded, had been disconnected when the power plant had been upgraded and never reconnected; a visual alarm bulb had burned out and had not been replaced.

Since the batteries were only designed to last six hours, by 4:40 p.m. they were essentially exhausted and the switching equipment began to shut down, disconnecting communications in and out of lower Manhattan and at the area's three major airports, including between control towers and airplanes. It was 10:30 p.m. before all service was restored. And in accord with Murphy's Law, the Chairman of the Federal Communications Commission was on one of the planes left circling the skies above New York when the control towers lost communications.

The next day, Bob Allen and Marilyn Laurie made an unpublicized visit to the central office and met with employees. The company's government affairs people spent the day fielding calls from senior officials at the Department of Transportation, the Federal Aviation Administration and the Federal Communications Commission. The company's media relations people could tell the media what happened, but *how* and *why* it happened were still a mystery. Somehow, triply redundant systems had failed. AT&T engineers descended on the switching center to figure out why.

Meanwhile, the executive responsible for sales to businesses felt strongly that his customers had been most directly affected. By late afternoon, he had talked his unit's media relations team into holding a conference call with business media so he could reassure his customers by explaining what he was doing. The media had other ideas—they wanted to talk about all the people stranded for hours at airports and on airless, foodless planes. Pressed to explain how triply redundant systems could fail, the executive speculated that the switching center technicians had probably disabled the alarms because they were loud and had a tendency to trip even when there wasn't a real problem.

The reaction was swift. As Marilyn later put it, "We got beaten up by the union and creamed by the press for blaming our employees." By afternoon the next day, in a second media conference call, the executive actually responsible for network operations explained the processes that had failed and exonerated the employees. But the damage had been done.

Follow-on media coverage clarified the facts but repeated the sharp criticism for initially blaming low-level employees. The FCC demanded a written report within 10 days; the chairman of the

House Commerce Committee announced he would hold hearings on the incident; New York City's mayor demanded that major communications companies back each other up in the case of outages; and AT&T ultimately lost the FAA account.

The contrast between the two network outages was striking. Surveys showed that in both cases, after an initial drop in public confidence, AT&T eventually regained pre-outage levels of customer approval. But in the second instance, it took longer to recover, perhaps demonstrating that Marilyn's approach was not a fluke. Bob Allen stood up and took accountability without pointing fingers at anyone else. The brash young business services president, by contrast, wanted to look "in charge" but he was too quick to point fingers.

It also demonstrated the limits of the management system Marilyn had adopted for her public relations organization. She had multiple internal clients, each with its own business goals, sometimes conflicting strategies, and varying levels of corporate loyalty. They all traded on the AT&T brand, but many of them put their personal brand first. Marilyn thought of the AT&T brand as a competitive moat separating the company from its competitors. It drove her nuts when business units drew water from the moat without replenishing it, through things like price cutting, or, as in this case, treating something like the power failure as a threat to their next quarter sales rather than a reputational issue for the whole company. She could not individually counsel all the business "presidents" created by the company's decentralized line of business structure. And she definitely didn't trust them to hire their own PR counsel.

So she had set up an organization of small PR teams dedicated to each business. The members of each team were co-located at the business's headquarters, attended the business head's staff meetings, and participated in the development of business strategy. They also attended Marilyn's staff meetings and participated in the development of the corporate communications strategy. But she had advised the business unit PR teams to invest emotionally in their client's success. "It's a lot easier to be heard," she said, "when people feel you care whether they win or lose." The danger, as happened in the power system case, is that the business unit PR leaders identified so closely with the business unit that they lost a broader perspective, or they allowed themselves to be browbeaten into doing what their client wanted.

Sensing the pressure public relations people feel to please their internal clients, she cautioned her people not to let their interest in advocacy swamp their sense of what is open and honest. "We must not end up distorting information because we're trying to make it look pretty" she said, "or because we're trying to avoid a problem." She offered two reasons. "First, it's the right thing to do in serving the interest of our ultimate client—the public. And second, the truth always comes out. If you look like a liar or a dissembler in the process, no one will ever trust you again."[63]

If that reasoning wasn't enough, Marilyn had control over the salaries and promotions of all 500 people within her organization, whether they were on her payroll or a business unit's. It was usually enough. Managing her colleagues in senior management, however, was a little more difficult.

September was usually the month when the AT&T board of directors held an off-site retreat, preceded the evening before by a dinner of all the company's senior officers and their spouses. In 1991, it happened just after the New York power outage. "But the subject seemed to be off limits," Marilyn recalled. "I finally leaned over during dinner and whispered to Bob Allen, 'we *have* to talk about this.'"

---

[63] L. J. McFarland, L. E. Senn, and J. R. Childress, *21st Century Leadership: Dialogues With 100 Top Leaders*, p. 126.

After dinner, she cringed as Allen got up and said to the group: "Marilyn says we *have* to talk about the service failure." The officers rather awkwardly left their spouses behind and trooped into another room. "Only then, as we faced each other in privacy, did the pain, anger, and shame of what we felt was happening come out," she recalled. "The core of our identity was reliability. Our personal pride was built around flawless service. We were all feeling a terrible sense of loss . . . and we were in denial. We didn't see what we didn't want to see. And until we faced up to the unthinkable truth—that we had a systemic problem—we couldn't act on the root cause."

The public gave AT&T the benefit of the doubt twice because it had a hundred-year record of reliability. "That, to me, suggests the first pillar of trust—consistency, consistency, consistency," Marilyn later said. "If you don't do what you're in business to do over the long pull . . . nothing else matters. And if you stumble, you'd better pick yourself up in a hurry and restore that consistency, because it's the core of what people believe when they believe in you."

Following that uncomfortable evening, the company's senior team resolved to recapture the exceptional reliability standards for which the company had been known. "That was the triggering of the quality movement at AT&T," Marilyn later said. "And in good old AT&T style, once we decide to do something, stand back because the whole ship is turning in that direction." Indeed, the company hired dozens of quality professionals and began a massive retraining effort. Marilyn oversaw development of an internal communications program called "Ask Yourself," which stressed individual accountability for protecting the company's customers. "It was delivered in a dialog manner with lots of conversations led by senior officers to explain not only that quality was everybody's job, but that there could never be enough rules to stop these things from happening if individual employees didn't hold themselves accountable for the kind of service the old Bell System had stood for," she remembered. "It was Angus MacDonald reborn in 1990."

Marilyn had used the service crisis as an opportunity to refocus the company on one of its sources of strength. She could have been following the playbook of the canniest of politicians, Rahm Emanuel. "You never want a serious crisis to go to waste," he told a conference of corporate executives just before his boss President Obama assumed office. "Things that we had postponed for too long, that were long-term, are now immediate and must be dealt with. This crisis provides the opportunity for us to do things that you could not do before."[64] He was talking about crises that would confront the new president when he took office in a few weeks, e.g., recovering from the Great Recession, the cost of healthcare, etc. None of these crises were of Obama's making but they would soon be his to deal with.

But there's a corollary to Emanuel's maxim: If you are prominent enough and in crisis, you can be someone else's lever. Marilyn learned that too. For example, in the late 1980s, when smart mobs were still using the U.S. Mail and door-to-door canvassing, one of the most prominent single-issue groups of all dragged AT&T into the most divisive national debate since the Vietnam War—abortion.

---

[64] Reported by Gerald F. Seib, "In Crisis, Opportunity for Obama," *Wall Street Journal*, Nov. 21, 2008, https://on.wsj.com/3bkQJfT.

CHAPTER ELEVEN

NO GOOD DEED . . .

Prior to divestiture, in AT&T's golden monopoly days, the company decided to move out of its old headquarters in lower Manhattan to a new building it would construct on Madison Avenue in Midtown. Marilyn's predecessor Ed Block proposed using the proceeds from the sale of the old headquarters to fund a foundation. Seeing an opportunity to get a handle on contributions the company was already making from operating budgets, the company's chairman and board of directors approved the proposal. So when Marilyn took over as senior vice president of public relations, she also found herself chair of the AT&T Foundation. It was a plum job in many ways, making her a player in her hometown social and political scene. But it also contributed to one of the earliest and ugliest headaches she would face in her AT&T career.

Long before she even arrived at AT&T, one of the beneficiaries of the company's charitable contributions was an organization dedicated to women's health and family planning. Since the mid-1960s, the company had been giving Planned Parenthood $50,000 a year to fund educational programs to prevent teen pregnancies. But by the late 1980s, Planned Parenthood had moved beyond family planning and contraception advice to become an outspoken advocate of abortion rights. Its corporate donors came under the guns of pro-life advocacy groups like the Christian Action Council. And because of AT&T's size and prominence, it soon found itself in the Council's crosshairs. By 1989, the Council had generated 60 letters a day protesting the company's support of Planned Parenthood. It did no good to explain the company was not contributing to abortion advocacy but to an educational program that, ironically, could help prevent abortions. "Money is fungible," was the reply. "You're killing babies."

"[The] letter-writing campaign raised our consciousness more than our defenses," Marilyn later said. In December of 1989, the AT&T Foundation approved another $50,000 grant for Planned Parenthood's program to prevent teen pregnancies. Marilyn thought that would send a message to the Christian Action Council—and to Planned Parenthood—that "we were not backing down." But she was concerned enough about the growing protests to have Reynold Levy, the president of the Foundation, discuss the situation with the organization's president, Faye Wattleton.

Levy called Wattleton to warn that Planned Parenthood had become so identified with pro-choice advocacy, it was becoming difficult to explain the company's financial support as anything but an endorsement of its political position. He admitted that some of the protest was organized by the Christian Action Council, but he said the company was also hearing from customers and employees who had not taken a stand one way or the other on the issue of abortion but were troubled that it appeared the company had.

In response, Wattleton offered to mount a pro-choice campaign that would generate more letters of support than the right-to-life group's letters of protest. He politely declined the offer. And, while he had intended the call as an early warning that Planned Parenthood might at some point have to find another donor to replace AT&T's $50,000 grant to prevent teen pregnancy, Wattleton expressed no concern about the money. On the contrary, she said if AT&T didn't renew its grant, it would be a body blow to the pro-choice movement. Even *she* didn't think AT&T was neutral on the issue.

Meanwhile, the *Chronicle of Philanthropy* praised the company's December decision to continue funding Planned Parenthood despite a boycott threat. But when the story was routinely excerpted in the company's daily news summary for employees, it generated megabytes of email split between condemning the company for supporting abortion and praising it for being pro-choice. "What opened our eyes was that both sides thought we'd taken a stand on abortion," Marilyn remembered.

She didn't want the company to be part of the national debate on abortion. But it began to dawn on her that was exactly where she was. "After talking with lots of people and doing intense soul-searching, we concluded that our support of this teen program through Planned Parenthood was being perceived as a pro-abortion stand by a growing number of customers, shareowners, and employees on both sides of the issue," she said. "We had never taken a stand on abortion. We didn't believe we *should* take a stand. And we weren't going to be *pushed* into taking a stand." But she had to admit Planned Parenthood had projected itself into the center of the debate and dragged AT&T with it.

"The misperception that the corporation had taken a position on abortion because of contributions to Planned Parenthood was becoming widespread and unshakeable." Marilyn took the matter to the Foundation's trustees on March 7. After lengthy and heated discussion, future funding was terminated by a vote of ten to one, with one abstention.

Marilyn expected blowback but she later admitted that she had "seriously underestimated the enormous depth of emotion surrounding the abortion issue." It's fair to ask how she could have missed this. Marilyn—embarrassed and more than a little insecure, given subsequent events—later agonized over the same question. "You must remember, we'd set aside our emotions to focus intellectually on the issue. We had deliberately desensitized ourselves from our emotions, from our pro-choice biases, to reach the best, logical corporate conclusion," she said. "Confronted by moral absolutism, we responded with intellectual absolutism."

The Foundation staff had a detailed communications plan. Notify the Christian Action Council and Planned Parenthood to allow them to communicate the company's neutrality to their constituencies. Respond to the media, but also try to minimize the coverage. Put out any fires quickly. And don't miss the opportunity to protect the Foundation's reputation by promoting its other programs to prevent teen pregnancy.

"We thought we knew the risks," Marilyn said. "The Christian Action Council had promised in initial discussions that they wouldn't take the credit or seek publicity for our decision. And we'd worked with Planned Parenthood for 25 years. We'd given them $1,200,000 since the mid-'60s. They were nice, thoughtful, committed people— people like us. How could they publicly castigate their oldest corporate friend, especially with AT&T's record?"

Most importantly, Marilyn and the Foundation staff thought because they were AT&T, their liberal friends would give them a get-out-of-jail-free card. In reality, it worked the other way. Because they were AT&T, Planned Parenthood could not allow their decision to go unchallenged as they had for Union Pacific and JCPenney just months before.

Levy immediately notified Planned Parenthood—by letter—of the decision, even though no grant request was pending. Thinking like a philanthropist, he wanted to give its leadership maximum notice to plan their next budget. But he was not thinking like a public relations person. Obviously, this issue was too sensitive to handle by mail. He later realized he should have met face-to-face with Wattleton. After all, their respective organizations were a 10-minute walk from each other.

Because the Foundation staff considered the Christian Action Council an interested party, they also mailed them a letter the day after Planned Parenthood's went out. They hoped getting the word to them quickly might defuse a shareowner anti-abortion resolution at the company's annual meeting, less than a month away. The Christian Action Council responded almost immediately, thanking the Foundation for its decision and promising to notify its constituents by sharing AT&T's letter. There was no mention of publicizing the Foundation's decision.

A week passed with no word from Planned Parenthood. Levy called a senior Planned Parenthood executive. He was angry about the company's decision but said they would not react as its opponents would. No boycott. But he also mentioned that Wattleton had been on vacation when the Foundation's letter arrived.

The very day Marilyn was scheduled to review the Foundation's decision with the AT&T directors at a routine meeting of the board's Public Policy Committee, the *Washington Times* ran a story on the Christian Action Council's success in reversing corporate support for Planned Parenthood. It was on page C3, and AT&T was only one of several right-to-life victories the Council claimed. But it quoted the letter the Foundation staff had sent them. Planned Parenthood was outraged to learn the company had sent a letter to its opponents. The directors on the Public Policy Committee asked Marilyn why they had not been consulted. "Because it wasn't a change in policy," she told them a little uncomfortably.

Wattleton was now back at her desk and fuming. The Foundation staff heard Planned Parenthood might boycott AT&T after all. In an effort to calm the situation, Levy called a friend who was on Planned Parenthood's board, pleading the company's position. Meanwhile, Wattleton sent a blistering letter to Bob Allen, calling the decision capitulation to an extremist minority and asking for a personal meeting. Marilyn called Wattleton, telling her AT&T's Chairman wouldn't be meeting with her, re-explaining the company's position, and pointing out that the Foundation had given Planned Parenthood more than a year to replace the company's donation. Wattleton said this wasn't about the $50,000.

She talked about how betrayed she felt that AT&T had notified the Christian Action Council, how angry she was that the company had called her board member, and how furious she was that Marilyn had not accepted the supportive letter-writing campaign she had offered back in December. She made it clear Planned Parenthood would not suffer the public loss of support of a company like AT&T without a response. "My explanations fell on deaf ears," Marilyn later said. "In listening to Wattleton, I was hearing the voice of an angry warrior." Wattleton ended the conversation saying Planned Parenthood would react "visibly."

Two hours later, Marilyn received Planned Parenthood's four-page press release calling AT&T's decision "corporate cowardice." In colorful prose, it said, "AT&T, a major American concern, has been brought to its knees by a fringe group, and has allowed fanatics to dictate its corporate policy. . . . We did not think that AT&T would cave in to a threatened boycott by a small minority and turn its back on these necessary programs."

The release called on the pro-choice public to write protest letters to Bob Allen. It announced Planned Parenthood's intent to run full-page newspaper ads and roll out a direct mail campaign to 600,000 supporters. It also asked supporters to donate AT&T stock and proxies to give Planned Parenthood greater influence over the company. In addition, it announced it was cancelling a $350,000 contract with AT&T for telecommunications equipment.

Planned Parenthood's ads were created by The Public Media Center, a San Francisco agency schooled in the kind of guerilla communication that exploits emotions, further polarizing opposing groups. "You have to be willing to point a finger at enemies and call them what they are," the agency's executive director told clients.[65] And that's just what Planned Parenthood's ads did with the headline "Caving in to extremists, AT&T hangs up on Planned Parenthood." The full-page ads ran in the *New York Times*, *USA Today*, *Investment Banker*, and the *Los Angeles Times* (just before the annual meeting in Los Angeles). An ad also ran in the *Star Ledger* in New Jersey—a jab at AT&T in its home state.

The ads themselves included two coupons. Clip one and send it to Bob Allen to cast your vote for choice. Clip the other and send Planned Parenthood a donation to make up for AT&T's cowardice with your dollars. The ads claimed the company's decision sent a message that education and family planning are unworthy of support, knowing full well that AT&T had contributed $6 million to such programs over the last two years.

The Planned Parenthood news release and ads awakened media interest. Stories once buried in the back pages now moved to the front section. Newspapers ran the ads with their stories as art, a bonus for Planned Parenthood and a double body blow to AT&T. Columnists and editorial writers ate up the controversy, with thoughtful opinion divided. A *Boston Globe* column, headlined "AT&T's Scarlet Letter," concluded "AT&T" now stands for "Abortion, Timidity and Teeming millions more unplanned babies."[66] Raymond Coffey of the *Chicago Sun-Times* took the company's view, pointing out AT&T had no obligation to fight someone else's war.

65 Kim Foltz, "The Media Business: Advertising Agency with a Cause," *New York Times*, May 21, 1991.

66 "AT&T's Scarlet Letter," *Boston Globe*, Mar. 29, 1990.

National television came on board late but made up for lost time. *CBS This Morning* invited Faye Wattleton and AT&T to debate the issue. Marilyn was still trying to minimize coverage. Debating Planned Parenthood might only encourage the interest of other TV news shows and bring the issue to far more people. AT&T declined to appear leaving Wattleton unchallenged. She was telegenic, poised, articulate. A black woman fighting for women's rights against a cowardly corporation, too cowardly, in fact, to send a spokesperson. Marilyn belatedly realized she'd "lost an opportunity to set the record straight in a rapidly spreading controversy."

Unlike Wattleton, Marilyn had not been on countless talk shows. But the company needed a TV spokesperson. Clearly it needed to be a woman speaking for the Foundation. So, the buck was hers when NBC's *Today* show came calling. She would not agree to a one-on-one debate. "I was not going to be positioned as going to war with one of America's most popular, charismatic female leaders," she remembers. "My job was to correct the disinformation about our decision. And to make sure the public understood how active we are in family-oriented philanthropy." She would follow Wattleton. Live.

On the day of the broadcast, Marilyn was in Los Angeles for the company's annual meeting. She crawled out of bed at 3:00 a.m. only to discover she didn't have a working hair dryer. It was not a good sign. "I'm no dummy at public relations, so I knew I would lose," she later said. "And I did." Rational explanations about the need for corporate neutrality don't make for good TV. But phrases like "caving in to extremists" and "corporate coward" are perfect sound bites laden with emotion. "That hit home when the producer [of one of the network news shows] said he felt sorry for AT&T," she remembered. "He said we couldn't win. Our message was too subtle, too intellectual. People understand arguing a position, he said. They don't understand arguing a non-position."

Meanwhile, thousands of letters and phone calls poured into AT&T headquarters every day. Ironically, Planned Parenthood's campaign showed how divided public opinion was. Calls and letters supportive of AT&T slightly edged out the critical. But Allen fielded as many questions on Planned Parenthood as on earnings at the pre-meeting news conference, and the abortion issue dominated the meeting itself. The shareowner resolution—which prohibited support for any organization involved with abortion—was resoundingly defeated with 95 percent of the vote.

National and local press coverage, which had increased as a result of the ad campaign, picked up even more because of the meeting. But the press had expanded the story to talk about a number of corporations caught between warring special interests.

While AT&T suffered relatively little financial damage, the reputational cost was harder to measure. Marilyn had learned a hard lesson in the political and social environment that she had, perhaps unwittingly, helped shape in her work on the first Earth Day. "Today's political landscape is increasingly dominated by single-cause groups, confrontational minorities that have gained power far beyond their numbers," she wrote. "They do not aim to win over public opinion or build a consensus. They aim to defeat a candidate or block an action. These groups exercise negative political power for causes on the left as well on the right."

The public has high expectations of a company as big and as central to their lives as AT&T. Such a company is a useful lever for small groups with a big issue they would like to bring to public attention. As soon as AT&T told Planned Parenthood's opponents of its decision to stop making an annual donation, it became a lever both sides would pull. They felt they had to. On Planned Parenthood's side, for fear others would follow AT&T; on the Religious Right's, in the hope they would. "These were the kinds of issues to be fudged if possible—in such a way that you don't become a target to be used by both sides," she said. "You'll die on the battlefield of highly emotional, conflicting values."

That's not to say Marilyn believed companies should shun controversy, avoid risks, and keep their heads down. As part of its family-oriented philanthropy, the AT&T Foundation continued to fund organizations that were arguably "controversial," such as the National Organization for Women's Legal Defense and Education Fund and the Children's Defense Fund.

Marilyn believed corporate responsibility is central to *all* a company's activities. In fact, AT&T's own research showed that people judge a corporation "responsible" in terms of how it treats its employees and customers even before asking how it impacts the community at large. In that context, "self-interest" has a broader meaning than doing good to do well. And it can become entwined in what some might call "controversial issues."

For example, in the 1990s, AT&T was attacked by the Religious Right for its inclusive employment policies. It was the first major American corporation to include sexual orientation in its formal diversity policy, back in 1975. The company's diversity training included a module on creating a productive and supportive working environment for gay, lesbian, bisexual and transgender employees. Many of its employees celebrated Gay Pride Month, just as they do Hispanic Heritage Month or other cultural and ethnic commemorations. This caused members of the Religious Right to accuse the company of everything from "indoctrinating" its employees in "aberrant lifestyles" to "encouraging immorality." They wrote hundreds of letters every year protesting the company's inclusive employment practices. Rev. Donald Wildmon of Tupelo, Mississippi, who founded the American Family Association, even backed a long distance reseller called LifeLine which he promoted as a "Christian alternative" to AT&T.

But despite the Religious Right's indignation, the company refused to cave on its diversity policy—just as it wouldn't cave if the Ku Klux Klan were to mount a boycott effort. Not because these efforts have no economic impact, but because the issue is so fundamental to AT&T's self-interest, and there is no room for compromise. To compete in an industry whose principal engine is human creativity, AT&T had to attract and keep the best talent available without regard to race, gender, disability, religion, sexual orientation, or any other irrelevant circumstance.

On the other hand, Marilyn's personal experience in the environmental movement taught her that single-issue groups can sometimes be right. "As I look back to 1970, when I was much younger and less apt to look at more than one side of an issue, I can't find one sorry prediction that has not happened," she wrote. "Oil spills, pesticide scares, trash piling up in urban and rural communities and washing up on beaches around the world, smog beyond reasonable tolerance, toxic waste leaks, the disappearance of magnificent species of land and aquatic life, a weakening of the ozone layer—such 'scare tactics' are common contemporary news."

One of the first initiatives she brought to the AT&T board was a restatement of the environmental policy she had first articulated in 1971. "As a matter of policy, AT&T should be committed to the protection of human health and environment in all areas where it conducts operations," she said. "And implementation of this policy should be a primary management objective and the responsibility of every employee." She made the case that such a policy would not only enhance the company's reputation and build employee pride, it would also improve the quality and cost of its operations while enabling it to build the kind of relationships to prevent unnecessary constraints on the business.

Anticipating how stakeholders will perceive and react to an institution's decisions is fundamental to the practice of public relations. But it assumes at least some distance from the operating decision. "I doubt an objective PR counselor coming in at the end of our decision-making would have missed the fact that we looked to the pro-choice movement as if we had 'caved in' and that principle would get washed away in an ocean of abortion emotions," Marilyn later said. "But then it is very rare—philanthropy may be the only routine example—for a public relations organization to both make a business operating decision and implement it."

Sadly, in that observation, Marilyn would soon be proven wrong.

CHAPTER TWELVE

MONKEY BUSINESS

"After all is said and done, public relations is everybody's job in the company," Marilyn once said. "That's why I think ultimately the single most important stakeholder group is your own employees, because if they're not doing the right thing, then the company is not doing the right thing."[67] As a result, she didn't consider employees a captive audience for corporate propaganda. She genuinely wanted to help them understand where the company was going, where it was winning, where it was losing, and how their job fit into it all. She believed free and open internal communication was critical to accomplishing that.

AT&T was one of the few companies that was nearly always in the news. So a daily electronic newsletter ran excerpts from that day's media stories about the company, both positive and negative. When the company made major announcements, she did her best to ensure that employees were told at the same time as the media. Periodic employee broadcasts put the chairman in front of all employees to answer their unfiltered questions. Senior leaders of the businesses and divisions met with employees in large town hall meetings and in smaller coffee klatches to brief them on the business and to answer their questions. Supervisors at all levels were trained, encouraged, and equipped to do the same with their teams. And the first rule of all these initiatives was candor, no matter how uncomfortable it might make some feel.

Straight talk was especially true of *Focus*, the company's all-employee magazine. Mailed to the homes of all 300,000 employees so their families could understand the company's business goals and

---

[67] Arthur W. Page Center oral history.

performance, *Focus* had garnered shelffuls of awards for writing and design. More importantly, in Marilyn's view, it had a unique voice in the world of internal publications—employees actually read it because the magazine was studiously candid about the company's performance and printed employee letters that were often critical of senior management. Occasionally, that would raise someone's hackles, but Marilyn did a reasonably good job of insulating the editors from executive complaints and meddling.

Among all the company's employee communications programs, editing *Focus* magazine was a coveted assignment and always went to the organization's best writers and most skillful team leaders. The annual budget was more than $1 million, including design and printing, which were done by outside companies. Production schedules were tight, and the staff was used to working late hours when deadlines loomed. In fact, the magazine's editorial staff prided itself on being a self-managed team. What they wrote for the publication was reviewed by subject matter experts for accuracy and by the law department for potential legal issues, but no one else saw the magazine in advance of publication.

Occasionally, the staff had to pull an article at the last minute because a technical reviewer raised issues that couldn't be resolved by the press deadline. That's what happened as the September 1993 issue was going to bed. A one-page article at the back of the magazine had to be pulled and the editors decided to substitute a fun "quiz" on AT&T's international business.

The production manager, a young African-American employee new to the magazine staff, called the outside designer in Manhattan and asked him to prepare a layout for the article, using the rough copy she faxed to him. The designer, in turn, asked a cartoonist he had used many times in the past to prepare some suitable illustrations. These were the days before broad use of email attachments, so everything had to be faxed back and forth between the designer, the artist, and the production manager.

Later that day, the cartoonist had faxed some illustrations to the designer, who pasted them into a typeset layout, which he copied and faxed to the production manager. The fax she received was dark and blurry, but she approved the layout.

That issue went into the mail on Tuesday, September 15, and a copy, delivered by messenger, landed in the editor's inbox the next morning. She was already deep into making assignments for the next issue, but she picked it up and began thumbing through. When she got to the fun "quiz" on the inside back cover, her heart dropped. A cartoon showed people on the phone around the world—a man wearing a beret in France, a woman in wooden shoes in the Netherlands, and so forth. But in Africa, it showed a monkey on the phone—a clear racial slur equating black people to monkeys.

Ashen faced, she rushed to her boss's office, showed it to him, and asked if she was overreacting. "I don't think so," he said. "But let's check." They both walked down the hall to the office of an African-American colleague and showed her the cartoon. They didn't have to ask if they were overreacting. She was aghast.

It was too late to recall the magazine; it was already in the mail to the homes of 300,000 employees, 15 percent of whom were African American. After a quick series of consultations, they decided to follow the crisis management playbook—admit the mistake before someone else makes a big deal of it. Accept responsibility and apologize. The magazine staff's apology ran in that morning's issue of the company-wide electronic newsletter.

When she saw it, Marilyn followed up with her own apology the next day:

To All AT&T People:

I am appalled and personally deeply sorry about the racist illustration that appeared in the September issue of Focus. I am aware of how much this has angered, hurt, and embarrassed people in AT&T -- particularly our African-American colleagues and their families. I deeply regret this not only because people have been hurt, but also because we try so hard . . . to accurately portray AT&T as a caring company that respects and values all of its employees.

Finally, while the staff of Focus magazine takes full responsibility for the illustration, the illustrator is not an employee, but a freelance artist hired by our design firm. Unfortunately, AT&T employees who have the same name as the illustrator have been receiving phone calls from offended employees.

-- Marilyn Laurie
   Senior Vice President
   Public Relations and Employee Communications

If the last sentence of Marilyn's letter showed how angry AT&T employees were, the rest didn't come close to communicating the embarrassment, anger, and sadness she herself felt.

Once people had seen the cartoon, Marilyn's apology was deemed insufficient. So, the CEO issued another one, but many AT&T employees—African American or not—were by now embarrassed or, in many cases, enraged. The cartoon became a lightning rod for every diversity grievance employees harbored. They shared their outrage with outsiders ranging from the NAACP and the Southern Christian Leadership Conference to Rev. Jesse Jackson and Rev. Al Sharpton.

In a final stroke of bad luck, all of this broke on the front page of the *Washington Post* on the weekend of September 17, just as the Congressional Black Caucus's annual Legislative Weekend was getting underway at the Washington Convention Center. More than 2,000 public officials and African-American leaders, ranging from members of the Nation of Islam to the NAACP were in town to discuss race relations. The organizers had arranged for the *Washington Post* to be delivered to every hotel room door in the city. The front page included a copy of the cartoon, about five times larger than the original version in *Focus* magazine, under the headline, "AT&T Apologizes For Racist Cartoon." Speaker after speaker at the conference used the cartoon as an example of corporate America's sorry diversity record.

The weekend of September 17 was also when the AT&T board held its annual retreat at the Greenbrier Resort in West Virginia. "I was frantic. That may be an understatement. I was practically suicidal," she later recalled. "I knew that, within 12 hours of the *Post*'s front-page story, it would be everywhere. You didn't have to have any experience in public relations to know what any freshman in a PR class at Northwestern University could have told you—you had a crisis on your hands." Plus, it was the second time a full-blown crisis had blown up during one of the board's retreats. Once again, Marilyn was under a microscope.

She tried to arrange for Bob Allen to meet with representatives of the company's black employees on the following Monday. "But my advice was not considered objective at the Greenbrier," she said. "So the board called in Vernon Jordan." Jordan was a leading figure in the civil rights movement and a close advisor to both President Bill

Clinton and the Reverend Jesse Jackson. The *Financial Times* called him "the most connected man in America."[68]

"I can't say I was excited about that," she later said, "because you know I'm back into this area of you didn't have to be a Rhodes scholar to know what to do." But Jordan—whisperer to the powerful—came in and said, "Don't worry. It will blow over."

Marilyn was flummoxed. "Now, he may have meant 'over the long term.'" Marilyn said. "But it dramatically slowed down any response. And made my job almost impossible." Isolated at the Greenbrier and told not to worry, Marilyn spent most of her time on the phone. She consulted outside PR counselors and African-American executives and leaders within and outside the company. She ensured that all employees who dealt with customers—from telephone operators to salespeople—had talking points on the crisis and on the state of diversity in AT&T. She had her staff draft sample letters managers could send to constituents who had questions. And she started and ended each day talking to her people about the crisis.

She tried to convince Allen the company's response had to be tied back to its diversity policies because what was being called into question was whether or not the company was racist. She proposed establishing a task force to look at the company's hiring policies, promotion policies, and minority purchasing. But as she later admitted, "Vernon Jordan's 'it will blow over' led to 'don't overreact'."

Meanwhile, managers were asking for advice on how to handle employees' anger and embarrassment. In response, Marilyn sent an email to all managers at fifth level and up, she said, "Many of you have asked what you can do to help during this difficult time. . . . The best thing you can do is take every opportunity to meet with your people,

---

[68] Verjeet Indap, "Vernon Jordan: 'It's not a crime to be close to Wall St.'" *Financial Times*, Aug. 17, 2018, https://on.ft.com/3bkRJRb.

listening to their concerns about the illustration and the larger issue of the diversity climate throughout our organization. . . . Every time you meet with employee groups, let them talk about the deep-seated feelings the *Focus* illustration tapped, and solicit their suggestions on ways we can move forward and accelerate the pace of diversity in our company." In addition, she told the executives to express their own feelings of embarrassment candidly and to recognize the hurt and pain people feel. But "don't say you know how they feel unless you're black," she warned. "There is no way someone who is white can know how it feels to be black."

Eventually Allen was called to testify before the Congressional Black Caucus, whose chairman dismissed all of his explanations and apologies as "bullshit." The NAACP announced a boycott of AT&T. And negative media stories increased while AT&T people of color felt increasingly alienated.

Marilyn finally convinced Bob Allen to go on a road tour to show how seriously the company took the problem and to rebuild bridges with employees who were people of color and with African-American leaders at organizations such as the NAACP, the Urban League, the Southern Christian Leadership Conference, and the Rainbow/PUSH Coalition. Allen was not a natural salesman and disliked the superficiality of politics. As far as he was concerned that's just what this was—a political game. So Marilyn made sure he was accompanied by the highest-level available African-American AT&T executive. But, in most cases, the black executives felt as "used" as Allen did.

Marilyn also asked every senior executive who had a relationship with African-American businesses or institutions to pitch in. For example, she asked a senior AT&T executive who was a long-time member of the United Negro College Fund's board of directors to call the presidents of all the historically black colleges to explain what happened, remind them of the company's past support, and ask for their help. The company's head of purchasing reached out to the company's minority suppliers. The advertising people called on minority media. Even Spike Lee, who was under contract to direct some AT&T television commercials had to be assuaged.

AT&T had been a generous corporate donor to all these organizations. And compared to other large corporations, it had a pretty good record on inclusion and affirmative action. At one point, 25 percent of all African Americans with PhDs in electrical engineering had received financial support and mentoring from AT&T. The company was a pioneer in minority purchasing and spent more than $1 billion a year with firms owned by people of color or women. Even during the extensive downsizing of recent years, AT&T took pains to ensure that the company's diversity profile wasn't adversely affected. In fact, it improved. Admittedly, there were only six black executives in top positions, but one had just been made president of a major business unit.

One senior business unit executive, who had been mentoring two dozen African-American management people for several years, scheduled a meeting with them and asked Allen, who was on his diversity road tour, to call in. When it was Allen's turn to speak, he started by saying, "I thought you knew we are better than this."

Maybe he was channeling the litany of diversity accomplishments he had been fed to use with outsiders. But, although he couldn't see them, the expressions on the black faces around the table amounted to a silent rebuke. It was clear to these African-American management people that their CEO—and probably his whole top management team—just didn't get it, didn't understand what it was like to be black in this day and age. And they certainly didn't understand the levels of hurt the company had tapped into or they would never think, much less say, "I thought you knew we are better than this."

So the road trip was only successful in convincing Allen that this crisis may have started in the PR shop but the fuel feeding it was deeper in the company. Among AT&T people of color, the incident had ignited fumes of discontent that so few of them were moving into higher ranks of management. Allen returned to his office determined to do something concrete about that.

Marilyn drafted a letter over Allen's signature to be sent to employees' homes, outlining some of the actions already taken to make the company more inclusive at all levels and asking them to call a special hotline set up to collect their suggestions on further actions. The letter went out on September 17. Within two weeks, the hotline had received more than 4,300 calls.

It didn't surprise her that media coverage dragged on into October. After all, every initiative the company took, every meeting Bob Allen had with African-American leaders, gave the media an opportunity to write about it again. But what she found most troubling was the number of customers and employees who were so upset they were taking the time to call and write about it. Bob Allen and other officers were getting an average of 40 letters a day about the cartoon. And employees were sending about a dozen letters a day to the company's electronic newsletter. This was actually worse than the Planned Parenthood debacle. And she couldn't see an end to it.

Marilyn's embarrassment and sadness had edged into humiliation. And her anger was now tinged with searing frustration at losing so much time in addressing the issues underlying the crisis because Allen and the board accepted an outsider's prediction that it would "all blow over."

In discussing the controversy at one of Bob Allen's staff meetings, she uncharacteristically began to cry, prompting Allen to uncomfortably call a break "until Marilyn is less emotional." Just a week later, in a meeting with the cross-organizational crisis team, she broke down again as she fought off efforts by one of the company's federal lobbyists to fire the magazine's editors. Crying in public is embarrassing for anyone. Doing it in a business meeting was mortifying for Marilyn. It was also demeaning because it revealed the little Jewish girl from the Bronx, all grown up, but not all that tough and fearless.

Marilyn knew no one on her staff was racist. It was even possible the guy who drew the cartoon wasn't racist, but simply clueless. He claimed he just liked to draw gorillas and put one in every drawing he could. The whole thing was an inconceivable series of mistakes or what the engineers call "process errors." But real people were deeply hurt. Among those people were the editors of the magazine, who she knew and respected. The editor-in-chief, in fact, had once been Marilyn's executive assistant, as personally close to her as her long-time secretary. But she couldn't put their pain and embarrassment—or her own—ahead of employees who are much more vulnerable.

One of the things destroyed in all this was the credibility of the magazine she had once been so proud of. She doubted it could ever be restored. Besides, its own staff had been exploring the possibility of replacing the print publication with an even more ambitious electronic vehicle. It made no sense to continue torturing the company for the sake of a publication that would probably disappear in months anyway. She knew what she had to do.

On October 4, nearly three weeks after the racist cartoon first appeared, Marilyn announced that "we have decided to cease publication of *Focus* immediately, and the senior editors of the publication have been reassigned." She was candid about the reason. "Because [of the offensive cartoon] it has become clear that *Focus* magazine has lost credibility with a significant number of AT&T people." She told her own organization in a breaking voice that "it was all about accountability, and there is no way to go part way on issues of this kind. This was in my shop. The accountability is mine."

She promised that whatever replaced the print magazine would reflect the input of a "reader's panel" of diverse employees and the company would solicit bids from minority suppliers in the production of whatever new employee communications media replaces *Focus*.

```
Finally, a personal note. Our employee
publications -- especially Focus -- have always
reflected an openness and a level of candor
unique in industry. I believe they contributed
to the development of a more responsive,
customer-focused culture at AT&T. I will always
be proud of them and the people who produced
them.
```

Shifting her attention to the damage Bob Allen's reputation had suffered from the whole incident, she called her PR team leaders together "to discuss how the chairman is spending his time and how to make him more effective." She didn't have control over his entire calendar, but between media interviews and speeches, her organization accounted for a significant chunk. For example, Allen typically gave five or six speeches a month, about forty percent to outside audiences. She wanted to focus his messages to differentiate him from other CEOs. She asked the speechwriting team to help Allen "embrace diversity as a business issue, not just a social issue." And she directed them to ensure that his employee addresses "embody a greater sense of urgency."

Privately, she also offered Bob Allen her resignation. He refused to accept it and, in a kind of by-the-way criticism, told her he disagreed with her decision to shutter the magazine. But he had come to agree with her initial counsel that the company had to address the underlying grievances employees of color harbored. So, on the same day, Allen announced the formation of a "diversity team" composed of the company's five most senior officers and employees of different ethnic and racial backgrounds. He charged the diversity team with "greatly accelerating the pace of diversity within AT&T" and to complete their recommendations before the end of the month so he could review them with the public policy committee of the company's board of directors. "Only by making diversity an integral part of the fabric of our business," he wrote, "will we bring about the true changes we need to be successful in the global marketplace."

By the end of the month, Allen received the diversity team's recommendations. It included specific goals to improve diversity at every level in the company and called for progress to be reviewed by the board's public policy committee. It committed to increasing purchases from minority firms by more than 10 percent a year. And it proposed the hiring of an outside consultant to study what the company could do to retain African-American talent and to make recommendations on increasing the employment of minority groups.

In the coming weeks, an occasional media story about the cartoon still popped up now and then. A few college student groups demanded that their school drop AT&T as their long distance carrier. And no one could ever predict when someone like Reverends Jackson or Sharpton would show up outside the company's New York office with a few picketers.

But for the most part launching a new diversity program with concrete goals and closing *Focus* significantly dampened the furor. And over time the diversity of the company's upper ranks even improved. Marilyn later admitted the whole episode was "personally painful" and "a nasty lesson."[69]

---

[69] Arthur W. Page Center oral history.

An interesting corollary to the *Focus* crisis showed that it was about more than a racist cartoon. It was the inevitable result of AT&T's failure to address the legitimate needs of an entire segment of employees. At about the same time the cartoon ran in *Focus*, a nearly identical drawing by the same cartoonist appeared in the alumni magazine of Rutgers University.[70] It illustrated a story about Rutgers graduates around the world. France was represented by a man in a beret and Nigeria was shown with a pennant-waving monkey. There was no public outcry. Indeed, as far as we know, there wasn't one letter of complaint.

---

[70] "Alumni Facts, Feats, Phenomena," *Rutgers Magazine*, Summer, 1993, p. 41.

CHAPTER THIRTEEN

LESSONS LEARNED

Success or failure, Marilyn always wanted to do a postmortem to figure out what went wrong or what could have been done better. She seldom lacked material suitable for dissection and analysis. As AT&T's chief communications officer, Marilyn arguably weathered more crises than any of her peers, with the possible exception of those in the West Wing of the White House. In the process, she learned some foundational lessons in the practice of public relations. Her rules of crisis management are a good example.

```
Tell the truth, tell it fast, take
responsibility, fix the problem quickly. And give
something back.
```

Those rules worked when the unthinkable happened and AT&T's network went down for eight hours. The company's reputation quickly recovered from what Marilyn described as "betrayal of customers' trust" because it was forthright in explaining what happened, took responsibility for it, kept everyone affected updated as it worked to fix the problem, and took concrete steps to repay customers for the inconvenience they experienced.

But as Marilyn discovered, there is always an exception that proves the rule—some crises are fueled by passions that have little to do with you. "When you're involved in a highly-volatile social issue, don't expect reason to carry the day," she said. "People are divided along emotional lines. And if you don't acknowledge that at the front end, you're not likely to satisfy anybody."

Two of the crises Marilyn faced fell into that category—the Planned Parenthood controversy and the racist cartoon that made its way into an employee publication. At first, she dismissed them as equivalent to acts of God that no one could have been prepared for. "If you stumble into a hot cultural issue," she said, "it doesn't matter how big you are, you're a little rowboat in a stormy sea." In time, when the heat of those crises had dissipated, she conceded her initial explanation, while technically accurate, was too simple and self-serving. She thought long and hard about everything that had happened in both crises.

On Planned Parenthood, she committed her conclusions to paper for a speech she delivered to other senior public relations executives later that year. In part, it read:

> What is so obvious now is that we had no exit
> strategy, let alone one up to the demands of
> single-cause politics. And once our decision was
> made, all the bottled-up emotion escaped. The
> staff moved immediately to execute this
> distasteful decision, not stopping to thoroughly
> assess the implementation options. We didn't
> fully examine such issues as timing, phased
> withdrawal, or the various ways we could
> communicate our decision. We didn't ask
> ourselves all the "what if" questions and plan
> the "what then" responses.

> To this day, I believe that the principles
> underlying our decision were sound. Planned
> Parenthood proved it had become political to the
> core in the very way it reacted to our decision.
> But being right often isn't enough. Sometimes it
> isn't even relevant. Reason doesn't often
> triumph over emotion. And it stands very little
> chance in the emotion-charged world of single-
> issue politics.

> Carrying out corporate social responsibility
> today is not a mellow, do-good activity, but a

complex, risky undertaking requiring the most
sophisticated stakeholder management and PR
strategies. Our position is as Peter Drucker has
described it: "Community responsibility, that is
concern for a healthy and viable community, is
not 'philanthropy' for the pluralist
institution. It is self-interest."

But we must more carefully define that self-
interest. We have an obligation to help society,
but we are also obliged to protect our companies
from attack. In the case of Planned Parenthood,
the organization's politicization of an issue of
individual conscience put it outside of AT&T's
values. We've reviewed the other non-profits we
support and have concluded that none fit the
Planned Parenthood mold.[71]

She sent the speech to Bob Allen, who sent it back with a
handwritten note: "Great paper. Excellent introspection."

Marilyn fully expected the lessons resulting from that
introspection would be valuable guidance should another crisis
rooted in a social issue ever occur. "I tried to apply them to *Focus*,
which was the next time it happened," she said. "And to my grief, I
couldn't get the others on the senior team to understand these
lessons." Her C-suite colleagues considered the racist cartoon
equivalent to a regrettable typographical error for which everyone
had apologized and that the reaction would "blow over" in time.

But Marilyn was convinced that concerns about racism
expressed by employees of color went further than that single cartoon

---

[71] These paragraphs and earlier quotes in this chapter are from a speech Marilyn Laurie
gave at the Golden Workshop on June 20, 1990.

and were an indictment of the company as a whole. And a significant proportion of the general public was inclined to agree with them.

"I mean, to me, *Focus* was such a clear rerun of the Planned Parenthood problem. But the senior managers took it on its own terms and we made the same mistakes all over again. That was my worst hour as head of PR." Marilyn's personal pain was not only because the crisis originated in her own organization, but also because she couldn't get her C-suite colleagues to see the lessons learned before. "AT&T in many, many areas was not learning, not listening, not adapting to the outside world very effectively," she said.

When the furor over the racist cartoon in *Focus* magazine subsided, Marilyn engaged in further introspection. She started 1994 by pulling together a cross-section of public relations people to conduct a postmortem on the *Focus* magazine crisis and what lessons could be drawn from it. She got an earful of often conflicting advice.

Some PR people complained that it took too long to recognize the cartoon was a serious crisis; others said the initial email apologies just drew more attention to the racist cartoon. Some of the African-American PR people were offended that they were not used more as company spokespeople; others who were put in that position felt they were being used as "token blacks." And even in the midst of the ongoing crisis, several people complained that a high-ranking black executive in government affairs was running her own parallel crisis management effort. Others jumped to her defense and explained that she didn't feel like a real partner with PR in handling the crisis.

Practically everyone agreed that the PR department made a mistake by focusing on the so-called "process error" rather than on the impact on black employees. "White people just don't get it," many of the black PR people said. "You can't be really objective about this because you're black," some white PR people retorted.

Most troubling was the number of employees who said their hesitancy to speak up when they thought the department wasn't responding appropriately wasn't fear of retribution, but concern for loss of reputation. "Pushing too hard will get you labeled as a noise-maker," one employee said.

For her part, Marilyn admitted that she didn't fully appreciate the reaction within her own organization both on how the cartoon made its way into the magazine in the first place and on how she managed it once it happened.

```
I did not listen as quickly as I should have to
one of my managers who was much more in touch
with the black community, and had trouble
getting through, and probably never lost the
view that the reason she wasn't being heard was
because of hierarchy.
```

There were moments when Marilyn felt the *Focus* postmortem was being executed on someone who was still alive. Nerves were still raw, but the message that came through loudest was the echo of something AT&T's first PR officer had said 68 years earlier: "Public relations is 90 percent doing and only 10 percent talking about it."

Employees were calling for the head of the magazine's editor. "I defended the editor. And by doing so, I prolonged the crisis," she said. "I knew as a professional that one of the rules of crisis management is to take accountability for having done the wrong thing. And while I tried to do that personally, I knew that the editor was . . . one of the most diversity-sensitive people we had in the entire company, a person whose values were a hell of a lot better than my friends' and probably mine most of the time. It seemed unthinkable to remove her. But ultimately I had to."

Marilyn said she learned a lot from both crises. Because most of the people involved in making the decision to stop funding Planned

Parenthood were pro-choice, they were blinded to Planned Parenthood's single-issue militancy and misjudged the organization's reaction. "We failed to prepare a rigorous exit strategy because we were captives of our own logic and misjudged the constituents' reaction to that logic. We were locked into reality."

In the case of the racist cartoon, because Marilyn knew no one on the *Focus* magazine staff was racist, her initial focus in dealing with the uproar was misdirected. "We were fixated on explaining how a racist cartoon could end up in our employee magazine," she said, "rather than addressing the pain it caused employees who felt marginalized and less than full members of the community."

In the end, both crises led her to an additional lesson in crisis management. "The worst judges of the public impact of their actions are the people at the center of the incident, even if they are public relations people," she said. "If anything like [the Planned Parenthood and *Focus* magazine events] ever happened again, I'd go for outside counsel because it's very difficult to manage an extremely complex and ever-enlarging crisis when you're in the middle of it and the cause." On the other hand, as Vernon Jordan demonstrated, not every outside voice deserves your ear. Some are tone deaf.

Marilyn believed the practice of public relations requires care and detachment in equal measure. She read somewhere that legendary White House reporter Helen Thomas said reporters must be detached—but they must care. She thought it was good advice for PR people too, but in reverse. "First, we must care. If you don't care about the success of the enterprise deeply, you shouldn't be there. Because much of what you do is to find inspiration in the enterprise that energizes [employees and customers]. To be cynical and apart is not right," she said. "But you also must be detached. Because if you become too absorbed into the culture, you lose your capacity to give equal weight to the public's expectations. You lose the capacity to look the CEO in the eye and say, 'I don't think so.' And if you get swallowed up, if you lose that detachment, if you lose that ear to the outside hum of the world, I think you lose your value." Clearly, detachment is impossible when you are the cause of a crisis. And just as clearly, counseling those who are in the middle of a crisis is impossible unless they believe you truly care.

Both require a high degree of toughness. Marilyn was a slight woman of steely character, who had the courage to resist the pull of seductively deceptive tides. "Our business is crammed with pressures to subtly shade the truth—whether to tell powerful executives what they want to hear, to deny that we live in a transparent society and agree that potentially damaging facts can remain hidden, or to hype a brand until the marketing bears little resemblance to its real capabilities. Avoiding the details of complicated financial transactions—managing phony grassroots support groups, starting rumors on websites or paid word of mouth—it's easy to just go along," she told her people. "Don't. You may be the only one in the room who isn't ready to go with the flow. You may not be expected to be tough at the time, but you'll always be expected to have been tough in hindsight! You'll never know how central integrity is until you've been through a few crises. And that may be too late."

Marilyn was no bleeding-heart Pollyanna. "The most important thing a company needs to do is to be successful," she said. "But who says that to get the bottom line where you need it to be, you can't do it ethically?" She knew companies sometimes get to the point "where they think someone is going to wipe them out if they don't take drastic steps, whether it's cutting employees, closing plants, or whatever." But even in desperate circumstances, she believed such actions could be done "with as much humanity and transparency as possible." And she expected the senior public relations counselor to point out, "If you cross this ethical line, the situation will become worse, not better."

Having the authority to issue that warning has to be earned. "If you have consistently supported the business, brought insights to it, motivated employees," she said, "then when push comes to shove, you have a chance of being believed when you say, 'Don't cross this line. The shit will hit the fan. And you will be sorry. *You* will be sorry. Not the enterprise in general. You.'"

In Marilyn's day, "reputational risk" had not yet made it to the top of exposures listed in many companies' 10K reports. Even today, many companies have drawn the wrong conclusion from their experience as a corporate piñata in the media. They have reduced reputational risk to two words: bad publicity. One large company caught up in the turmoil of the financial crisis of 2007–2008, griped, "We may be adversely affected by . . . negative publicity . . . regardless of the factual basis for the assertions being made." There's no question that negative publicity can lead to unwanted attention from the government, not to mention the tort bar. It can undermine employee morale and make customers skittish. It can sink sales, wreck careers, and move markets.

But in the crises Marilyn faced, she learned that reputational risk is the function of a company's actions, whether planned or in reaction to events over which it has no control. Turning up the public relations wind machine cannot blow bad publicity away. So-called "headline risk" is a self-serving cop-out. Negative publicity is not *sui generis* but the product of other risks. Damage to a company's reputation is the risk of other risks. It can't be managed directly.

The key to managing bad press—and reputational damage—is to pay real-time attention to the decisions, behavior, and events from which it flows.

That's why Marilyn put a senior public relations counselor at the right hand of every business unit leader. It wasn't to give them a personal press agent, but to make their PR counselors full-fledged members of the business's risk assessment team. She believed good PR counsel can help line managers find their way through the thicket of reputational issues embedded in their operations. She wanted PR counsel to help operational managers identify the stakeholders most closely affected by different categories of risk. She wanted them to help their clients understand stakeholders' changing expectations, as well as to assess gaps between those expectations and the business's current performance. And to help them prepare a response plan, ensuring that timely communications back up corrective actions.

Just as importantly, she believed integrating public relations people into a firm's risk management processes would also ground them in the reality of a company's business. It helped temper the urge to present the business aspirationally, as they wished it were, rather than as it really is, creating a gap between reality and reputation that exposes the company to even larger risk.

That ounce of prevention worked well during the company's most serious network failure. But it wasn't foolproof. For example, in the second network failure, one business unit's PR counsel failed to focus his client on the full scope of the problem and the associated public interest issues. Worried only about a small segment of customers and looking for a scapegoat, he blamed employees for what was clearly a systemic failure, adding a whole new dimension to the crisis. "It was as if God was punishing us for not having learned our lesson well enough," Marilyn later said. "The media and public reaction to a leader blaming it on the little guy was the exact opposite of the Bob Allen response in the first crisis. And it triggered a tremendous amount of media hostility."

But even with the best risk assessment, not every crisis can be averted. They're sometimes the product of honest mistakes, unforeseeable circumstances, or just plain bad luck. Knowing this, Marilyn worked hard to get all her C-suite colleagues comfortable with the idea that if something is newsworthy, it will become public. And if it is going to get into the news, they might as well be the ones to put it there and at least have a chance to frame it correctly. This wasn't always a popular position. Most lawyers, for example, have been trained to admit nothing and, given a chance, to suggest everyone take the Fifth. Senior executives are seldom eager to admit a mistake. And the best of us can only see what we want to see.

Of course, few liars make it to the top of companies like AT&T, but in the fog of a crisis it is difficult to distinguish the truth from speculation or wishful thinking. You never have all the information you need, and all the information you get will be colored by someone's agenda or biases, including your own. Marilyn believed senior public relations counselors need skepticism and honest self-knowledge in equal measure.

Finally, in any crisis, she encouraged her colleagues to focus on caring for those directly affected, followed in order of priority by employees, customers, and investors. And she advised them to be guided in this, as in all things, by what served the public interest. On that foundation, Marilyn's rules of crisis management came naturally.

CHAPTER FOURTEEN

COMPUTER DAYS

Marilyn was not a digital native, but she was usually the first of her peers to try some new technology, often before it had been completely debugged.

By the 1990s, all AT&T officers had a personal computer on their desk, but few did more than use it to track the company's stock price, and their secretaries had to turn it on in the morning and log off at day's end. But Marilyn had had a personal computer at home since 1983. "I talked [the Bell Labs] management information systems division into letting me borrow one as a 'human factors trial'," she remembered. "And I promised to document the travails of the naive user. Little did I anticipate how many travails there would be." As at seemingly every important event in her life, she committed the whole experience to paper.

> My new personal computer had been installed at
> home while I was at work. Rushing through the
> last of the day's chores, I drove home, tore up
> the stairs, and entered the guest room to
> respectfully greet the high technology addition
> to the household. I looked at its clean lines,
> blank screen, blinking modem, and wondered
> . . . is it on? How do I tell if it's on? A
> little shaking, a little listening, a little
> staring at the screen . . . . It must be off.
> How do you turn it on? Is the switch under the
> keyboard like an electric typewriter? No. A knob
> somewhere like a radio? No. A toggle switch on
> the big white unit holding up the screen? No.
> Damn. How do you turn it on?

Some fifteen minutes later, I try the switch on
the back and am rewarded by the first flickering
green characters. After logging in and seeing
that it recognized my password, I try to shut it
off. The installer has left painstaking
instructions citing commands to follow. So far
so good. We seem to be at the last stage of
shutdown. By this time, I'm annoyed and
surprisingly frustrated. I can't wait to be free
of this intense concentration on unfamiliar
procedures. The machine asks: Do you want to
continue? No. No. A thousand times, no!

The damn machine is still on. I want to pull the
plug. I'm scared. It will break and everyone
will condemn me for breaking my new machine the
first night. I'm so tired. Why won't it let me
go? What am I doing wrong? Wait a minute. It's
not asking me if I want to continue using the
computer . . . . It must be asking me if I want
to continue SHUTTING DOWN the computer. I try
again. Do you want to continue? YES! Free at
last. My first experience has ended. I've turned
the computer on and off. Done absolutely nothing
in-between. Total elapsed time . . . 30 minutes.

Marilyn eventually mastered a succession of personal
computers, laptops, and Blackberries. She sent terabytes of email.
But she still did most of her more thoughtful writing—such as the
saga of turning her first PC on and off—in her cursive script on lined
paper. And it was in that medium that she tried to articulate the
rationale for AT&T's multiple forays into the computer business.

"While many people, including me, wrote endlessly about the
seam between computing and communications," Marilyn said, "we
didn't seem to have any kind of clear vision about how to exploit that

seam and understand what [customers'] real needs were at the seam." Indeed, the company's initial computer announcement, back in 1984, was entirely opportunistic. Settling the antitrust case meant the company could sell computers; it designed and built computers to run the phone network; so why not sell them? Furthermore, its computers were optimized to run on the UNIX operating system. UNIX was developed at Bell Labs, ran on different makes of computers, and, thanks to free licenses, was used in virtually every university computer lab in the country. When computer science graduates showed up for work at most companies, their first question was, "Where's my UNIX?"

Marilyn considered the engineering vice president behind the 1984 computer announcement "a dynamic, somewhat arrogant, certainly heavily opinionated, and widely considered difficult personality." But he had sold Jim Olson on a strategy he outlined on a napkin—to use UNIX's software dominance as the snow plow for hardware sales. It would take a while—and untold billions—before they realized that the money to be made in the computer business would not come from hardware, which was quickly becoming a commodity, but from software, which the company had already given away. Multiple versions of the UNIX operating system were developed by organizations ranging from the University of California, Berkeley, to Microsoft, IBM, and Apple.

After AT&T's less than successful entry into computers in 1984, responsibility for the business moved from division to division through a succession of leaders—at one point, even with two CEOs—but it was always behind the curve. "It's hard to understand how so many people could have missed the boat over so long a period of time," Marilyn said. "I think there was a real problem in the executive suite not being schooled in the computer business, and not having the computer business in their gut or in their work experience."

That might have been part of the problem, but as events would prove, what AT&T lacked was more than a golden gut attuned to computers. It was that no one had a clear vision of how AT&T could exploit the seam between computing and communications.

In 1987, the head of business long distance services had estimated that about half the unit's biggest sales involved moving large amounts of data around the country and giving its customers online access to it. For lack of a better term, he called that data networking. But real data networking was more than moving data on the network. And it was more than manufacturing computers, as the equipment people thought. Data networking also requires sophisticated routing systems, specialized software, and consulting services capable of tailoring it all to a customer's specific needs.

But that's not the path the company followed. In 1988, after trying mightily to go it alone in the computer business, without a single profitable quarter in four years, and still convinced that it needed to have a better computer capability, the company decided the only way to stem its losses was to buy a company that knew what it was doing. A number of companies were considered. As Marilyn later recalled, most of the senior leadership team thought it was a bad idea to buy *any* computer company; some thought if AT&T were to buy a computer company, it should be a company like Hewlett-Packard. Only one person thought it should be Dayton, Ohio-based NCR. That person was Bob Kavner, the executive committee member responsible for the company's existing computer business.

Kavner was the son of a factory worker, the first in his family to attend college, and eager to enter the white-collar ranks. As he later recalled, "the two people [in the neighborhood] who wore ties were the optometrist and the accountant. So I said, 'I'll be an accountant.'"[72] Trim, articulate, and very smart, he turned an internship at the Coopers & Lybrand accounting firm into a full-time position, ultimately working his way up to audit partner while still in his mid-30s. He served clients such as Columbia University, the Metropolitan Museum of Art, and AT&T, then the world's largest company. Bob Allen brought Kavner in to replace himself as the company's chief financial officer in 1984. A Ferragamo tie more stylish than the typical AT&T executive, he proved masterful in charming both financial analysts and reporters. After a few years in that role, Kavner was put in charge of the company's multimedia products and services, including computers.

He played the role of a high-tech CEO, wrestling with the UNIX software cult, dealmaking with startups, investing in promising ventures, and giving speeches. Lots of speeches. Marilyn's people even arranged for him to give a keynote at COMDEX, then the industry's largest trade show, where he acknowledged the Las Vegas setting by doing a brief tap dance before speaking.

Kavner and Marilyn both considered themselves change agents. She was scrappy by nature; he had seen how other companies operated and considered AT&T ponderous by comparison. AT&T had built a culture exceedingly good at repetitive action to meet a known demand without the complications of competition. But when demand was uncertain, changeable, and competitive, the culture was too damn polite. "AT&T managers were very skilled in not telling people what they thought they didn't want to hear," Kavner recalled.

Kavner asked Marilyn to accompany him to a Sun Microsystems meeting. He was a member of Sun's board thanks to AT&T's 20 percent ownership of the company. The other members of the board

---

[72] Samantha Stainborn, "Robert Kavner Alumnus Profile," Adelphi University website, Aug. 22, 2012, http://bit.ly/2S6oB8I.

were Silicon Valley titans like the venture capitalist John Doerr and John Hennessy, the president of Stanford University. The evening before their meeting, the board members usually all gathered for dinner at a Palo Alto restaurant with company CEO Scott McNeely.

Marilyn was a little surprised when McNeely arrived with his shirttails hanging out, greeted everyone, ordered a drink, slumped into a chair, and pulled a crumpled sheet of paper out of his pocket. "These are the challenges the company—and I—need your help on," he said. That kicked off a discussion about whatever was bedeviling him, whether succession planning and retaining talent or inventory control and technology trends. "McNeely opened discussion in a vulnerable way and without even hinting at his preferred solution," Kavner remembers. By contrast, the next day's board meeting was more of a fiduciary exercise, hearing from the audit and compensation committees, listening to product development plans, and so forth. The board's real contribution came the evening before.

Marilyn couldn't help noticing how different it all was from AT&T's board meetings, which were tightly choreographed.

It all led her to believe AT&T needed someone to drag the company into the future, despite the kicking and screaming it would provoke. She thought Kavner might just be the one to do it. For his part, Kavner desperately wanted to turn AT&T's foundering computer business over to someone who was already living in that future. His infatuation with NCR was a combination of its early development of UNIX-based computers, its strong management team, its success in making the leap from cash registers to computers, its deep international presence, and its relatively affordable price. NCR's stock had been depressed since the 1987 stock market crash, making its market capitalization less than $4 billion. Allowing for a 50 percent premium, Kavner thought he could get the company for around $6 billion—a lot of money, but not beyond the reach of a company with a market capitalization of $30 billion.

But NCR resisted AT&T's advances for more than two years. Then, in early November of 1990, the *Wall Street Journal* reported that the two companies were discussing a merger. Six days later, Allen called NCR's CEO Chuck Exley and asked for a meeting on "an urgent basis." Exley agreed to meet that afternoon at an airport hotel in Cincinnati. Allen flew in from New Jersey on the AT&T jet; Exley drove his wife's car. Allen made his pitch in a half hour meeting over coffee and cookies—$85 a share for the company and AT&T wanted Exley to stay on as CEO. Exley made it clear that AT&T's offer was unwelcome, but said he'd discuss it with his board.

One week later, the NCR board of directors not only said "no sale," it also enhanced the "golden parachutes" Exley and his top officers would receive should there ever be a change in control. A little more than a week after that, on Sunday, December 2, Allen increased the pressure on Exley and his board by going public with an offer to buy NCR for $90 a share in AT&T stock.

When it became clear in mid-November that this would not be a friendly merger, Marilyn began looking for outside help. One of the first people she interviewed was Gershon Kekst, founder and chairman of Kekst and Company, which had already done work for AT&T's investor relations people in the finance division. Although not as well known to the general public as other PR firms, Kekst was the one name many lawyers and bankers would suggest when a CEO called in a panic, looking for PR help. That was partly because he had been on one side or the other of some of the biggest, nastiest takeovers in the world. But it was also because he left those corporate battles with the respect—if not appreciation—of the parties on both sides of the fight.

Marilyn anticipated a lengthy and possibly messy period of courtship with NCR. If that was the case, she wanted Kekst at her side. Furthermore, she needed the help. "It fell to me to do the communications around the deal," she said. "And it was astounding to me that I couldn't get a clear, two sentence answer to, "What is the benefit of this deal?" So she poured her frustration out to Kekst over lunch in the Grill Room of the Four Seasons restaurant and then in his office just a few blocks away. As was his style, Kekst said little except to ask for clarification or more detail. Finally, Marilyn asked him a question, "What would you do if you were me?"

"I'd get the best PR agency I could find," he replied. "You need someone who has done this before."

"How about you?" she said.

"Oh, we can't take your account," Kekst said. "We already represent NCR."

At that moment, Marilyn realized just how difficult the upcoming battle would be. She eventually found experienced outside public relations counsel. But there were moments when she suspected she had been of more help to Kekst than he could ever be to her. Nevertheless, when the NCR merger was behind her, she retained Kekst herself just to keep him away from competitors.

Meanwhile, she still didn't have a compelling rationale for wooing NCR. So, she did what PR people often have to do. She wrote something and brought it to Kavner and Allen, saying, "Is this it? Does this sound like what you have in mind?" She ultimately framed an argument around the concept of NCR being "transaction intensive" and therefore a networking company. But up to and including the day she retired, Marilyn would say, "To this day, I'm not sure what the real reasons were, what the logic was. Because it was never offered up to me in any way that was coherent."

Exley must have felt the same way because he said the proposed combination "makes no business sense," was "a desperate attempt to salvage AT&T's disastrous foray into the computer business," and that his company's shareholders and other stakeholders "are best served by continuing to build NCR's enormous inherent value as an independent company." Meanwhile, NCR's outside legal counsel met with Allen separately and told him he could have the company for $125 a share.

Most financial and industry analysts were fairly confident AT&T's real intent was to get NCR to the bargaining table. But at least some warned that a protracted hostile acquisition could be a disaster. "AT&T needs NCR's management; that's why they're buying the company," said one telecommunications analyst. "This deal isn't like buying a cellular business franchise where any management will do."[73] And Bob Allen was determined to keep NCR's management. As Marilyn put it, "We had the romantic belief that the culture of just about any company that wasn't AT&T was going to be more entrepreneurial and successful, and that if we integrated it too quickly, we would squelch whatever it was that had made them a success." Unfortunately, what AT&T didn't realize was that NCR itself was in the middle of a major turnaround trying to get into the next generation of technology.

NCR's turnaround efforts essentially ground to a halt when Allen flew to Cincinnati with his initial offer. The months that followed could have been drawn from *Barbarians At The Gate* with AT&T in the unaccustomed role of barbarian: it launched a proxy battle to replace NCR's directors; Allen and Exley both appeared before the other's board of directors; they both made the rounds to

---

[73] Carla Lazzareschi, "AT&T Poised for Hostile Takeover of NCR Corp.," *Los Angeles Times*, Dec. 6, 1990.

their companies' biggest institutional investors, many of whom owned both stocks; NCR's local and national media branded AT&T as a "predator;" Ohio's lieutenant governor suggested AT&T "reach out and touch someone else;" and two Dayton banks took out full-page newspaper ads with the phone numbers for MCI and Sprint.

It wasn't until May 1991 that the two companies reached an agreement for AT&T to acquire NCR. The price was $7.48 billion in AT&T stock or $110 a share, a price the company said was affordable because of the rise in AT&T's share price over the previous months. Nevertheless, it was a 132 percent premium over NCR's market value before AT&T started its hostile offer. Allen and Exley both appeared to be buoyant at the deal's closing.

Before the news conference announcing the deal, Marilyn warned Allen he had to reassure Kavner, who had been the architect of the deal but would soon be out of a job. "Kavner's done a good job," Allen said. "And I expect he'll continue to play an important role in the company." Marilyn warned him reporters would want to know more than that. "Well, that's what they're going to get," he said. As it turned out, it was the fourth question asked at the news conference. Allen accused Marilyn's people of planting the question. But he did reassure Kavner privately that he didn't have to worry about his job, even though Allen said he was sincere in his desire to keep Exley on board and to give him all the autonomy he wanted.

Nevertheless, after watching over the merger transition for four months, Exley retired, $35 million richer thanks to his new AT&T shares. His successor, drawn from NCR's executive ranks, lasted six quarters. The company itself was part of AT&T for only five years, though in all that time, it retained its autonomy, even when AT&T puts its own man in the CEO position. As for Bob Kavner, he became group executive for end user products such as telephones and answering machines.

Decades later, Kavner admitted his infatuation with NCR was ill-fated. "In hindsight, I may have been too focused on rescuing AT&T's own computer business," he later said. "And I was wrong to think selling a broader line of servers and desktops was the way to do it." Plus, fighting AT&T off for nearly a year put NCR behind the curve in the fast-moving computer industry. It also put AT&T behind the curve in the communications industry.

As Marilyn saw it, the hostile takeover was never really resolved, even after the acquisition closed. "By not integrating [NCR] immediately, we never absorbed them into what could have been an AT&T networking strategy," she later observed. "Technology was moving so fast, it required hands-on leadership," she said. "Bob [Allen] was looking for a solution through structure. But it never got computing integrated with communications. It never got new devices integrated with the people doing the more traditional devices."

To Marilyn, the problem was leadership. "There are times in the history of a company when the leader has to be part of the team, not above the team," she continued. "And I think this change in the nature of the company, which had always been governed differently by its chairman, became the undoing of AT&T."

The seam between communications and computing that Marilyn had identified went unaddressed by both AT&T and NCR. Today, we call that seam the internet. And more than a little ironically, it became the source of Bob Kavner's fortune after he left AT&T in 1994 and made early investments in companies like Pandora Media, Earthlink Networks, Overture Services, and Ticketmaster-Citysearch.

CHAPTER FIFTEEN

INTERNET AND WIRELESS

AT&T's offices in Basking Ridge were spread across seven long, low-slung stone structures set into the rolling pastures of a former 200-acre farm just off New Jersey's Route 287. Each structure was four stories tall, with parking underneath and offices above. The buildings were interconnected by long hallways. But getting to the far end of Building Seven from the far end of Building One could take so long some people went down to their car and drove themselves over.

At the center of the complex was Building Four, which housed a two-story cafeteria with wood-burning fireplace. The executive offices, which ran along the perimeter of the building on the third and fourth floors, were connected by a wide spiral staircase. In addition to executive offices, the third floor also housed the company boardroom, with a battleship of a table that could seat two dozen people in plush leather swivel chairs, and a smaller "Anteroom," with a round table about 15 feet in diameter that could seat about 15 people in equal comfort. Allen's immediate reports usually met in the Anteroom and Ian Ross was famous for observing that "nothing good ever happens in the Anteroom."

Perhaps. But it was definitely the scene of some lively discussions. "I was yelling and screaming all the way through [the 1990s]. I yelled out at a meeting of the management executive committee that I thought we were reliving what was going on at IBM [at the time]," Marilyn remembered. "The company's loosely-knit, heavily-political, and lengthy decision-making cycle was corrosive to our competitive capability. We needed a tight-knit team where anyone who practiced politics was shot in the head. While it may not have been obvious to the senior team, it sure as hell was obvious to the employees who were saying it in spades."

AT&T needed a team of commandos who spent less time worrying about the turf they stood on than the turf they could win from competitors. AT&T didn't have many of those kind of senior executives—what got them their plush offices in the days of the Bell System monopoly were management skills. AT&T now needed people with leadership skills who were hungry to do something new. If those weren't the kind of people the company could grow, it could hire them. With Kavner sidelined in an ill-defined role, Marilyn thought Alex Mandl might be that kind of executive.

Marilyn was arguably more attuned to office politics than most executives but was initially misled by Mandl's early initiatives as CFO. In those early days, he seemed to be following the standard CFO playbook of cutting costs and focusing everyone on the bottom line, or in his case a trendy new measure called Economic Value Added.[74] But over the two years Mandl was CFO, she began to realize the depth of his strategic thinking. He quickly understood what levers controlled the company's performance and how their leverage could be increased. And when he was made head of the company's core communication services businesses in mid-1993, she saw how much he could get done and how quickly he could do it.

Mandl was Austrian by birth and still retained a bit of an Arnold Schwarzenegger-like accent after more than three decades in the United States. He had come to the U.S. with his father Otto when his parents divorced. Otto became headmaster of what was then the Happy Valley School, in Ojai, California, which Alex attended as a

---

[74] Economic Value Added is basically net operating profit after taxes in excess of the cost of capital. Many consider it a better indicator of economic performance than earnings, as measured by generally accepted accounting principles, because it includes the cost of the debt and equity required to produce it.

teenager. From there, he attended Willamette University in Salem, Oregon, where his father took a teaching position. He then enrolled in the University of California, Berkeley, where he received an MBA, despite having to navigate clouds of tear gas released outside the business school to disperse students protesting the Vietnam War.

One of his first hires for communication services was a guy who got into Harvard with perfect SAT scores, graduated *cum laude*, and then became responsible for Microsoft's Outlook and Exchange software, despite having majored in literature and American history. Tom Evslin was as unassuming as he was smart. Mandl charged him with pulling together an internet strategy. As Evslin later admitted, "There were people who said it would take us four to five years to do it because we had to be up to AT&T standards."[75] In internet years, that's about the time between now and the day the sun burns out. Evslin launched AT&T WorldNet in seven months. And when he realized average customer acquisition costs were greater—and far less certain—than offering five hours of free web browsing and totally free email service to AT&T customers, the service began acquiring 100,000 customers a month. Plus it had unmatched reliability.

To Marilyn, Evslin's success was less a matter of computer savvy than heart. Because of the inexorable pressure to meet the quarter's earnings expectations, "AT&T people had a loss of heart to grow markets," she said. "If [the company] were a human being, you'd say it is a person who has lost self-esteem and ambition." Evslin clearly had heart and ambition, and the success of WorldNet was, in her words, "dazzling."

But in keeping with her compulsion for constant improvement, she also thought he made a fundamental mistake. "Tom Evslin created an offer that promised to bring people internet service with

---

[75] Kevin Maney, "Former Execs 'Walk All Over' AT&T," *USA Today*, Sept. 24, 1998.

real AT&T quality and reliability," she said. "But he entered the market at a very low price point that ultimately restructured the internet access industry. He bled margins out of the internet access industry to the point that no one was making any money, including Evslin. We have deep pockets so we could afford that strategy. But the AT&T brand does not require you to go in at a price point way under everybody else in the industry. People will buy the brand for a few pennies more. That's the power of the brand."

Many will argue with that analysis. After all, Evslin's free offer was only a lower-cost means of acquiring customers. After a year, its price was about the same as the competition. And no one who understood the internet believed the price of access would be the source of real earnings. That would come from advertising, assuming you could attract enough eyeballs.

But Marilyn's point was that the brand would justify a premium. In any case, the dial-up service Evslin was offering was supplanted by broadband access before the decade was out. And while AT&T WorldNet service is still available, its quality isn't anything to brag about, and its customer base is growing about as much as that for people who still rent their phone.

If Marilyn thought the company's approach to the internet was flawed, she still admired the aggressive way Mandl seized the opportunity. And she was especially impressed by Mandl's approach to the company's re-entering the wireless business.

AT&T had abandoned the wireless business as part of the 1984 divestiture of its local telephone companies, much to the dismay of many executives. The decision was based on a mix of assumptions, ranging from the short-sighted belief that mobile telephony was a "local service" best left in the hands of the local telephone companies, to the mistaken belief, based on a McKinsey & Company study, that it would never be more than a niche service.

Less than a decade later AT&T realized its mistake. Early in 1991, Allen told the board, "Wireless communications in its broadest form is—or should be—our territory. We need to be a player—both to seize the growth opportunity which will inevitably come, and to protect our core carrier business." To Marilyn, it was a no-brainer, much more obvious than buying a computer company. "Everybody knew [wireless] was critical for our future. It was a growth path," she said. "Plus, it involved things we understood—spectrum, regulation, customers who were already our customers."

But the only way back into the wireless business was by buying or partnering with an existing wireless company. McCaw Cellular was by far the best candidate in terms of geographic coverage, quality of service, and depth of management talent. The company was publicly-owned, but the McCaw family held 60 percent voting control. The company's chairman, Craig McCaw, had inherited a small cable television system in Centralia, Washington, from his father when he was still in college. He operated it from his dorm room at Stanford University, using its cash flow to buy other cable systems in remote areas until he had the 20th largest carrier in the U.S. From that base, in the 1980s, he used the systems as collateral for billions in loans to snatch up undervalued cellular licenses across the country, building one of the most innovative, but heavily indebted, companies in the industry. Buying McCaw Cellular would be only a little less difficult than getting one of Craig's kidneys. Besides, in 1990 he was the highest paid CEO in the country.

In September 1992, when Mandl was still CFO, Allen asked him to take charge of reviving moribund discussions the company had already had with McCaw about a partnership. Mandl quickly got McCaw's agreement to form "a strategic alliance" by making a small investment in the cash-strapped company. But defining the terms of a partnership proved complicated and contentious. There were so many moving parts, it was difficult to ensure each partner was being treated fairly. When Mandl was appointed head of the company's communications services business in mid-1993, the discussions were still eating up a lot of paper but getting nowhere. So Mandl got on the phone with Bob Allen and, in a 20-minute phone call in which Allen asked fewer than five questions, convinced him the company should give up the idea of an alliance with McCaw and just buy the whole company. It took a bit longer, and $12.6 billion, to convince Craig McCaw.

It was a Friday in August 1993 when a deal looked within reach, and Mandl asked Marilyn to bring her team into the New York City offices of the company's outside law firm, Wachtel Lipton, to make arrangements for an announcement as early as the next Monday. Marilyn, in turn, dispatched the corporate jet to pick up a key player who was Mandl's primary PR counselor, but was now on vacation with his family in Vermont's Great Northwoods at a place with a single landline and no wireless or email service.

She tasked him with writing the news release and key talking points that would guide all the media relations, employee communications, and community relations people after the announcement was made on Monday morning. Craig McCaw would become AT&T's largest individual shareholder and would join the company's board; the name of his company would change to AT&T Wireless; and its operational headquarters would remain in Redmond, Washington. But one of the remaining questions was to whom McCaw's president Jim Barksdale would report. Barksdale, the former chief operating officer of Federal Express was beloved at both his former and current companies. In fact, walking into Wachtel Lipton's offices, he was stopped by a FedEx deliveryman who recognized him and wanted to say, "Hey."

Laurie consulted with Bob Allen and HR head Hal Burlingame and was told that, while Barksdale wasn't crazy about the idea, he would report to Mandl. Allen didn't intend to make the NCR mistake all over again.

No one went home all weekend, nor did they get much sleep. Marilyn and members of her team went in and out of conference rooms as both companies' lawyers and investment bankers slogged through the laborious task of preparing the official documents, not to mention pulling a fine-tooth comb through the communications material based on them.

The announcement went out before the markets opened on Monday morning, August 16, followed by a news conference from the Art Deco building in downtown Manhattan that used to be headquarters of the old Long Lines division that built and operated the company's wired network. After making the announcement and answering questions from media gathered in the building auditorium, Mandl and Barksdale went upstairs to jump on a conference call with the financial analysts who followed the two companies.

Marilyn and the officer who had prepared the communication material went to her office to listen to the conference call. As they listened on her speakerphone, Marilyn worked through the papers in the blue plastic briefcase that seemed to follow her everywhere. At some point, a shadow fell across her desk. It was Bob Allen, holding a copy of the Q&A in his hand. "This says Barksdale will report to Mandl," he said. "Tell me I'm looking at an early draft." Before she could answer, they both heard someone on the conference call ask who Barksdale would report to. "Jim will report to Alex," the moderator said. Neither Barksdale nor Mandl said anything.

"Jesus Christ, Marilyn," Allen said. "You were in the board meeting when we discussed this. We had it all worked out. Now . . . . " He literally ran out of words, turned and walked out of her office, with a final and declarative, "Fix it," as he stepped through the doorway. "He's really angry," Marilyn told the PR officer who wrote up the Q&As. It was the first and only time he had heard Allen curse or Marilyn say anything so obvious.

She *had* been in the board meeting when Barksdale's reporting relationship had changed. But she had somehow failed to pass that information on. He chalked it up to the frenzy of the past few days and ran back to his office to correct the Q&A. In time, he would learn it was more than a question of her bandwidth.

In any case, Barksdale reported to Allen and coordinated with Mandl. But true integration would have to wait. "The market McCaw [and later, AT&T Wireless,] played into was very much an if-you-build-it-they-will-come market," Marilyn observed. "They were always behind demand. Consequently, they built a culture of 'the demand will always be there.' There was nothing in McCaw that recognized it had to be better than other people's mousetraps, and you've got to keep doing that. That's marketing—constantly staying on top of how people's needs change, and how to satisfy them better and differently. So yes, McCaw has been a great success story. But that's just chapter one." In chapter two, Barksdale found himself petitioning Marilyn for permission to use the Cellular One name in its advertising, rather than AT&T. Denied.

Despite getting the reporting relationship he wanted, Barksdale left less than a year later to join an internet startup called Netscape, which many analysts considered the "hottest product on the web."[76]

---

[76] Barksdale took a nominal salary of $1 a year while at Netscape. When the company was bought by America Online in 1998, his equity stake was worth an estimated $700 million. Barksdale and his wife plan to give their wealth away before they die.

He was replaced at AT&T Wireless by a McCaw veteran. When Netscape went public later that year, Barksdale's 12 percent equity in the company was worth more than $100 million. Mandl took note.

CHAPTER SIXTEEN

BREAKING UP AGAIN

If divestiture unleashed AT&T's competitive juices, it had the same effect on the supposedly happy-with-their-local-dial-tone-monopoly telephone companies spun off as part of the deal. From the first conference call to begin planning for divestiture, the local Bell phone companies tried to revise the deal AT&T had reached with the government. They argued they needed to keep the Yellow Pages business and AT&T relented. They said mobile telephony was a local service they should have and AT&T relented. They even argued about where to paint the yellow lines to separate AT&T equipment from theirs in switching centers they would both occupy. And behind the scenes, each local Bell company approached its members of Congress about passing legislation that would let them offer long distance service.

The leadership of the local Bell companies had always bristled at direction from "195 Broadway," even though most of them had had a tour or two there. But this was not simply an exercise in churlishness. AT&T's interests had diverged from those of its former subsidiaries. They found themselves at loggerheads in front of state regulatory commissions on such issues as the price for carrying long distance calls on local networks. Plus, most of the local companies' senior officers were convinced AT&T would eventually be competing with them on their own turf. And they were determined to compete in long distance before that happened.

Bob Allen first heard about their attitude in the spring of 1984. Some AT&T Network System executives returned from a meeting with fairly high-level officers of one of the Bell telephone companies and reported they had been told, "We believe AT&T tanks are right over the hill waiting to attack our local market as soon as the breakup is complete." Allen called such talk "paranoid," but he also remembered how it felt when he was CEO of one of the soon-to-be-divested Bell telephone companies. "Being told they couldn't be in the long distance business drove a lot of emotional behavior," he remembered. "The glamorous high-margin business went to AT&T and they were left with the ugly, low-margin utility business." [77]

There were solid business reasons to hang on to Network Systems while trying to heal the rift with the local telephone companies. "The old Western Electric crew may have been the only unit that really understood their costs," Allen said. "They were a stand-offish bunch, but they knew what they were doing, and they almost always produced at least the earnings they said they would. We needed that kind of support as we worked to improve the other equipment businesses." Allen knew AT&T had no plans to enter the local telephone business. Until that changed, he believed the relationship with the local phone companies could be managed.

The leaders of AT&T Network Systems were not so sanguine. They had fought to keep the Western Electric name on the grounds that even that minimal move would provide some insulation from the fear that buying equipment from AT&T Network Systems was filling a future competitor's coffers. Ed Block, who was still corporate vice president of public relations and brand management, turned them down on the grounds it was a bad solution to an imaginary problem. All businesses would go to market as AT&T, but they could put "Western Electric products" in small type on their business cards and advertising. When Marilyn took Block's job in 1987, Network Systems President Wayne Weeks took another run at the issue.

---

[77] This and later quotes are from Bob Allen's oral history in the AT&T Archives and History Center.

Rather than sending him a memo, outlining why she couldn't make an exception to the corporate identity standards, she made an appointment with him.

Weeks was an engineer trained at the U.S. Naval Academy and raised in the proper southern town of Thomasville, Georgia. He was unfailingly polite around women and enjoyed a good dirty joke with his male colleagues. Tall, thin, and a chain smoker, he had the pasty complexion of someone who hadn't been outside in a long time, which was not true because he was a dedicated gardener and hunter. When necessary, he could be as polished as any of the "suits" at AT&T, but his natural gait was a loping stride, and he never completely lost his lazy, country accent. So, while he was considered a tough, disciplined boss within Network Systems, he was generally underestimated in the Shangri-La of AT&T's executive offices.

Marilyn showed up on time and found Weeks behind his desk reading the *New York Post*. She tapped on the door jamb which caused him to look up, put down the paper and stand, raising his hand in greeting with a hearty, "Howdy, pardner. Come on in." He sat back down, and Marilyn took one of the visitor chairs in front of his desk. He noticed she had a thick binder with her, which he did not consider a good sign because he was famous for saying, "AT&T people give good binder, but never get anything done." When he was part of the team planning divestiture, he had run a small pool within his group betting on "vinyl futures," meaning the number of binders that would land on their desks from other groups that week.

Not appreciating any of this, Marilyn ran through the whole binder, explaining the various corporate identity systems different companies used, which one AT&T had selected and why, how much progress the company had made in building public unaided awareness of its name, and finally why Network Systems couldn't change its name to Western Electric. Weeks didn't argue. In fact, he didn't say anything until Marilyn asked, "Is there anything else I can do for you?" His answer probably came more quickly than he intended, "Yes. Get out of my office."

Weeks gave up on changing the corporate identity system, but he redoubled his efforts to convince Allen that Network Systems should be spun off as a separate company. It was not a new idea. In fact, it was one of the things Tobias had discussed with Marilyn in their "door-closed, feet-on-the-desk" meetings.

In fact, Tobias had somewhat gingerly made the argument to Olson and then a little more forcefully to Allen. In fact, he wrote a lengthy paper in August 1990 arguing that "a highly-integrated vision encompassing all of AT&T would be an oxymoron." For example, he argued, "Ownership of some businesses may preclude us from being successful in certain other businesses." An accompanying chart showed that Network Systems' operating income had declined by a third in the past two years. The solution, he felt, was to lessen AT&T's ownership of Network Systems by merging it with other global players and retaining a small, minority interest.

Allen wasn't convinced, but he allowed his management executive committee to discuss it at length, once in 1994 even going around the table and asking everyone what they thought. Weeks had retired by that point, and Tobias had moved on to become CEO of Eli Lilly. But Bill Marx, who had replaced Weeks, and Vic Pelson, who had replaced Tobias as head of Communication Services, both said spinning off Network Systems would not only resolve the Bell companies' misgivings, but it would also turbocharge AT&T's stock price. Marilyn, perhaps sensing there was enough energy behind an idea that clearly made Allen uncomfortable, later claimed she and he were on the same page. "The things Bob had to say and the things I had to say were very similar," she said. "I was worried about the implications for Bell Labs, which received the bulk of its funding for product development from Network Systems and all of its research money from AT&T." She clearly had misread Allen's true feelings.

About a year or so later in late June of 1995, Bob Allen called Marilyn to his office. As she climbed the circular staircase to his office on the fourth floor, she wondered what this was about. Her curiosity only peaked further when Allen pushed the button under his desk to close the door behind her. She took her seat in front of his desk, pen poised over her pad of paper.

"We're going to make some changes," he told her. "But before I tell you about them, I want you to know only a handful of people inside the company know about this. And I want your word that you will tell no one—not your husband, not your secretary, not your executive assistant, no one on your staff, no one."

When she agreed, he told her he had been speaking to the board since March about restructuring the company. He was going to ask the board of directors to split the company into three parts—a communications equipment company built around what used to be Western Electric, a computer company built around NCR and the parts of AT&T it had absorbed, and a communication services company, which would carry the AT&T name.

He had decided the timing was right about a year earlier when he had been persuaded that the company's full-throated opposition to telecom reform was beginning to sound whiny and shrill. Instead of arguing against opening the long distance market, the company now argued *for* legislation to open local markets to competition.

Allen didn't know if the legislation would pass, but the company's change of position would make it even more difficult for Network Systems to sell equipment to the local phone companies if it were still part of AT&T. And if the legislation did pass, the equipment market could explode, making a stand-alone company like Network Systems very successful. Plus, it was time to face up to the fact that the NCR acquisition had not only failed to fix the company's computer business, it created problems of its own.

Allen explained he had initially confided in only the company's chief counsel and chief financial officer because the legal, regulatory, and financial implications were so significant. They in turn had hired outside law firms and investment bankers, and no one was brought on board unless he personally approved. But she needed to know what was going on should any leaks develop and, obviously, to figure out how to announce this to the world once they had a concrete plan and the board approved it.

Marilyn went back to her office and immediately began writing a list of everything she had to do. She had still never written a news release, though she had edited quite a few. But she had a very capable staff to do that when the time came. She thought her greatest contribution would be thinking through the implications for everyone who would be affected by what would come to be known as "Trivestiture," i.e., splitting AT&T into three companies and spinning them off to sink or swim on their own. It turned out to be quite a lengthy list that filled several pages in the stream of consciousness flow of her cursive handwriting.

She knew each constituency would have unique concerns, but two overarching issues would probably be front and center. "I knew the restructuring would probably involve job losses. We wouldn't need a central staff of 28,000 people to coordinate all our business units, and the businesses spun off would probably sell nonstrategic divisions and do their own downsizing to try to become more competitive," she said. "We'd been through it before, and I knew it was a powder keg."

Harkening back to her concerns about the 1984 divestiture, she said, "The only other issue that worried me as much was whether or not Bell Labs' fate would trigger some kind of public concern."

Marilyn and Burlingame, who had also been brought in to the small group planning what was now being called "Trivestiture," drilled the finance people about the size of any potential "force reduction," and they were told that, while there would undoubtedly be some, they couldn't speculate about the number because that decision would ultimately be made by the three resulting companies, which didn't really exist yet. The closest they could get was:

```
It is the marketplace that ultimately determines
the size of a business. Each of these businesses
will operate in hotly-competitive markets. So,
while it is too soon to determine an exact
impact, it would be safe to say the combined new
businesses will have fewer employees than the
current AT&T does today.
```

That was just one of the issues, like the division of assets, debt, and patent rights, that would be addressed after the announcement. The same thing applied to Bell Labs. Neither issue turned out to be much of a problem in the days immediately after the initial announcement. But as Marilyn said at the time, "I've learned there's no such thing as an issue that can't come back to bite you later."

On Friday, September 8, Marilyn got Allen's permission to bring two of her key public relations officers into the circle of now 40 people who knew what was going on. One was a man who was the primary PR counselor to the head of communications services. The other was a woman who was the primary PR counselor to the head of Network Systems. Both had worked in each other's jobs earlier in their careers. And neither knew why they had been called to Marilyn's office. In fact, until they met coming off the elevator in the executive area neither knew the other would be there.

"You going in to see Marilyn?" she asked.

"Yup. You too?" he said.

"Yes. What do you think this about?"

"I'll bet she's going to tell us we're changing jobs," he replied. Marilyn was a big believer in moving people around as part of their career development.

When they sat down in Marilyn's office and the door snapped closed behind them, they weren't prepared for what she told them. It wasn't about them. It was about recreating AT&T.

She started with the need for secrecy. Then she outlined what was about to happen and reminded them about secrecy again. "The tentative date to make this announcement is Wednesday, September 20," she said, "assuming the lawyers and investment bankers can finish their work by then and the board approves the plan."

Meanwhile, she explained everyone had to continue doing their work as usual while preparing everything necessary to make the announcement. She gave them a white paper she had written and typed herself, analyzing the likely concerns of key constituencies. She had also taken a stab at writing the key messages the company needed to get across. But they were to produce everything else—timeline, news release, talking points, speeches, constituency letters, employee communications, etc. Not trusting email, they agreed to shuttle material back and forth on floppy disks.

They decided to split the work between them. The corporate PR officer, who was closest to the financial and legal teams fleshing out the restructuring plan, would take the lead on drafting a timeline and writing all external material. The Network Systems PR officer, whose business unit's employees would be the most affected, would take the lead on all internal communications. Marilyn would provide input, review their work, and run interference with the lawyers and accountants. They used the key messages Marilyn had written, which went through surprisingly few changes, as their lodestar.

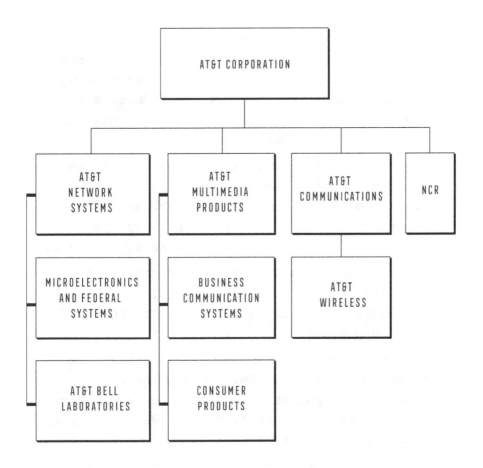

AT&T IN 1995

In September, the company announced it would break into three companies. NCR would regain its independence, and the other equipment companies would be spun off as a separate company eventually known as Lucent Technologies. AT&T would retain the communication services companies, including wireless, as well as part of Bell Labs, which would become a new AT&T Labs.

This restructuring is a bold strategic move that
will realign AT&T's current businesses to take
full advantage of changes in the fast-growing
global information industry. We undertake this
restructuring from a position of strength. AT&T
has never been stronger.

The restructuring will improve each business's
current capabilities and better enable it to
create long-term value for shareowners. Each new
business will have a sharper focus on its
individual market and clearer strategic intent.

The restructuring will eliminate strategic
conflict between businesses (e.g.,
simultaneously selling to and competing with
service providers).

This will not only remove complications from
sales to existing markets (e.g., the local
telephone companies), it will open new markets
(e.g., competitors of AT&T's current service and
equipment businesses).

It will accelerate decision making by greatly
simplifying our corporate structure. It will
give each business unit financial flexibility
appropriate to its market and opportunities
(e.g., capital structure and cost structure).

This restructuring resolves thorny public policy
issues which limit our business flexibility
(e.g., European concerns about vertical
integration, the strictures of the FCC's
Computer Inquiry II ruling, the McCaw Consent
Decree, etc.).

Throughout the transition and beyond, AT&T and
these new companies will meet all existing

```
commitments. We will not miss a beat in serving
customers. We will communicate openly and
honestly with employees. We will always act in
the best interests of AT&T's current
shareowners.
```

The weekend of September 16 and 17, 1995, Bob Allen and his wife Betty were guests of honor at the New Castle, Indiana, high school homecoming. Allen had graduated from the school and was the local boy made good. As chairman and CEO of AT&T, he traveled by corporate jet and golfed on national television with stars of stage, screen, and Wall Street. But he had never lost touch with his old friends in New Castle and, as he waved to them from the football stands as New Castle's high school team played Kokomo, few would guess that he had a care in the world.

But over that weekend a now expanded team of PR, financial, and legal people were putting final touches on the documents that would be reviewed by the AT&T board of directors and then announced to the world in less than five days. Miraculously, security had held. There had not been a single probing question from any of the reporters and investment analysts who had full-time jobs covering the company's every move, reflective moment, or hiccup.

The AT&T board met at 8:00 a.m. on Wednesday, September 20, as planned. Marilyn was up to review the communications plan by 8:30 a.m. And by 9:05 a.m., the board voted, and Marilyn made a phone call releasing information to every conceivable constituent—almost simultaneously.

"We had worked with Bob on a major explanation of this as a letter, and I got approval from the lawyers to share it with employees five minutes ahead of the news release so that we could get to them first," she remembered. "So the letter went out first. Then the news release. We posted the announcement on the internet immediately. At this point, I got all our PR staff together."

"About an hour before the announcement, we told all our officers to be ready for a 10:00 a.m. conference call with Bob Allen," she said. "By 11:00 a.m., the people who had been briefed at 10:00 a.m. were out contacting stakeholders and delivering the key messages we had prepared earlier. This went on all over the world for the rest of the day."

By noon, Rick Miller, who had replaced Alex Mandl as chief financial officer, held a conference call with the financial analysts who followed the company. And by 2:00 p.m. employees were able to view a taped message from Bob Allen, followed by a live news conference from New York. That afternoon, letters went out to shareowners and retired AT&T officers, and AT&T PR teams in every major U.S. city reached out to their local media, government officials, and community leaders to answer questions. A full-page ad ran in major newspapers across the country the following day. It was a classic example of what Marilyn called "turning on the wind machine."

The initial media reaction was very positive. All of the messages Marilyn and her team of two had crafted appeared in one form or another in both the print and TV coverage so the small PR team that had pulled off the announcement felt good. The stock gained $10 billion dollars in value in a single day, which made everyone feel good.

No one was happier than Rick Miller, a proverbial "numbers man" who had made his reputation helping Penn Central come out of bankruptcy and leading Wang Computers into it. He did not normally find enthusiasm contagious. Thin, angular, and gray in hair and pallor, he was all edges and seemed too ascetic to get excited about anything but balancing his check book.

But when he had come to lunch in the executive dining room on September 20, after briefing the analysts, he told Allen his meeting had gone very well. "They just thought we should move faster to establish the equipment company," he said. Then, in an almost off-hand way, as he reached for the pickles and remembered the 2:00 p.m. news conference to follow, he added, "why don't we say we'll do the IPO by the end of the first quarter?"

Thus were sown the seeds of a public relations crisis that would ignite a national debate on downsizing and make AT&T and its chairman the symbol of corporate greed.

CHAPTER SEVENTEEN

WHEN THINGS COME APART

"On September 21, the real work began," Marilyn remembered. "We have a set of corporate values and we really did our damnedest to follow them through the entire process." It would not be easy. Just separating the books of the three companies and giving them each their own balance sheet was a monumental task. Together they had revenue of $80 billion, debt of $20 billion, 300,000 employees, and facilities in all 50 states and around the world. They had contracts with each other, shared intercompany debt, and used each other's intellectual property.

Restructuring meant divvying up almost a hundred billion dollars of assets, not counting the second largest private pension fund in the world and intellectual property that had been accumulating at the rate of one patent a day since the 1920s. Plus, each of those 300,000 employees would be affected in one way or another. "When you restructure, it's very easy to lose track of your budgets and your financial commitments. When people change jobs, customer contacts can go down the drain," Marilyn said. "We were determined that no commitments would fall in the cracks as we moved forward."

On September 25, the board created a steering committee of Bob Allen, Hal Burlingame, John Zeglis, Rick Miller (who had replaced Alex Mandl as CFO), and Marilyn. Their job was to resolve conflicts so issues wouldn't bounce back and forth around the company waiting for a decision.

The fourth quarter of 1995 was a blur. Financial analysts were almost euphoric about the restructuring announcement. They hailed it as a bold, decisive, gutsy move that would allow AT&T to exploit the changing landscape of the telecom industry. Some said it was the most constructive move the company had made since divestiture, creating tremendous shareholder value by unshackling each of the new businesses from common ownership so they could focus on their individual markets without internal conflicts. Some analysts said that Wall Street had underestimated AT&T, and the sum of its parts would turn out to be greater than the whole. Some columnists wrote the restructuring was appropriate given changes in the telecom industry. They pointed to the 1984 breakup as a past acceptance of change that had paid off for shareholders. AT&T's stock had greatly outperformed IBM's, which had resisted change a decade ago.

Allen was widely applauded for having the insight, fortitude, and optimism to tackle the future. Of course, he was also criticized for past failures such as the purchase of NCR, which had lost half its value since he bought it. But AT&T's stock price continued to rise on the positive noises, especially about the new communications equipment business, which was unofficially being called everything from Newco or Equipco to S&T, for Systems and Technologies.

The steering committee met almost daily, and Allen gave the members assignments. For example, Marilyn was told to pull together a team that could work with a corporate identity consultant to come up with a suitable name for Equipco. She also had to figure out how to divide the company's $19 million art collection, eight miles of documents in the company's archives,[78] and—not incidentally—her own 500-person organization.

As a rule, people followed their jobs. But some people were in corporate jobs dedicated to one or more of the new companies. And while each company had a CEO, a CFO, and a chief counsel, few of them had ever held that role in a public company. Burlingame had to

---

[78] In the end, it was decided to keep the AT&T Corporate Archives intact, giving Lucent (Equipco's eventual name) free access to all the material placed in it up to the date of the split. Lucent decided to establish its own archives as part of its launch.

help Allen figure out who would be the CEO of Equipco (or whatever it was to be called). Zeglis was given the task of sorting through the company's treasure trove of patents and other intellectual property and assigning each to the appropriate company. He was also working with Miller to divide the pension funds, corporate debt, and other financial assets and obligations between the three companies.

Somewhere along the line, Miller decided if they were going to launch Equipco's initial public offering at the end of the first quarter of 1996, they might as well put the cost of restructuring in 1995. That way AT&T, Equipco, and NCR could each start the new year with a clean balance sheet. Of course, those costs would have to be announced on the first business day of 1996, January 2.

It would be tough. Each business would have to estimate all the costs involved at the same time they were pulling together their fourth quarter results. The total cost would probably depress AT&T's overall results for the year, but that wouldn't surprise the financial community. They would see it as a once-in-a-lifetime opportunity to clean the company's books of obsolete equipment and facilities. Low-performing divisions could be sold off. Each company's workforce could be resized to the new competitive environment, and the separation charges could be wrapped into one magnificent write-off that would give all three companies as close to a clean slate as the accounting rules would allow.

By then it was obvious to everyone that the restructuring would result in fewer jobs. No one knew how big a reduction would be required, but outside the membership of the steering committee, a rift began widening between human resources and public relations on one side and the financial and operational people on the other. The bean counters called the HR and PR people "bleeding hearts" who didn't understand the realities of running a business and were overly concerned about not being "nice." The PR and HR people accused the financial and operating people of focusing too much on Wall Street and not taking the human impact of downsizing into account. Not to mention the negative press that would follow.

So on November 15, in an effort to get ahead of the need for layoffs, AT&T announced a voluntary buyout offer to more than 75,000 management employees, about half the people in the company's management ranks. "The point of our buyout offer was compassion and respect for people," Marilyn said. "It was not [about saving] money. The idea was to offer a buyout to as many of our managers as possible so we would have fewer people to terminate involuntarily. You may lose more good people than you want this way, but it makes it easier for those people who are ready to leave to go. And it gives the people who don't want to make the journey to a new company—which is something we learned about in 1984—a way out. Nevertheless, we got creamed for it in the media. Next thing we knew people thought we were forcing 72,000 layoffs." Marilyn's media relations people tried to explain that the company didn't expect more than 10 percent of the eligible employees to take the offer, but the 72,000 number was just too headline-worthy, and it continued to be cited.

Marilyn began to hear rumblings that some senior executives thought the announcement could have been handled more deftly. Some thought making the voluntary offer now, instead of in January when it would be part of a larger announcement, just drew unnecessary attention to the likelihood of layoffs. This was just inviting the media to take two swipes at the company rather than one. Marilyn countered that it was part of the company's commitment to transparency. Once the company knew it had to eliminate some jobs, it had an obligation to let employees know and give them an opportunity to figure out what they wanted to do. But even some board members asked her if she had considered retaining an outside public relations firm to help. There would be points in the coming months that she would have welcomed help, and in fact sought it. But for now, she thought she had everything under control.

"We moved on," she said. "We continued to get leadership teams in place, and we started the roundtables for 28,000 staff people. Roundtables required everybody in the organization to have a resume and a supervisor's assessment. A group of people who were dealing with a particular unit in the organization would meet in a room with all the resumes, all the assessments, and the new organization design for their group. Every person being discussed needed to have someone in that meeting who knew them personally. Otherwise, the roundtable could not proceed."

Once the unit's supervisors had all that information and everyone was present, they worked together to decide who had the best skills to fill the jobs on their unit's new organization chart. The process began November 20 and went through most of December. "We couldn't stop for the holiday season," Marilyn said. In fact, in public relations, everything was on a low boil in the whole month of December. "We were in a blackout period because we filed for the IPO of Equipco in December, which meant we couldn't say anything about the part of the company being spun off. The lawyers were all over us because we were so visible. We couldn't even do employee broadcasts. We had to be mum and the media was totally confused by our silence."

Meanwhile, the financial people were working around the clock to size the earnings charge the company would take on December 31, 1995, and announce on January 2, the first business day of 1996. The cost of reducing staff would be a relatively small part of the write off, but it would have great symbolic value to Wall Street, which had never really abandoned the notion that the company was bloated and slow-moving. Miller wanted the biggest number of job eliminations he could get out of the three new companies.

Marilyn tried to convince the lawyers to delay the announcement to mid-afternoon so it wouldn't be the first thing employees saw when they returned from the holidays. "I fought the good fight not to make the announcement at 8:00 a.m. on January 2," she said. "I lost. There seemed to be a little bit of legal wiggle room that could have given us a half-day longer to delay. Ultimately, the new CEOs decided that wiggle room was not worth wiggling in."

Marilyn had a long-standing vacation with Bob planned for the week between Christmas and New Year's Day, which was typically a very quiet period in the company. She had put in so many hours over the last few months, she needed to clear her head and reconnect with her husband. The drafts she had seen of the coming announcement looked reasonable to her, and she trusted her staff to work with the legal and financial organizations on the announcement of the restructuring charge. So she packed her bags and took her family to an ecolodge in the rain forests of Costa Rica.

She didn't know that Miller had asked her staff to find out if the number of job eliminations he expected to announce would be the largest in business history. He was bummed to find out that IBM, Sears, and General Motors had all announced greater job cuts than the 40,000 he had in mind. In the days leading up to New Year's Day, the announcement Marilyn's team had drafted changed significantly. The headline and the whole release now led with the number of jobs being eliminated. It wasn't broken down by the three companies being created, which would have made AT&T's portion only 17,000, but it was all lumped together and attributed to AT&T, which of course was taking the charge since the other two companies didn't exist yet.

Marilyn's people argued vociferously that leading with job eliminations would make it the point of all the coverage and few reporters would distinguish between eliminating jobs and cutting employees. The human resources people supported their argument, but the finance people were focused on Wall Street. To them, a big number of job cuts was a dog whistle with a melody of higher earnings to come. They would not be deterred. In fact, one member of Marilyn's team—ironically the woman destined to be senior vice president of public relations at Equipco—argued so forcibly, she was banned from future meetings. The corporate officer Marilyn had left in charge folded like a tent. In hindsight, Marilyn later admitted that not being in the room when all this was being argued was a big mistake. "PR simply didn't have the influence it should have had at a critical moment," she said.

"Arthur Page used to say that, 'All business in a democratic society begins with public permission and exists by public approval'," Marilyn later reminded people. "Well, in January of 1996, we rediscovered just how important 'public permission' is."

As designed, the announcement suitably impressed Wall Street. AT&T's stock price increased four percent by the end of the day. The next day's news coverage was relatively straightforward and neutral, although most newspapers led with the 40,000 figure. The *New York Times'* headline was typical—"Job Cuts At AT&T Will Total 40,000, 13% of Its Staff."[79] And as if taking its cue from the company's CFO, the story's opening lines said, "The AT&T Corporation announced the biggest single job cut in the history of

---

[79] Edmund L. Andrews, "Job Cuts At AT&T Will Total 40,000, 13% of Its Staff," *New York Times,* Jan. 3, 1996.

the telephone business yesterday, and one of the largest corporate workforce reductions ever."[80]

Some of the stories included many of the messages the company was trying to get out about the generous financial and job-hunting support affected employees would get. For example, the *Washington Post* quoted the president of the nation's largest outplacement firm calling the downsizing "a 'textbook example' of how to do a layoff in today's economic climate."[81] The *New York Times* quoted Allen, acknowledging "how wrenching it will be for employees and their families," and then added that the company really had little choice but to slim down "in response to changes that are expected to rock the communications industry over the next few years."[82]

Some media stories focused on the generous benefits package offered to departing employees. A number reported on the centers the company had set up to help laid-off employees in their job searches. A few reported that more employees than expected had taken November's voluntary buyout offer, reducing likely layoffs.

As Marilyn and her people logged off their PCs that night, they felt the announcement had gone about as well as they could have hoped. But as it turned out, they had focused too much on the newspapers that were tucked into the seat pockets of the limousines ferrying AT&T executives. They took too much comfort in the fact that most of their "messages" made it into print, albeit at the end of long stories. They should have paid more attention to the TV evening news, which was how most people heard about the downsizing. Ironically, she had argued that point early in her AT&T career.

---

[80] Andrews, *New York Times*, Jan. 3, 1996.

[81] Kristen Downey Grimsley, "AT&T Promises Aid to Laid-Off Workers; Package Reflects New Trends in Downsizing," *Washington Post*, Jan. 3, 1996.

[82] Grimsley, *Washington Post*, Jan. 3, 1996.

The television news anchors tied AT&T's downsizing to feelings of insecurity and fear rattling working people in every community. For example, for Tom Brokaw on NBC, "jobs" became "people." On his evening newscast, he announced, "40,000 *people* lost their jobs at AT&T today ... If what happened today to 40,000 workers at AT&T is any kind of barometer of what's ahead, it will be another long, anxious year for the American middle class."[83]

On one level, objective economic data suggested everything was fine—inflation was at historically low rates (2.7%), unemployment had declined in the last four years and was at relatively low levels (5.8%), stock prices were at all-time highs (the Dow had added 1,000 points in the last 12 months). But the statistics could not show that many Americans were feeling increasingly worried, frustrated and angry. More than 3.25 million people had lost their jobs in 1995, one out of every 20 workers—a level that had become the norm for the previous five years. In the last ten years, more than one-third of Americans (35%) had either lost their own job or an immediate family member had. Almost one quarter (22%) of Americans worried they would lose their job in the next twelve months.

Despite low inflation, real incomes were being squeezed; all but the top 10 percent of wage earners had seen their real income decline. Optimism about the national economic outlook had taken a negative turn in December of 1995 and Americans were even more pessimistic about their personal financial situation. Only three out of ten believed their children would be better off than they were.[84]

---

[83] *NBC Nightly News* with Tom Brokaw, January 3, 1996.

[84] This economic data were widely available from public sources such as the Bureau of Labor Statistics. The public opinion data is drawn principally from a national poll conducted by the *New York Times* from December 3 to 6. It formed the basis for a seven-part series, "The Downsizing of America," which ran from March 3 to March 10, 1996, and put a human face on the issue of job losses.

All this was knowable, but it had not figured into the planning of AT&T's announcement. "We ran afoul of a national wave of public sentiment that was very angry at the way we were restructuring to compete in the business conditions we faced," Marilyn later admitted. "The wave washed over us beginning on January 2 when we made our downsizing announcement."

She never forgave herself for not seeing it coming, which after all, she considered one of her prime responsibilities. And it particularly galled her that this was AT&T's third entanglement with a social issue percolating just outside the periphery of her senior colleagues' tight focus on the company's stock price.

"The downsizing crisis was an exact replica of the principles gone wrong," Marilyn said. "If you were watching the outside world, you would have recognized that the issue of corporate downsizing was coming to a head. And yet the downsizing was done in a way that refused to give a nod to public sensibilities and concerns—not that counsel wasn't offered." Indeed, in Marilyn's absence, her people were either ignored or steamrolled.

"I do believe that the financial people at the time thought the downsizing would be helpful to the stock, just as we were accused by the media," she later admitted. Little did she know she would have one more time at bat, this time facing off with Bob Allen himself.

CHAPTER EIGHTEEN

PAYING THE PIPER

While breaking AT&T into three more-focused companies struck most savvy observers as a great idea, at least in theory, the AT&T board of directors understood just how complicated it would be in practice. The 1984 divestiture, after all, had taken two full years to pull off. While Trivestiture would arguably be simpler, carrying it off in less than half the time would be no walk in the park.

That's why the board gave a special grant of stock options to the members of the steering committee. The options could only be exercised if the company's stock price increased about 20 percent in four to six years. The size of the option grants was not insignificant—from options on about 300,000 shares for Marilyn and Burlingame to about 850,000 for Allen. But valuing what those options would be worth several years out was more art than science. The standard method uses a formula created by three academics,[85] which in the case of Allen's option grant produced a value of $10.8 million.[86]

Surprisingly, no one remembered it would be reported as compensation when the company made its filings for 1995 to the Securities and Exchange Commission. AT&T was traditionally one of the first companies to make that filing because it had to send a copy to shareholders at least 10 days before its annual meeting, which was always held in April. With more than 3,000,000 shareowners, the company needed to file its proxy with the SEC in February to be

---

[85] The formula, developed by three economists—Fischer Black, Myron Scholes, and Robert Merton—but known as the Black-Scholes formula, calculates the theoretical value of options using current stock prices, expected dividends, the option's strike price, expected interest rates, time to expiration, and expected volatility.

[86] AT&T's 1996 Proxy, filed on February 26, 1996, p. 37.

sure there was enough time to print and mail it on schedule. Compensation for the CEO of AT&T would come out right on the heels of its downsizing announcement.

A draft copy of the compensation section went to Marilyn every year and she discovered that the special bonus showed up in it. Although the bonus consisted of options that couldn't be exercised for four years, Marilyn immediately realized revealing them in a period of such economic anxiety would be a public relations disaster.

She went to Allen and warned him about the potential impact. Allen was not a greedy man. His salary, bonus, and usual stock awards totaled about $7 million, and were quite modest compared to that of his peer CEOs. But Marilyn was quite sure total compensation of $16 million, after adding the hypothetical value of the special option grants, would create a furor. "There must be a way to rescind the grant until this has blown over," she said.

"But none of us will get any of it for four years and, even then, not unless the company's stock price continues to go up," Allen countered. "Plus, I'm taking a 20 percent cut in base pay." He couldn't understand why people wouldn't get that, and he refused to make some symbolic action for the sake of "optics." He wasn't going to call a board meeting to do it. So, the proxy went out the way it was.

The best Marilyn could do was to prepare a letter to employees over Allen's signature explaining his compensation. The letter went out on the same day the proxy was filed, knowing that the media would jump on the compensation section as soon as it hit EDGAR the SEC's web-based database of corporate filings.[87]

Uncharacteristically, the letter also took a swipe at the news media, which she would later come to regret. There was no question

---

[87] Development of EDGAR (Electronic Data Gathering Analysis and Retrieval) began in 1984 and by 1995, 92% of all public companies were using it.

the tsunami of media coverage had defined AT&T as the most prominent example of greed-driven downsizing, but Marilyn would later have to admit that the company had given them an invitation to do so when the release of Allen's salary followed so closely on the heels of the job cuts announcement. The *New York Times'* coverage was typical, even quoting from Allen's letter to employees:

> Robert E. Allen, AT&T's chairman and chief executive, and the man who ordered 40,000 people cut from the company's payroll, received stock options last year that increased his total pay package to $16 million from $6.7 million.

> Executives of the AT&T Corporation say Mr. Allen's actual pay is much less, because he and other top executives cannot cash in their options for at least four years. Mr. Allen, in a long and testy message to all company employees on Monday, said he had actually taken a 20 percent cut in cash compensation and was "in line with CEOs of comparable companies."

> In the last several weeks, AT&T and its layoffs have come under a torrent of hostile coverage on television, newspapers, and news magazines that have highlighted the company's cutbacks as a sign of deeper troubles in the American workplace.

> Mr. Allen, in a message to all of AT&T's 303,000 employees, lashed out against what he called "relentless" and "inaccurate" news coverage and defended his business judgment, his salary, and his empathy for the "painful results" of AT&T's job cuts.

> "Restructuring to get to a strong future does unfortunately require force reductions," he

said. "I'm not immune to the emotions they
engender. I'm deeply saddened by the pain and
loss this is causing some of our people and
their families. But in the end, concern isn't
enough."

News stories like that were bad enough, but if AT&T public
relations people thought they had dodged a bullet when they
announced the restructuring charges on Jan. 2, they were soon to
discover that Pat Buchanan, a conservative Republican running for
president in the New Hampshire primaries, had reloaded his guns.
Buchanan had made fighting the loss of American jobs one of the
central themes of his campaign and relentlessly attacked Bob Allen
as a "bloodless, corporate butcher," who "laid off forty thousand
workers *just like that*" while "making $5 million a year" and seeing the
value of his company "stock [go] up five million" on the news.

Buchanan had tapped into working people's very real fear and
anger by making Allen into a symbol of corporate greed. And now he
had even more to work with. When he won the New Hampshire
primary, pundits credited his attacks on corporate downsizing. "We
gave Pat Buchanan the issue on which he built his damn campaign,"
Marilyn said at the time.

Far from coincidentally, media coverage of AT&T's downsizing
increased and became increasingly critical, with six negative stories
for every neutral one. For example, *Newsweek*'s Allan Sloan wrote
that, while AT&T's downsizing made sense, AT&T's executives
should share in the pain. In reporting the story, Sloan even schlepped
out to New Jersey so he could look Allen in the eye when he asked if
it was "fair" to draw a million-dollar paycheck when workers were

losing their jobs. Allen just glared at him and said it wasn't his job to decide what was "fair."[88]

The Council of Institutional Investors, which represents over 100 public and private pension funds, prepared a report which concluded that Allen's compensation was, at best, insensitive and, at worst, undeserved, considering the merely average performance of AT&T stock in recent years. The Council's report came against the backdrop of an article in *Fortune* by one of the most respected business writers of all, Carol Loomis. Titling her piece, "AT&T Has No Clothes," Loomis documented how, since divesting its local telephone companies, AT&T had "lurched from one strategy to another . . . and specialized in huge write offs tied to downsizings."[89]

Little of this surprised Marilyn. When the bean counters ignored PR advice not to highlight the elimination of 40,000 jobs as part of AT&T's 1996 restructuring, they stumbled into the miasma of job insecurity that had fallen on the country. "We didn't have the biggest downsizing in that particular period," she later recalled. "But because we released the information in a way that played to Wall Street, there was no place to go but down. It was ugly."

And even Marilyn herself couldn't convince her CEO that accepting a big option package on the heels of the downsizing announcement would make him look greedy and out-of-touch. "When the big guy takes the cash while the little guy loses his shirt, it is seen as failing a test of character," she later told a group of public relations executives." And I can tell you, don't hold your breath for those kinds of failures to be forgiven by the public."[90]

---

[88] Allan Sloan, "For Whom Bell Tolls," *Newsweek*, Jan. 15, 1996.

[89] Carol Loomis, "AT&T Has No Clothes," *Fortune*, Feb. 1996.

[90] From remarks Marilyn Laurie made when inducted into the Arthur W. Page Society Hall of Fame in 2002.

Despite the company's efforts to soften the blow for people laid off—from generous separation payments to grants for education and starting a business—the company was demonized. "The senior team thought we had a defensible argument based on reason," she said. "It's irrelevant. In a highly-politicized and emotional social issue, that's not what carries the day. What carries the day is values. And we flunked on values." In the final analysis, employees and the public did not get the attention they deserved in the decision process. And then the company gave them reason to believe shared sacrifice was not in the executive lexicon. If that was not obvious to most of Marilyn's C-suite colleagues, it certainly occurred to the people who reported to her.

Herb Linnen, a crusty ex-AP reporter turned AT&T's media relations director in Washington, D.C., sent her an email warning that the negative chatter within the Beltway was a big deal. In response, she wrote:

```
Herb --

This IS a big deal problem we're facing. The
challenges to AT&T's core reputation as a caring
employer, a socially responsible company that
cares about its communities, [and] a well-
managed company with a compelling vision of the
future . . . are very threatening. I haven't
seen anything like this in all my time at AT&T.
The business has work to do . . . and so do we.
I haven't discussed this broadly because I don't
want anyone to panic. We are doing some extra
integrated planning, prevention, and containment
work. See what happens in a week or so.

-- Marilyn
```

On January 22, Marilyn called her officers into a meeting and declared a "PR Crisis" due to "the national debate and an avalanche of negative reaction to the downsizing along with the equally negative *Fortune* article, the dropping stock price, and upcoming negative financial articles." But events took an apocalyptic turn when *Newsweek* took a second bite at the apple with a February 26, 1996, cover story proclaiming Allen a "Corporate Killer."[91]

Marilyn first heard *Newsweek* was working on another story about corporate downsizing because a woman who worked in the company's Washington, D.C., office was married to Evan Thomas, one of the magazine's assistant managing editors. She carried their pillow talk into the office and tipped her boss off who quickly called Marilyn. Since the company had already had its say with *Newsweek*'s Allan Sloan—in an encounter that neither he nor Allen had found particularly satisfactory—Marilyn decided to maintain a low profile and hope AT&T would be only mentioned in passing.

Marilyn would see even worse later, but *Newsweek*'s cover on Monday was a nightmare. It looked like a parody put out by some slightly addled college kids. Mugshot quality photos of four CEOs—IBM's Lou Gerstner, Digital Equipment's Robert Palmer, Scott Paper's Al Dunlap, and AT&T's Robert Allen—appeared on a black cover under the words "Corporate Killers."

The story inside was actually not as bad—it repeated much of Sloan's prior story, including the previous Allen quotes, and added about eight people to its list of "hit men." Sloan had succeeded in getting only one CEO to present the opposing point of view—"Chainsaw" Al Dunlap, the cost-slashing CEO of Sunbeam. And Marilyn later learned Dunlap's submission had been so disjointed

---

[91] Allan Sloan, "Jobs—The Hit Men," *Newsweek*, Feb. 26, 1996.

that Sloan, a master of arguing both sides of any issue, had been forced to edit it heavily. But the cover was over the top.

When Allen saw it, he called the *Washington Post*'s CEO, Don Graham, who counted *Newsweek* in his media empire. Graham did what any CEO in his position would do—he sympathized and passed the buck. By the end of the week, Allen had received a fax from Richard Smith, *Newsweek*'s chairman and editor-in-chief:

```
Dear Mr. Allen:

Don Graham has told me of his conversation with
you and of your deep concerns about our cover on
this week's issue. First, let me say that I take
those concerns very, very seriously. While the
subject matter of the story is obviously a major
topic of national debate, I sincerely regret any
misunderstanding of our intentions caused by the
cover itself. . . . Had we been more sensitive
to the possibility that the cover choice would
distract readers from the seriousness of the
story, we would have chosen a different
approach.

As the person responsible for the magazine's
operations, I wanted to let you know just how I
felt. Beyond that, I genuinely hope that you
will consider writing a piece for the magazine
about the painful and difficult issues involved
in corporate restructuring.

-- Yours sincerely,
   Richard M. Smith
```

Allen passed the fax along to Marilyn with the notation "I got his attention, anyway!"

Marilyn took up Smith's invitation, and six weeks later Allen's essay ran in *Newsweek*'s "My Turn" column. Entitled "The Anxiety

Epidemic," it said, "downsizing is a necessary evil, but business needs to do more to ease the pain."[92]

These were essentially the same arguments that Allan Sloan had made in his two previous articles on the subject. But rather than being pleased to see his ideas embraced, Sloan was incensed. He felt that, by giving Allen a turn in the magazine's pages, his editors had implicitly distanced themselves from the story. The cover had not even been his idea. He felt if Allen had a bone to pick, he should write a letter to the editor like everyone else.

Apparently, at least some of *Newsweek*'s readers felt the same way. At least partly to mollify Sloan, the magazine ran four letters in its next issue—all taking issue with the Allen piece. AT&T's own research was more positive. Over 60 percent of *Newsweek* readers read at least some of Allen's "My Turn" column. Of the 65 percent who had an opinion of the column, positive reactions outnumbered negative by two-to-one. In fact, 20 percent said it made them feel more favorable towards Bob Allen.

Marilyn had copies of Allen's column mailed to 5,400 business and community leaders. But she was fighting an uphill battle. In March, the *New York Times* ran an unprecedented seven-part series on "The Downsizing of America." Not to be outdone, *Businessweek* followed with its own cover story on "Economic Anxiety."[93]

Bob Allen, who had more in common with Mister Rogers than Gordon Gekko,[94] was now the personification of cold-blooded corporate greed. Marilyn found stories that Allen was cold and aloof particularly galling. She knew he personally replied to all the letters

---

[92] Robert E. Allen, "The Anxiety Epidemic," *Newsweek*, Apr. 8, 1998.

[93] *Businessweek*'s cover story appeared on Mar. 11, 1996.

[94] Gordon Gekko, a character in the movie *Wall Street* famously said, "Greed is good." Mr. Rogers is Fred Rogers, the host of a popular public television program for pre-school children.

he received from spouses and children whose wife, husband, or parent had been laid off. And she had been with him when, at her suggestion, he took the corporate jet to Homestead Air Force Base in the days after Hurricane Andrew tore across southern Florida.

Homestead had been ground zero when the fast-moving Category 5 storm made landfall, leveling entire neighborhoods, tossing boats and mobile homes into the air, and leaving more than 250,000 people homeless and three million without power from Key Largo to Miami.

The destructive power of 165-mile-per-hour winds was evident as the corporate jet approached the military airfield. The control tower was silent, every window blown out, and the runways were littered with debris, including overturned aircraft. But Allen had not come to check on the company's facilities or equipment.

On this particular day, Allen's mission was simply to check on as many local AT&T people as he could. About 259 AT&T employees had lost their homes and nearly all their possessions in the storm. The company had provided counselors, temporary housing, and cash advances for affected employees. But Marilyn knew that seeing the CEO in person, stepping through the muck and debris, would signal that the company was with them for the long haul. And though the initial crisis period was over in about three weeks, AT&T's support continued through 1992.

"I will never forget Bob Allen tearing up as he stood in the home of one technician," a local employee remembered. "As we stood in soaked and mildewing carpet, in what was left of his home, the service tech was explaining to Bob how he protected his company van in the storm. Bob couldn't believe the man's dedication and pride in his van, when all he owned had been destroyed. And then his wife offered them refreshments from her hurricane supplies."

Allen's emotion in those encounters was genuine. Marilyn's problem, and his, was simply that he couldn't display it on demand in front of a reporter. To him, that would be phony.

CHAPTER NINETEEN

THE LONG ROAD BACK

Marilyn did her best to remind shareholders about the purpose of restructuring the company in its 1995 annual report, which arrived in their mailboxes just as all the negative downsizing coverage was peaking. The chairman's letter at the beginning of the report put it all in the context of a "continuing journey" which admittedly had some bumps, but gave shareholders a 19-percent annual return since 1984. It reminded them that restructuring was "designed to make the company's businesses more responsive to customers and more agile competitors in their markets." And it emphasized the dramatic changes in customer needs, technology, and public policy that had made restructuring necessary, as well as the speed with which the company was implementing the plan.

By early March, six months after the announcement, AT&T had chosen a CEO and a board of directors for its $20 billion spin-off, now called Lucent Technologies. It had filed Lucent's initial public offering, and its executives were on the road telling their story and getting their people aligned with its mission. NCR had a new CEO, had reclaimed its name, and had launched a new product line which was doing quite well.

AT&T had named Alex Mandl president and appointed him to its board; it had mailed its proxy and been drawn kicking and screaming into the debate about executive compensation; and it was still in the turmoil of downsizing. "Whenever you're in crisis, and certainly whenever you're restructuring, I believe employees are your most important constituency," Marilyn later said. "We focused on employees by fanning out AT&T's leadership in face-to-face meetings all across the country." In a 90-day period in the spring following the downsizing announcement, Allen and other senior officers met with more than 10,000 employees in 70 meetings across the country. Ninety-four percent of employees said they found the meetings informative; 75 percent said the meetings had given them greater confidence and trust in the company's senior leaders.

But if employee attitudes improved following direct contact with senior leaders, consumer attitudes, which were largely formed in the crucible of negative media coverage, had declined precipitously. The proportion who thought AT&T was "well managed" fell from 65 percent prior to the downsizing announcement to just 47 percent in March. Not surprisingly, only 24 percent thought the company "treats employees well." Nearly half of consumers said that the layoffs had negatively impacted their feelings about AT&T. Most troubling, nearly a third (32%) thought the layoffs would decrease the quality and reliability of the company's long distance service.

Shaken by the backlash and still feeling queasy about the numbers in the January downsizing announcement, AT&T's human resources department quietly revisited the downsizing estimates. Whereas the original estimate was that as many as 30,000 people across the three new companies could be surplus once their jobs were eliminated, the HR people now decided the number would be closer to 18,000, based on new estimates of the number who would take voluntary offers and—most significantly—a more realistic view of the number who would find work elsewhere in the company.

Originally, the planners had assumed there would be an insignificant number of job openings, but they had not taken the company's normal attrition rate into account. After years of downsizing, AT&T's employee population skewed much older and closer to retirement than average, and the company's younger employees had plenty of opportunities elsewhere as the telecom boom began to pick up steam. Every year, about 14 percent of

AT&T's employees took jobs at other companies, retired, or died. Marilyn had the new numbers worked into speeches and interviews, but many reporters accused the company of manufacturing either the first 40,000 estimate because it was trying to impress Wall Street or the second 18,000 because it was trying to backtrack in the face of withering criticism.

Marilyn knew the real cause was wishful thinking bordering on incompetence, but that was hardly a good defense. "In the tremendous haste to get the downsizing done, the company never really closed down the commitments individual units were to make and how they would be tracked," she said. "It was absolutely hopeless. We took heat for the 40,000 [positions to be eliminated]. And then we didn't take [the positions] out. So, it was a double disaster."

Of course, the company also had its defenders—some were organized and equipped by Marilyn's people, others jumped in on their own simply because they saw larger issues in play. Columnists such as William Safire at the *New York Times* and George Will and James Glassman at the *Washington Post,* Robert Samuelson in *Newsweek*, and Michael Prowse in the *Financial Times*, wrote contrarian stories that defended the company in some respects. Even ex-Mayor-turned-columnist for the *New York Post*, Ed Koch, weighed in with a surprisingly nuanced survey of think tanks.[95]

---

95 William Safire, "The Great Disconnect," *New York Times*, Mar. 11, 1996; George Will, "Wall Street Is Partners With Main Street," *Los Angeles Times*, Mar. 3, 1996; James K. Glassman, "Jobs: the (Woe Is) Me Generation," *Washington Post*, Mar. 19, 1996; Robert Samuelson, "The Politics of Self-Pity," *Newsweek*, Feb. 26, 1996; Michael Prowse, "Blame Consumers," *Financial Times*, Mar. 18, 1996; Herbert Stein, "Good Times, Bad Vibes," *Wall Street Journal*, Mar. 14, 1996; Michael Hammer, "Who's to Blame for All the Layoffs," Manager's Journal, *Wall Street Journal*, Jan. 22, 1996; James Champy, "Jobs Die So Companies May Live," *New York Times*, Jan. 7, 1996; Marjorie Kelly, "Breakup, Resurgence of AT&T Offer a Lesson About Change," *Minneapolis Star Tribune*, Mar. 4, 1996; Ed Koch, "Is Downsizing a Disaster?" *New York Post*, Feb.

While welcome, all the to-and-fro of supportive columns tended to reinforce AT&T's symbolic role in the downsizing story. "Although the contrarian view supporting our actions was, by mid-March, in full flower in the media," Marilyn said, "the emotional view is what dominated the general news. No applause from Wall Street can overcome concern about the impact on our own people." And not all the "help" directed the company's way was an unalloyed delight. After lighting into critics who were demonizing American business for not understanding how the economy really works, *Businessweek* offered a suggestion: "Fire the CEOs whose strategic backfires lead to layoffs, as was the case at AT&T."[96]

Other suggestions were more well-intentioned. Some of the company's executives suggested doing a "better job" of describing all the support laid-off employees were getting—generous severance payments, funds to help start a business, extended health benefits, unlimited job counseling. The company had even established a nationwide job bank with more than 100,000 positions at other companies and had run full-page ads in major newspapers looking for more. "Wanted Good Jobs For Good People," was the headline and there was an 800 number at the bottom for companies who were "looking for skilled people." It was essentially a model downsizing, Marilyn was told.

"Problem is," she said, "nobody wants a model for downsizing. They don't want downsizing at all. We'll continue to force march reporters through our employee resource centers and package story after story on how we treat our people well. But we need a much bigger and better story based on where we're going and how we're

---

23, 1996. All demonstrate that having powerful people on your side is not always enough.

96 Keith H. Hammonds, "America's Hate Affair With Big Business: What Can Be Done," *Businessweek*, Mar. 4, 1996.

bound to get there—even if it includes some difficult and painful steps. And that destination needs to be seen as in the interest of customers and the nation."

Through all this, Marilyn discovered how lonely her job could be. Many of her colleagues in the executive suite either didn't know what she was getting so worked up about (which, on most days, was even the case with her top client, Bob Allen) or they couldn't understand why she couldn't fix whatever was wrong. They measured the depth of public relations problems in the column inches of the newspapers they read, especially the *Wall Street Journal*, the *New York Times* and *USA Today*, and they were incredulous that she couldn't schmooze reporters into line. But by the end of March 1996, more than half AT&T's media coverage was negative. Colleagues at other companies called to ask "how are you holding up" with a tone suggesting they prayed to never catch what she had. And her phone rang off the hook with experts of all stripes offering to fix things.

One high-profile PR counselor offered to host dinners for Bob Allen with the "people who run the New York media." Doubting that would accomplish much even if he could pull it off, she politely declined. Another advised, in all earnestness, that what she needed was to "put a stop to all these negative stories." Hello?

Marilyn tried to tell Allen that he had become the poster boy for a national issue—the greed of overpaid CEOs. "It's not fair. It's not right," she said. "But it's true. The issue is not going away. And it's embodied in you." She knew his friends in the tight-knit CEO community were sending him supportive letters, because he forwarded them to her. Jack Welch told Allen he was once called "Neutron Jack" because of his policy of cleaning house every year by making managers fire the bottom ten percent of GE employees and then firing the bottom ten percent of management himself. Welch said he lost the moniker when the stock went up. Others told Allen to keep a stiff upper lip; it was just his turn in the barrel.

"Baloney," Marilyn told him. "Easy for them to say. But the criticism we're getting is focused on *you* more than on the company. You have to play; you can't sit it out." Allen countered by saying, "I can't be someone I'm not. I will never be a table-pounding screamer or a high motivator of masses of people because of my rhetoric."

Marilyn assured him he didn't have to become a screamer or the reincarnation of Winston Churchill, though he could use coaching on delivering his message and expressing his true feelings. Beyond that, short of giving back his special options as a dramatic indication that he "gets it," she gave him two options.

First, he could become an active and visible spokesman for customer choice, leading the charge to open local markets to fair competition and discussing the company's vision in terms of customer benefits. To back that up, Marilyn's team would develop a state-specific agenda of speeches, employee town meetings, and editorial board visits. They'd ghostwrite articles for him on the benefits of greater customer choice based on new research they'd field. He'd spend even more time with consumer groups and with employees to rally them around entering markets to give customers greater choice.

They'd also step up community-oriented philanthropy focused on kids, education, and technology. And he would personally deliver the most significant grants. He would champion new ideas on worker training and other approaches to deal with employee dislocations. But the larger issues of corporate restructuring and downsizing would be shifted to third parties.

Alternatively, she said, he could keep his head down, make sure the business made its numbers, avoid any pay issue next year, and—if he was lucky—someone else would take his place as the symbol of corporate greed. In both cases, she'd look for opportunities to associate him with positive news. The second strategy, she said, was "risky but viable." He said he'd think about it. He probably did, rolling an unlit cigar in his mouth, but he never said which path he wanted to follow, which told her all she needed to know. He was either in denial or hoping the problem would go away on its own.

Meanwhile, AT&T was suffering from a "gang mentality" among the media who were portraying the company as uncaring, unfocused and poorly managed. AT&T and its chairman had become symbols of irresponsible downsizing and corporate greed. Attacking those issues head-on was a suicide mission that would only cement the company's position as the principal villain in the national soap opera. As it was, AT&T had been forced onto "the slippery slope of reactive communications." The only way off that slope was through "extreme message focus," using the "new AT&T" as the platform. What had been lost in the last 90 days was the concept that Allen and his senior team were indeed building a new company.

The key to restoring Allen's reputation, Marilyn believed, was to show how everything Allen was doing—even the distasteful things like laying people off—was in the interests of building a stronger, more competitive company. "Leaders can be flexible, adaptable, willing to change," she said. "But in the end, they can't be perceived to be erratic because you can't trust someone you can't see on a reasonably predictable path."[97]

Marilyn shelved plans to stage a worldwide coming out party for the "new AT&T" later in the year in favor of a strategy she called "Rolling Thunder":

---

[97] Arthur W. Page Center oral history.

1. Confine communications to a few approved key messages. Tie every major announcement to the achievement of our vision.

2. Anticipate and defuse ancillary issues that put us back in the headlines.

3. Rally employees around our vision of the future through proactive communications and executing our [business] strategy.

4. Go directly to key stakeholders with messages that put our [business] initiatives within the context of long-term goals.

5. Raise the visibility of senior executives' engagement internally and externally.

6. Focus on the future, articulating a clear and compelling vision for the new AT&T.

She was determined to put the AT&T wind machine on high throttle. But she realized her strategy had an important missing element—the evasive "mission" Marilyn had spent so much time and energy seeking was still as illusory as a unicorn. The closest she had come was "AT&T's mission is to be the global leader in enabling customers to reap the benefits of information technology." It was accurate, if not terribly compelling. Her strategy depended on it but, man, was it vague.

So she looked for ways to bring the company's mission and values to life. Her director of employee communications suggested giving all employees a paid day off from work to volunteer in the community. The program, "AT&T Cares," was modeled on a similar initiative at Ford and could donate one million hours of community service within a year. Marilyn thought it was a brilliant way to reconnect employees with the company's past tradition of service to the community. Research also suggested the program would boost employees' spirits, while increasing people's regard for the company.

She sold the idea to Bob Allen and his senior team, all of whom promised to participate. On the day the program kicked off, in fact, Allen drove to the city of Newark, New Jersey, to work alongside Habitat for Humanity volunteers. Marilyn helped paint benches in New York's Central Park. Others helped wire local schools for internet service. In all, more than 5,000 employees donated a day of work to non-profits in 25 cities across the country, earning positive stories in places like the *Wall Street Journal* and the *NBC Nightly News*.

Marilyn also surveyed employees to find out what would make them feel that they had a stake in the "new" company they were building. The survey offered examples ranging from a "founder's bonus" to "stock options." Most employees said they had no idea what stock options are, but since the top officers get them, they must be good so that's what would mean the most to them. She took that data to Bob Allen and Hal Burlingame for discussion in the management executive committee, which agreed that giving rank and file employees an option on 100 shares of stock would increase their sense of ownership in the "new" AT&T. Allen then took the plan to the company's board, which quickly approved it.[98]

And to send a strong signal to the staff at headquarters that the company was serious about changing the culture, she lobbied Allen to close the executive dining room. She didn't have to twist his arm. Few officers were eating there regularly since most of them worked through lunch and ate cafeteria sandwiches. Seeing Bob Allen in line

---

[98] AT&T's shareowners approved a grant to each employee of 100 stock options, which at the stock's peak in mid-1999 was worth about $2,000. Before they could be exercised, however, the stock price declined below the strike price and never recovered. In September of 2002, the company offered to exchange the options for a smaller number of restricted shares, which were to be held for three years before they could be sold.

to get a sandwich probably said things were changing more loudly—and persuasively—than anything Marilyn could write for him to say.

Marilyn also packaged AT&T Foundation cash grants with product and service donations to create the AT&T Learning Network—a $150 million program to bring the benefits of information technology to primary and secondary education over the next five years. AT&T Wireless, for example, agreed to equip schools with cellphones that could be used in an emergency or to improve communications on field trips. AT&T's consumer long distance business agreed to provide schools with free internet service. And the unit providing long distance services to businesses agreed to host websites teachers could access to develop online lesson plans.

The Foundation staff redirected a good chunk of new educational grants to preparing teachers to use new media in the classroom. They funded the development of new course curricula and started a program to bring the best teachers from every state to AT&T Labs for summer workshops, all of it under the "AT&T Learning Network" umbrella. By 2001, the AT&T Learning Network had been recognized and honored by many of the country's most significant educational organizations. Marilyn had Bob Allen announce all this at a New York City news conference.

Creating the AT&T Learning Network also positioned Allen to play a major role in an Education Summit in May that would bring together most of the country's governors and CEOs from 44 major companies. A pet project of IBM CEO Lou Gerstner, the Summit was designed to discuss ways to raise the basic skill levels of high school graduates. Normally Allen had little patience with politicians, who he generally considered "grandstanders." He also didn't consider it particularly productive to spend a day listening to speeches he could just as easily read in a fraction of the time. But he was genuinely interested in the subject—one of his daughters was studying to be a teacher and his own mother had taught school—so he took the company helicopter to IBM's Executive Conference Center in Palisades, New York.

Allen was coming out of a workshop on educational standards when he saw a familiar face coming around the corner. Leslie Stahl, a correspondent for the *60 Minutes* television news magazine, was a casual acquaintance who had sat next to him at several dinners when Tom Wyman, an AT&T director, had been CEO of CBS. Assuming she must be doing a report on the crisis in American education, Allen smiled and stopped to shake her hand. Then he saw the camera over her shoulder and the microphone in her hand.

"Mr. Allen," she said. "I wonder if you would respond to the charge that you got a big pay package for millions and millions of dollars when you're laying off thousands and thousands of people?" Like a deer in the headlights, Allen mumbled something about it not being the right time or place to get into such a discussion. Stahl whispered "I know, I know" sympathetically and plowed ahead with her questions.[99] When Allen finally got away and found a quiet corner, he called Marilyn.

"I'm dead," he said.

He wasn't dead yet. There was still more pain to endure. The AT&T Annual Meeting would follow within weeks, just in time for the media, the company's unions, and pundits of every stripe to take a few more swings at him.

AT&T's 1996 annual meeting was held in the Miami Convention Center, and Allen gamely started the day with an early morning news conference, where he was pelted with questions about his compensation. Then he faced an auditorium of angry shareowners, most of them retirees, who lined up outside four

---

[99] Lesley Stahl, "Easy Money in Hard Times," *60 Minutes*, Apr. 7, 1996.

oversized phonebooths to ask questions, or to simply say their piece into a telephone handset that amplified it throughout the hall. The audience applauded wildly whenever anyone said anything critical about him and laughed derisively when he tried to defend himself.

By contrast, Evelyn Y. Davis, the septuagenarian annual meeting gadfly, provided comic relief. Proud of her multiple facelifts, but too vain to admit she had become hard of hearing, she delivered her remarks in a shrill voice still accented by her native Dutch. Commandeering one of the telephone booths, she began by complaining that the date of AT&T's annual meeting conflicted with that of another company, forcing her to choose between the two. Allen said he expected the other CEO to send thanks. At one point, when Allen tried to refer one of her questions to the company's president, Alex Mandl, she screamed "I vill not deal vith vun of your flunkies!"

Mandl smiled gamely, shifted in his chair a level below the podium and probably thought to himself that, if all went well, he would not be anyone's "flunky" for much longer.

CHAPTER TWENTY

UNPLANNED DETOUR

The opening ceremonies of the 1996 Olympics in Atlanta were held on Friday, July 19, in warm, but not oppressive weather. AT&T executives and their guests were cosseted from the crowds and the humidity in a three-story tent constructed in the middle of Centennial Park around the main entertainment stage. AT&T was a major sponsor of the games and the company's sales teams were entertaining business customers before shepherding them to waiting buses for the ride to Olympic stadium.

Bob Allen should have been in a good mood, but he was standing off by himself noshing on hors d'oeuvres, when Marilyn told him the French media were reporting the company's head of European operations was leaving the company. She asked him if it was true and, if so, what she should tell her media relations people to say.

"If he wants to leave, let him leave," he said. That wasn't exactly what Marilyn was asking, but she took it as an answer. She didn't know until much later that Allen had earlier heard from Burlingame, reporting on a meeting he had just finished with Alex Mandl.

Mandl had become Allen's heir apparent when he was appointed president just months before. But in recent weeks he had been approached about a job at a small startup. He had thought Barksdale was smart to make the move to Netscape, and that it had made him a multimillionaire in practically no time only confirmed his initial opinion. Plus, now that he was the company's chief operating officer, the full weight of competing with AT&T's former telephone companies was hitting him. Allen was just 61. There was a good chance that long before Allen stepped down, the former Bell phone companies would get into long distance and clean AT&T's clock, leaving Mandl holding the bag.

On the afternoon of the Olympic opening ceremonies, Mandl had dropped by Burlingame's office, closed the door, and slumped onto the couch. Whenever executives closed Burlingame's door upon entering his office, he knew they were in there to complain about someone or something.

"Hal," Mandl said. "I've been thinking a lot. I can't sleep at night." Assuming this was the beginning of another "why doesn't Bob like me" discussion, Burlingame leaned forward.

"What is it?" he asked.

"I'm leaving the company. I have a chance to run a small startup and build something from the ground up. It doesn't compete with AT&T, and it's too good an opportunity to pass up," he said.

Burlingame had heard this story before, not from Mandl, but from others. It was usually a ploy to renegotiate their compensation. "Alex, we just made you president a few months ago. You have a real shot at succeeding Bob as Chairman. If it's money . . . . "

"Hal, they're offering me a $20 million signing bonus and 18 percent of the equity."

Even Burlingame was impressed. No public corporation could match that. He knew it was similar to Barksdale's package at Netscape so it was probably true. This was no negotiating ploy. But coming on the heels of the previous six months' misadventures, Burlingame knew this would be big trouble.

"Alex," he said, "You know you can't tell me something like this without my doing something with it." Mandl said he understood and left. Burlingame asked his secretary to find Allen.

When Allen returned from Atlanta on Monday, July 22, he called Mandl into his office. He did not try to convince him to stay. Nor did he try to hide his irritation that Mandl had entertained outside offers just four months after being named the company's president. Most of their discussion was about how and when to make the announcement. Allen asked for a few weeks to get his ducks in a row, and Mandl gamely went along.

Although they never admitted it to each other, their announcement goals were diametrically opposed. Mandl naturally wanted to use the announcement to help launch his new venture, attracting potential investors and eventually customers. He had already hired a public relations agency to represent him. Allen equally naturally wanted to low key the announcement. While he knew it could not be positioned as "business as usual," he didn't want anyone doubting the company's ability to meet its financial goals or complete its restructuring.

Allen spent much of the next two weeks on the phone with members of his board. They were as shocked and disappointed at Mandl's decision as he was, but they went along with Allen's plan to handle it like any other senior level departure and to hire search firms to find someone who would be a good fit as AT&T's chief operating officer.

When Allen told Marilyn, she counseled him to address the elephant in the room—although he had never officially anointed Mandl as his successor, most reporters and financial analysts assumed the job would eventually be his. So, whoever Allen selected to replace Mandl also had to have sufficient standing to be seen as Allen's eventual successor.

That, of course, complicated matters for Allen. He wasn't close to retiring, especially not after the media beating he had taken and before he could prove he was right in restructuring the company. He didn't want to give the board a reason to hurry him out the door by engaging them in a search for his successor. Besides, he didn't think someone could come in and take right over as CEO.

Although the mantel had been thrust on him without warning when Olson died, Allen had spent several years as the company's chief operating officer; he knew the business inside and out; and he knew the ins and outs of the company's senior managers and board members. He wanted to find someone who could develop the same knowledge base by spending time in an operational role before becoming chief executive. So Allen and Burlingame would look for a chief operating officer with help from some search firms. There would be no talk of a board search committee.

Marilyn later said, "It's unclear how much of this was Bob's reluctance to leave and how much was his belief that AT&T is a company where it's treacherous to just come in from the outside and take over on Wednesday." Whatever the reason, she worried that Allen's leading role in the process, and the board's acquiescence to a more passive role, would be a problem. "It just wasn't justified by the kind of scrutiny the public always gives to any high-profile activity by AT&T," she said.

Furthermore, Burlingame and Allen had not exactly clothed themselves in glory with the outsiders they had already brought in. Except for Barksdale and Mandl, nearly all left richer than they had been on the way in, thanks to their separation agreements, not their performance. Marilyn took special pain editing the Q&A prepared as guidance for all the media relations people who would be fielding reporters' calls as well as for all the senior managers who reporters might interview: Mandl was leaving for an outrageous amount of money, his resignation would not affect the company in any way, and an external search to replace him as chief operating officer had already begun. Besides, the company had never told Mandl he would replace Allen because he wasn't slated to retire for four years.

In what would prove wishful thinking, the news release itself treated Mandl's leaving as kind of a sidebar.

> AT&T Chairman Robert E. Allen today announced
> changes in the responsibilities of the company's
> senior management, including a search for a
> successor to Alex J. Mandl, president and chief
> operating officer, who is leaving AT&T to become
> chairman and CEO of Associated Communications, a
> new venture company in the wireless
> communications business.

Marilyn also wanted to get the release out at the same time as, if not before, Mandl's new company so AT&T would have an equal shot at positioning the story with reporters. The fly in the ointment, though, was the PR agency Mandl had hired. It was a firm with a reputation for bare knuckle media relations. In fact, its CEO had gone around Marilyn to offer its services to Allen directly after the "Corporate Killers" cover story. His calls and letters to Allen didn't stop until Marilyn sent a blistering letter telling him she was fed up with his end runs. She suspected the temptation to leak the story to a favored reporter in advance of the official release time was going to be almost irresistible.

She agreed to release the news at 9:30 a.m. on Monday but warned her media relations team to be ready to go on Sunday evening at first hint the story had leaked. Much to her surprise, no reporters called on Sunday evening and there was nothing in Monday morning's papers about Mandl's resignation. Mandl's agency had kept its word.

Allen began an 8:00 a.m. meeting of the senior officers in the Anteroom on the executive floors of AT&T's Basking Ridge facility by announcing that Mandl had decided to resign to take a "once in a lifetime" position at a startup. He said Mandl's responsibilities would be split between Miller and Zeglis, while he conducted an outside search for a new president and chief operating officer. Then he asked Mandl if he wanted to say anything. About half the people in the room already knew of Mandl's decision. The others looked around the oversized round table for a hint of what this really meant. From Allen's expression and the curt way in which he announced the news, they could tell he found the whole episode a little distasteful. Even Mandl, normally confident and a bit brash, seemed uncomfortable as he expressed the customary words of mixed feelings. When Mandl finished, Allen thanked him and said he was sure he had other things he had to take care of. Mandl left the room.

At 9:02 a.m., 28 minutes before the news release was to be issued and even before the meeting in the Anteroom broke up, a Salomon Brothers research analyst named Jack Grubman—who had obviously been tipped off by Mandl or his PR agency—broke the news in what the *Times* called "a harshly negative note to his clients."[100] The note was picked up by the Bloomberg newswire and the games began.

Grubman, who *Institutional Investor* magazine perennially ranked as the number one or two telecom analyst, wrote that Mandl's resignation could cause "major" management disruption" and "may be an indication of deeper issues within AT&T." He concluded, "Needless to say, we remain cautious on the stock." AT&T shares dropped like a stone as soon as the opening bell rang on the New York Stock Exchange.

Mandl had already left the building to begin a media tour with his new PR representatives. By the time Marilyn caught up with him by phone, he swore that he had not told Grubman about his decision to leave. Considering how close the two were, that was hard to believe. Mandl had made a point of entertaining Grubman at his homes in New Jersey and outside Washington, D.C. Marilyn knew

---

[100] Mark Landler, "How Snap Analysis Spurred an AT&T Slide," *New York Times*, Aug. 21, 1996.

they had been trading industry gossip for years and that Mandl occasionally fed Grubman backdoor information about the company. Grubman was even on his telephone's speed dial. In any case, by early afternoon, Grubman issued a second note, suggesting that his initial assessment might have been overly negative.

But the damage had been done. Marilyn's strategy had been successful in focusing the media on Mandl's new compensation package. That was not exactly difficult—the media love to write about what people make. And they used the quotes she had quietly planted in the mouths of outside search firms, like, "Mandl will be the highest-paid American under seven feet tall."[101]

Still she was not able to defuse the impact of the Grubman-incited stock decline, which became a big part of the story. The company's protests that "nothing will change" were rebutted by a 2.5 percent drop in its share price on extremely heavy volume. The combination of the surprise announcement, Grubman's negative analysis of its significance, and especially the absence of any moderating comments, caused investors who were on the fence to put in sell orders before the markets opened for trading. The selling then fed on itself and it took days before the stock recovered.

By then, the media had set the storyline explaining the first day's share decline—Mandl was the apparent successor to Allen, he had been frustrated playing understudy to a CEO who showed no inclination to leave the stage, and the company was unlikely to find someone as capable who was also willing to sit in the warm-up pen. Sadly, Bob Allen—once again—became the story. *Fortune* magazine perhaps characterized it best as more "salt in [Allen's] wounds."[102]

---

[101] Dennis Kneale, Gautam Naik and Bart Ziegler, "AT&T Heir Apparent Switches to Tiny Firm Offering Huge Pay," *Wall Street Journal*, Aug. 20, 1996.

[102] Andrew Kupfer, "What, Me Worry?" *Fortune*, Sept. 30, 1996.

Marilyn had also been wounded. When Mandl had been made president, it led to a wholesale reshuffling of the top deck. All the operating heads then reported to him. And the management executive committee (MEC) on which Marilyn sat was replaced by a new office of the chairman, consisting of Allen, Mandl, CFO Miller, and Chief Counsel John Zeglis, who also became chair of a newly created executive policy council. Zeglis, Mandl, and Miller would report to Allen. Burlingame and Marilyn would report jointly to Zeglis and Allen. It was the first time she had not reported directly to the CEO since Olson held the office.

It was not a reflection on her performance, though some board members and senior executives didn't hesitate to express frustration with her inability to make the company look like an aerodynamic sports car, despite wheels that regularly fell off. They considered the negative publicity the company had received over the past few months a failure of perception—and therefore a PR problem—rather than a failure of strategy or execution, for which they would have shared responsibility.

Nevertheless, in the days ahead, she had as much access to Allen as she needed, and Zeglis was not the kind of manager who worried about subordinates going around him to his boss. "Nothing she sent to Allen came to me first," Zeglis later said. "I didn't think it was necessary and had plenty of other things to worry about."

But that was precisely the kind of thing Marilyn *did* worry about. When it came time to brief the MEC on the timeline for the Trivestiture announcement, she told the officer who had actually prepared the plan that Allen didn't want any non-members of the MEC in the room. And when she sat in on the board meeting to finalize the purchase of McCaw Cellular, she told the same officer the same thing. That officer later learned neither claim was true, and he remembered, somewhat ironically, that Marilyn had warned *him* that one of his subordinates seemed to be spending a lot of time with Mandl, potentially displacing him as Mandl's primary advisor.

She, like many of her male peers, didn't get to the inner circle of senior management without keen political instincts and careful maneuvering. She didn't brag about it, but she didn't see any reason to apologize for it either. It was only years later when he realized that, even at the peak of her career, she was still insecure enough to worry about subordinates getting between herself and her top client. It was one of the few indications of the toll her climb to the top had taken. She was, after all, human. She couldn't do everything. But something in her made her feel she had to at least appear that she could.

Marilyn didn't buy that the company was looking for a chief operating officer, not a future CEO. And she had very strong opinions about the qualities a future CEO should have. "I recall conversations with Bob when I said it seemed to me, from a public perspective, that the incoming chairman of AT&T would be expected to be very strong in at least two or three out of four areas," she later remembered. "And the areas I named were, considering the brand and customer franchise, marketing; considering our technology base, someone with real technical depth; considering the size of the company, someone who had long experience in a really big organization and could make an elephant dance; and then finally, someone who knew our industry, given the regulatory, legislative, competitive, and somewhat arcane interrelationships among the current cast of characters and the new entrants." She said you'd walk on water if you were expert in all four; if you were expert in two out of the four, she'd consider you qualified.

She wasn't sure Allen bought her premise. But it wouldn't completely surprise her if he hadn't. The big lesson she had learned in the Planned Parenthood and *Focus* magazine crises was that when you are the cause of a highly-emotional situation, you are probably not the best judge of what actions the public will accept. "By the time Alex left, and given the concern about the company's prospects, Bob's credibility had been so damaged he was no longer seen as necessary to a transition," she said. In other words, the whole rationale of bringing someone in for a period of "education" under Allen's tutelage was seriously flawed. "Hiring a candidate who would accept that kind of arrangement was a misjudgment on Bob's part, given the state of his own credibility," she later said. Nevertheless, that's precisely what Allen and Burlingame tried to do.

*   *   *

The afternoon of October 17, 1996, was unseasonably warm in New Jersey. Marilyn was sitting on the terrace outside her Basking Ridge office waiting for her vice president of corporate PR to show up for their meeting. When he arrived, she got right to the point.

"I just spent three hours with our new president," she said.

The media had been full of speculation about the search for Mandl's successor. The latest two names added to the list of potential candidates were Mike Armstrong, a former IBM executive and the current CEO of Hughes Electronics, and William Esrey, the CEO of Sprint. The others included George Fisher, the CEO of Kodak who had begun his career at Bell Labs and was on AT&T's board, and James McNerney, the head of General Electric's lighting division who was on everyone's list of potential CEOs while he waited for Jack Welch to pick his eventual successor. One favorite, James Barksdale, the CEO of Netscape, had publicly taken himself out of the running (although he had reportedly suggested he would take the job if AT&T bought his fledgling internet browser company). Such was the caliber of the talent Allen and his two search firms, Spencer Stuart and Korn Ferry, were reportedly considering.

The search itself had taken on new urgency ever since AT&T had announced in September that it expected third and fourth quarter earnings to be as much as ten percent below analysts' expectations because of intense price competition in communication services. Coming on the heels of Mandl's resignation, the change in earnings guidance underlined the importance of identifying and installing effective operating management. For the first time, Allen had even said he would step aside if that's what it took to find the right person for the job.

"So, who is it?" the corporate PR officer asked.

"I don't think you'll know his name, but you know his company," Marilyn said.

"What is it?" he asked, not really understanding why they were suddenly playing 20-questions.

"R. R. Donnelly," she said in the flattest tone he had ever heard from her.

"The Yellow Pages advertising people?"

"You're thinking of R. *H.* Donnelly," she said. "This is R. *R.*" As if that cleared everything up. Seeing that he was still drawing a blank, she helped him out. "The Chicago-based printing company. I think R. H. and R. R. were brothers or something."[103]

She was right—this well-read, usually well-informed officer gave up. "So, who is it?" he said. Again.

"John R. Walter. He's the president of R. R. Donnelly. He just led them through a major transformation from paper and ink to digital media. Bob's betting he can do the same kind of thing here."

She then told him the board members had met individually with Walter two nights before, followed by a group dinner at the Pierre Hotel in Manhattan. She, Miller, and Zeglis had met individually with

---

[103] R. H. Donnelly was actually R. R. Donnelly's son.

Walter the next morning. Her meeting, she said, had been the longest, and she came away impressed with his energy, self-confidence, and engaging personality. However, he was the darkest of dark horses. And Marilyn was smart enough to know that his appointment would not be received enthusiastically by the media, investors, and even employees, all of whom were expecting someone with more marquee value.

Furthermore, his appointment could still fall through. He had been offered the job informally, but he hadn't accepted yet. He and Allen were still dancing around the issue of when he would take over as CEO. Allen wanted to leave it open; Walter wanted a date certain. Of course, neither of them would broach the subject with the other; they were negotiating through Burlingame.

Nevertheless, Marilyn wanted someone to take a swing at preparing the communications plan for an announcement, assuming everything could be resolved by the following week. She gave him a slim folder which she said contained all the background information she had on Walter, who had been on both search firms' initial list of candidates, but had been the only one the board interviewed.

When he got back to his office, he was surprised to discover the folder contained exactly three documents—Walter's official Donnelly biography listing an impressive number of board memberships (three corporate and seven non-profit), a copy of a very favorable *Businessweek* article about him, and what appeared to be a report by author and educator Warren Bennis on Walter's "leadership style."

The corporate PR officer was sure the executive recruiting firms had prepared fat dossiers on Walter which he could get from Burlingame. Meanwhile, he went onto the internet to see what he could find. At Donnelly's web site, he downloaded the previous 11 years of their financial results. The first thing that jumped out was that, at about $6.5 billion in revenue, Donnelly was a much smaller company than AT&T. But its financial results looked very familiar—revenue in the latest quarter was down six percent; in the first nine months of the year, it had incurred restructuring charges of $560 million as it closed printing plants and wrote off part of the software venture touted in the *Businessweek* article; and excluding those charges and one-time gains, net income had declined 26 percent.

Not trusting himself to interpret these results, he returned to Laurie's office. "Marilyn," he said, "unless I'm missing something, Donnelly's financial results look an awful lot like ours with declining revenue, lower earnings, lots of write-offs, and layoffs." She looked at the material he thrust into her hands and said, "Let's find Zeglis." After scanning the material, Zeglis called the company's treasurer who had one of the sharpest financial minds around.

"I'm going to have some financial data faxed over to you," he said. "It's for a company whose chairman is being considered for our board. Could you do a quick analysis of its results, compare them to the S&P or whatever benchmark you think appropriate, and let me know what you think? I need it by the end of the day."

Marilyn never saw that analysis, but at 7:30 p.m. on the evening of October 22, 1996, the board unanimously voted to offer the position to John Walter, as recommended by Allen.

CHAPTER TWENTY-ONE

HEIR UNAPPARENT

Marilyn's announcement team met Walter for the first time on the evening he was selected. He was seated at the long conference table in the office across from Bob Allen's, sorting through all the material they had prepared in the past few days, including a detailed timeline, news release, letter to employees, and Q&A. Of all that, he seemed fixated on the fourth question in the AT&T Q&A: "Isn't R. R. Donnelly having serious problems of its own? Their third quarter earnings declined 26 percent. They recently had to write off $560 million in restructuring charges because of a failed strategy. If Walter couldn't solve Donnelly's problems, why do you think he can solve AT&T's?"

The answer to that question had come from eleven pages of material faxed to AT&T by Donnelly's corporate communications department. But Walter seemed less concerned with the answer than the question. "Who asked this?" he wanted to know. Marilyn explained that her team tried to think of the rudest questions reporters might ask to be sure they were equipped to answer them. "Well, it's wrong," he said. "Did this come from Donnelly's investor relations department? If it did, it's only because the head of that department knows I wanted to fire her. She's totally incompetent." The media relations people tried to change the subject, drawing his attention to other questions. "Let's change the question," he said as he started scribbling on the Q&A in front of him. When the meeting broke up at around 10:00 p.m., Walter was still obsessing about how his Donnelly record would be perceived. Ironically, the subject did not get that much play in all the reams of copy written about him in the following days.

At lunch the next day, just before the news conference, CFO Rick Miller was seated next to the public relations officer who had prepared most of the announcement material. Miller pointed out that someone had set the dining room table without any knives. "Do you think they're afraid to give us anything sharp?" the PR guy said. Miller guffawed so loudly it attracted Walter's attention.

Luckily at that point Tom Wyman, the chairman of the board's compensation committee, came into the room. He and Walter had known each other for some time. In fact, Wyman's son worked for Donnelly. After Walter and Wyman had slapped each other's backs for a few minutes, Walter asked to be briefed on the news conference. Marilyn looked at the PR officer who had prepared the material and, between bites of his sandwich, he ran through the agenda again, describing the setup for the news conference and reiterating the company's key messages—Walter's experience and leadership qualities would supplement the company's senior team, he had already proven himself by transforming a traditional business into a thriving, global high-tech company, Walter and Allen will partner closely, etc.

Nothing could have prepared Walter for the news conference that followed. The media arrived with a chip on its shoulder. Walter had not been on any of their screens as a possible candidate. Allen was reminded that he had said in one contentious interview that of course he would step aside if he found a "god." So someone from the national media actually thought to ask, "Is John Walter god?" And then, Walter was asked the most consequential question of all, "Who's your long distance company?" His answer: "I don't know."

No one was thrilled with the news conference. By the time everyone got off the elevator from the auditorium where the news conference had been held, "Chainsaw Al" Dunlap was on CNBC blasting Walter's appointment and asking why AT&T's board has not sought someone "with a proven record of wealth creation, which is what suffering shareholders are looking for." Further, AT&T's stock price was down half a point on volume of 4.8 million shares, about twice the normal volume. By the end of the day, it would be down nearly $2 on volume of 9 million shares.

Marilyn didn't realize how upset Walter was until the dinner she had arranged at the Olde Mill Inn, just across the highway from AT&T's Basking Ridge headquarters. It was supposed to be a celebratory dinner, but Walter understandably was not in a joyful mood. He was convinced his inability to name his long distance company had torpedoed any chance he had of establishing himself as the visionary CEO AT&T needed. And he blamed Marilyn and her team for not preparing him for the question. "The prep you guys gave me for that news conference was just awful," he said. "More than awful, it was appalling."

Everyone stared at their menu while Marilyn gamely offered that she and her people would work harder to get into sync with his expectations. "Just appalling," he continued. "I thought AT&T would have a real professional operation. All you guys did was point me to the elevator and warn me there'd be a lot of photographers."

In fact, Marilyn's team *had* warned him that the moment he stepped off the elevator to walk the ten yards or so to the auditorium, he would be confronted with a phalanx of about a dozen photographers, each flashing strobe lights into his face. They had experienced the scene before and knew it could be unnerving. On the other hand, they had also given him five pages of questions that were likely to come up. Admittedly, where he got his long distance service was not one of them.

Thankfully, at about that point, the waiter brought the wine list. Walter fancied himself an oenophile and he discovered a vintage to his liking. When the bottle was brought to him and uncorked, he swirled a sample in his wine glass, took in its bouquet, sipped, and ran it over his palate. "That's really exceptional," he said.

Then he told the waiter—a kid just trying to work his way through college—"You really ought to try it." The waiter demurred, but Walter insisted, pouring some into an empty glass. "Go on. Feel empowered," he said. Again, the waiter—now becoming embarrassed—said he really couldn't. It was against house policy to drink on the job. "Your only policy should be to please the customer," Walter said. Then, while the poor waiter tried to pour the rest of the wine so he could escape, Walter began a lecture on customer relations, employee empowerment, and winning organizations.

While all this was going on, AT&T's media relations vice president, Adele Donahue, was working her cellphone to get a handle on the tone of the next day's stories. She had been the steady, reassuring voice of AT&T through the turmoil of the past year. She brought a dogged intensity to representing the company and took negative media personally.

The issue this evening was John Walter's appointment and she was not optimistic. The *Wall Street Journal*, she reported, would carry three stories, including one on the impact on Donnelly. The *New York Times* would carry three, all on Walter. The *New York Post*, always a wild card, would probably be the most negative, focusing on the post-announcement nosedive in the company's stock price.

The search firms had worked their contacts at the various news outlets, providing enough background information on the search process to demonstrate it had been thorough and the board of directors had been deeply engaged. Two directors, in fact—Walter Elisha, the chair of the committee on directors, and Tom Wyman, the chair of the compensation committee—had met with Walter several times, reporting their findings to the other board members. In summary, she felt the coverage would be prominent, with a range of perspectives from critical to skeptical and wait-and-see. Everyone would play up the surprise of his appointment.

"Well, that positions me to exceed their expectations, doesn't it," Walter said. "Let's go around the table. What's your advice? If you were me, what would you do?"

One of Marilyn's senior officers offered advice that would unfortunately prove prescient. "Don't underestimate the complexity of the company," he said. "It's big, but worse, it's highly complex. Everything depends on everything else. At GE, the jet engine people don't particularly care what the lighting people do. But here if you change pricing by a quarter of a penny in a data service that only multinational companies buy, it has repercussions in consumer long distance." He was exaggerating, but not by much.

"I disagree," Walter said. "I don't need to get into the nuts and bolts of the business. In fact, I need to stay naive and push for simple solutions. AT&T needs leadership, not more management."

In fact, the company needed both.

Vying to outdo each other with metaphors, the next day's papers variously described Walter as "a bolt from the blue," "a distinct let down" (*New York Times*),[104] "a Telecom Novice," "found in the Yellow Pages," (*Wall Street Journal*),[105] and "heir un-apparent" (*New York Daily News*).[106] Morgan Stanley's research analyst headlined her investor note: "AT&T: My Mother Warned Me There Would Be Days Like This," but reiterated her strong buy on the stock. Most financial analysts expressed surprise at Walter's selection, particularly in view of his relative youth and lack of industry

---

[104] Mark Landler, "AT&T, In Flux, Goes Far Afield to Find a Leader," *New York Times*, Oct. 24, 1995.

[105] John Keller, "Bell Curve: A Telecom Novice Found in the Yellow Pages," *Wall Street Journal*, Oct. 24, 1995.

[106] *New York Daily News*, Oct. 24, 1995.

experience, but they generally adopted a wait-and-see attitude. The most positive story was what reporters call a "tick-tock," a moment-by-moment or day-by-day chronology of a major event. To put the search in the best possible light, Marilyn had asked Burlingame to quietly give a *New York Times* reporter a rundown of events leading up to Walter's selection.[107]

The negative media coverage didn't particularly surprise Marilyn. "There was very little we could do to head off the criticism," she later said. "It all played out along the dimension of surprise, and John's gaffe, when he didn't know who his long distance carrier was, sort of summed up his lack of experience in having to face the press— the big-time press—in the '90s when they were out for blood. They never gave him a chance to get off the ground."

Marilyn also surveyed employees following the announcement. Most rank and file AT&T employees either didn't have an opinion about his appointment (27%) or thought it was a good idea (38%). But among AT&T executives, 53 percent were unfavorable, citing especially his lack of industry experience.

Walter was true to his word—he made no effort to understand AT&T's complexity. When the head of Network Operations arrived in his office with a thick binder designed to explain how a telephone call made it through the network, he left perplexed. Walter essentially told him he didn't care. He wasn't going to do network planning; he was going to run the company. When a senior officer showed up to give him a tutorial on the charges AT&T paid local phone companies to initiate or complete a long distance call, which were the company's largest single expense, he never got off the first chart before being told, "Tell me what I need to know when I need

---

[107] Judith Dobrynski, "AT&T's Romancing of its New President," *New York Times*, Oct. 24, 1995.

to know it." It even took a while for Walter to realize that "R-box" did not refer to a make of tennis shoes but to the Regional Bell Operating Companies (RBOCs).

Walter brought one of Donnelly's PR people with him, putting him in a relatively undefined human resources job to facilitate "culture change." Marilyn met with Walter's sidekick in early November, just two weeks after his arrival. She was probably sizing up potential competition, since Walter had already loudly expressed his dissatisfaction with her organization's initial performance. But the ostensible reason was "to get a handle on Walter's expectations"—how many speeches did he give, how many media interviews did he do, how did he like to be briefed?

She was surprised to learn that Walter gave relatively few outside speeches, maybe half a dozen a year, and he did not do many interviews either, maybe one every other month. By contrast, Bob Allen gave about 24 major public addresses a year, not counting grace notes at various charity dinners. The interview requests were virtually endless. He could spend part of every day on the phone with one reporter or another. On the other hand, Allen required little handholding. He knew what he wanted to say, and he knew when it was important to take a direct hand in shaping it. Otherwise, he let his speechwriters assemble the wisdom of the organization on the subject at hand and present it to him for review, comment, and approval in a largely mechanical process.

Walter's sidekick told Marilyn Walter preferred an iterative process with very long lead time. He wanted to understand the "so what" of anything he was asked to do, starting with the business goal it served. He preferred in-person briefings on all this but if it had to be in writing, it couldn't go on for more than a page. He never spoke extemporaneously. He always wanted talking points even for small internal meetings. He always stayed on message, repeating the same points and anecdotes until his audience could get to the punch line before he did. Finally, he was highly critical, always looking for a better way to do things.

Marilyn was all for finding a better way to do things. In fact, she had driven her staff to distraction over the last year, searching for the silver stake that would put the stories of AT&T's alleged corporate greed and incompetence in their grave. But now she had an additional problem. Reporters had been pestering the company's media relations people to interview Walter. But the coverage of Walter's appointment had been so cheeky Marilyn had steadfastly maintained a position of keeping him under wraps through the first two months of his tenure, explaining he was "too busy." As the traditional lull between Christmas and New Year's Day arrived, she assumed they were out of the woods for a while.

She never expected Walter would celebrate the holidays by firing the head of the company's consumer long distance business. But that's what he did—or almost did—on Friday evening, Dec. 20, just before leaving for the holidays.

Consumer long distance was led by Joe Nacchio, who had been named one of the youngest officers in AT&T's history based on in-your-face marketing and incandescent competitiveness. Born and raised in Brooklyn, he wielded his hard-edged, percussive accent effectively in rallying his troops. He combined street smarts with near-encyclopedic knowledge of the telephone business. He was brash, fast-talking, and easy to slight. He expected people to show him respect but it was said the only thing harder than working for Nacchio was to have him working for you.

Nacchio had been openly derisive about Walter's appointment. Knowing that he now would never have a shot at the job himself, he commiserated with his friend Jack Grubman, who put him in touch with billionaire Philip Anschutz. Anschutz was looking for someone to turn the fiber optic cables he had buried along railroad rights-of-way into a business. By the time of the AT&T officer Christmas party in mid-December 1996, Nacchio was not-so-quietly bragging that he was about to leave the company to become CEO of a competitor.

Walter heard about that and also about the pot-shots Nacchio had taken at him. On Friday morning, December 20, just before lunch, he called Nacchio into his office and told him he had decided to put someone else in charge of the consumer long distance business. Walter left open what Nacchio would be doing. "Burlingame has some ideas," he said. In fact, Burlingame had no ideas. He had been told Nacchio was being let go and to prepare an exit package. Nacchio left Walter's office and the building for a previously scheduled lunch. Burlingame, who expected to meet with Nacchio to discuss the formalities of his departure, was dumbfounded. He spent the rest of the afternoon trying to track him down, finally reaching him late in the day and convincing him to come back to the office.

When Nacchio got there, he thought it was to discuss an interim position while he solidified plans for his new job. He and Anschutz had not yet completed their negotiations. Burlingame had to tell him there was no other job and the company planned to issue the news release that night. Marilyn could hear the screams from a floor away. "You mean PR is already drafting a release?" After a while, Burlingame's secretary, ashen faced, came down and asked Marilyn to join Burlingame and Nacchio. She agreed to postpone any news release for 24 hours to allow Nacchio to complete negotiations for his new position.

AT&T issued the release late Sunday afternoon, December 22, simultaneously with Nacchio's new company, Qwest. AT&T's release said simply that Nacchio was leaving to become CEO of Qwest and who was replacing him. But when Walter, who by then was back in Chicago, got on the phone with reporters, he made a point of saying he had "fired" Nacchio. The *Wall Street Journal* used the management change as the lede for a Christmas Eve profile of Walter that was relatively favorable to him, but less so to his boss, Bob Allen.[108]

Allen didn't think Walter had overreached. He knew how the media worked, and he himself had been caught off guard more than once. But he was worried that, when Walter was pushed into areas in which he wasn't yet competent (which after less than 90 days, was most areas), he was vulnerable to mistakes and to being misinterpreted. Allen asked Marilyn to "throttle back" the wind machine even more.

Marilyn thought a series of employee meetings would give Walter a feel for the company and, especially, show employees he wasn't the bozo the media had made him out to be. So in the first business days of the new year, she scheduled him to speak to a large group of employees at the company's main headquarters complex in Basking Ridge. When Walter took the stage, he started by waving a sheaf of papers at the group. "This is what PR wanted me to say," he said. "It's worthless. I don't think these PR people know anything." He threw the papers on the podium and walked out in front of it, saying "If they do to me what they did to Bob Allen, I'm in trouble."

When Marilyn heard about this, she put Shelly London, director of employee communications, on the case. London had come to public relations from sales where she had worked for some of the company's most difficult executives. She was bright, upbeat, and resilient. Marilyn told her to get as close to Walter as his Donnelly sidekick had been and to focus him on internal communications.

London quickly discovered Walter had a very short attention span and seldom read anything longer than a page. He was also

---

[108] John Keller, "Ringing Bell: AT&T's New President is Wasting No Time in Shaking Things Up," *Wall Street Journal*, Dec. 24, 1996.

hopeless with a script. He tended to lose his place and had a wooden delivery. But she quickly discovered if she turned his written remarks into a one-page diagram of arrows connecting boxes of memory-jogging phrases like "snake story," "off-line," "acronyms," and "Carpetland" to a central theme, he could spin a great story.

His favorite theme initially was about how much AT&T had to change, and those four phrases were his go-to evidence. (The snake story was Ross Perot's oft-repeated remark that, if a snake showed up in General Motors' boardroom, they would form a committee to study it rather than simply kill it; "off-line" referred to an AT&T habit of dealing with contentious issues outside a meeting rather than when they came up; acronyms referred to engineers' love of reducing everything to initials, turning them into words as if everyone knew what they stood for; "Carpetland" referred to the thickly carpeted, empty space on the executive floors at Basking Ridge.)

Realizing Walter's outsider status would last only so long, London developed a collection of these "mind maps" on different topics. And to give him a platform all his own, she had him launch a program called "You Own It" to encourage employees to take personal initiative in solving problems rather than foisting them on someone else or pushing them up the line. There was little evidence this would make any list of the company's top problems. But it resonated with rank-and-file employees.

The *Wall Street Journal* story about John Walter was even more consequential than anyone knew at the time. He told the *Wall Street Journal* he planned to "take command of [the company's] segregated advertising efforts." Since Marilyn had been the person who first drew the problem to his attention, as soon as the promise showed up in print, he put her in charge of the effort. As she remembered it, "He came in, he looked around, and he said, 'This is ridiculous. Marketing communications is fragmented. The brand is a disaster. You say you can do something about it—go do it'."

Thus, the executive vice president of public relations and employee communications became the executive vice president of brand strategy and advertising, reporting directly to Walter. The three officers who reported to her (one of whom would eventually replace her) reported to Zeglis for about a year.

And what a year it was.

John Walter lasted only nine months. Allen suspected he had scuttled a merger with one of the local phone companies by leaking it to the media when he discovered he was unlikely to have a role in the new company.[109] Plus, Allen had been hearing complaints about Walter from a steady stream of executives who said he was unable to focus on any subject for more than twenty minutes, was quick to criticize but offered no solutions. They said he still didn't have a grasp of the business' fundamentals and didn't seem to be making any effort to learn them. He had made little progress on basic operating issues—such as fixing the billing systems—despite his early expressions of disbelief at their inadequacy. And he particularly alienated the former McCaw Cellular executives by openly questioning the company's wireless investment.

By September, the board decided to let Walter go and to take a stronger role in finding, not a chief operating officer, but a new chief executive. By mid-October, the board chose someone who had been interviewed the first time around but was only interested in the top job—Mike Armstrong, a former IBM executive and current CEO of

---

[109] AT&T was plagued by leaks ever since the 1996 downsizing announcement. While John Walter was possibly the source of the leak about the SBC merger, AT&T Wireless employees may also have been the source. They discovered the company was having discussions with SBC when they were told to postpone their own discussions with the company about trading spectrum.

Hughes Electronics. Ironically, Armstrong arguably met at least three of Marilyn's criteria to become AT&T's CEO: as a top officer in both IBM and Hughes' parent General Motors, he had experience working in a large company; he understood the telephone industry because AT&T had been one of his sales accounts at IBM; and he understood technology from computers to rocket science.

CHAPTER TWENTY-TWO

REBUILDING A BRAND

Marilyn watched the corporate soap opera playing out in the media during the fall of 1996 with relief that she wasn't in the thick of it. She had not thought John Walter was as bad as he was portrayed, but she also knew he wasn't as good as the company needed. "John had a lot of strengths, but they weren't sufficient to rescue a company like AT&T," she later said. "It was Bob Allen's finest hour, in my view, when nine months later, he took the hit for saying that John was not up to the job."

On the other hand, she thought Allen had no one to blame but himself. "AT&T is always supposed to be the gold standard whether it's corporate governance, customer service, or how it treats its people," she later said. "The process by which John Walter was selected didn't meet that standard. In fact, I was surprised we didn't get more heat on the corporate governance process in the media to begin with." In any case, although she suspected Walter might have had an ulterior motive for moving her out of public relations—his former PR counselor was waiting in the wings in Human Resources—she was delighted that her full-time job was caring for the AT&T brand. "Great job—steward of the brand," she said. "The AT&T brand is a living miracle, and it's been in my gut, as well as in my head, for 20 years." In fact, she believed a company's brand is the manifestation of its mission, an obsession of hers ever since Jim Olson had given her a copy of Ford's laminated card back in 1987.

When she was first given the brand job, she told *Ad Age* magazine, "The PR side of the business is really only a hop, skip and a jump across into the balance of marketing communications. I've always been a very loud voice on the need to systematically grow our brand. And now I have the incredible opportunity to actually put my energy where my mouth was."[110] Prior to breaking into three companies, AT&T's mission had to include everything from telephones to computers and everything in between; its customers ranged from individuals and businesses to governments and other communication companies. She knew the mission statement she had chipped out of the granite-like egos of a succession of business leaders was only a common denominator everyone could agree to but had little real meaning for customers. "Reaping the benefits of information technology" sounded good, but what did it really mean? Could the consumers apply it to their own lives? Could businesses? She remembered the old saw that if you asked a 19th century farmer what he needed most, he wouldn't describe a tractor, but a bigger horse that didn't eat much.

But Marilyn was no neophyte in advertising. She had managed small campaigns in her first real job out of Barnard, and at AT&T she had directed the creation of the "Knowledge Business" campaign for one of the company's toughest and most demanding clients, Arch McGill. Admittedly, that seemed like a lifetime ago, but more recently, in 1993, she had sent her people up and down the hallways of Bell Labs to get the researchers' predictions of products and services their work might make possible in five or ten years.

That led to the creation of a series of television commercials, directed by an up-and-coming director named David Fincher, that portrayed what an interconnected world would look like—in many cases, quite accurately. Narrated by actor Tom Selleck, the "You Will" campaign asked such questions as, "Have you ever renewed your driver's license at an ATM? Have you ever studied with a

---

[110] Kim Cleland, "People: AT&T's Laurie Connects with Brand from PR Post," *Ad Age*, Mar. 17, 1997.

classmate thousands of miles away? Have you ever installed a phone on your wrist?" The answer of course was "You will. And the company that will bring it to you: AT&T." The campaign was so successful, it was parodied on David Letterman's late-night television show. And the company was smart enough to let Selleck do the voice over for the spoofs. Nearly three decades after it ran, the You Will campaign even has its own Wikipedia page.

In 2016, the man who invented the World Wide Web, Timothy Berners Lee, conceded that "overall the ads were remarkably accurate in predicting the cutting-edge technologies of the coming decade," from intelligent personal assistants and electronic toll collection to home automation and video conferencing.[111] Marilyn was understandably proud of the campaign but, in later life, had to admit "the one [claim] that flopped is 'and the company that will bring it to you is AT&T'."

But "You Will" was just a corporate advertising campaign. The company's divisions were each going their own way and outspending the corporate effort 20-to-one, largely on price war advertising. The overall impression people had of AT&T was less about innovation and more about saving pennies. The president of one of the company's ad agencies had warned the company that they "would go out of business if they kept selling on price." He predicted that AT&T's aggressive strategy of promoting itself as the lowest-cost provider of telephone service was a "dead end." And he counseled it to "build a new relationship with customers on the foundation of its role in their lives."[112]

---

[111] Timothy Berners Lee, "We live in the future AT&T imagined in 1994" (sic), *Vox*, July 28, 2016.

[112] Peter Georgescue, *The Source of Success: Five Enduring Principles at the Heart of Real Leadership*, (New York: Wiley, 2005), p. 2.

As Marilyn saw it, her new charter was to penetrate the zeitgeist as the "You Will" campaign had and to bring all the company's business units under the same umbrella. However, 1997 was not 1993. Back then, business publications put AT&T and Bob Allen on their covers with headlines like "Could AT&T Rule The World?" and "1-800-GUTS: AT&T's Bob Allen Has Turned The Company Into A World-Class Risk Taker."[113] More lately, the same publications had run covers screaming "Why AT&T's Latest Plan Won't Work" and "AT&T: When Will The Bad News End?"[114]

"We're moving from a product-facing organization to one that's customer-facing," she told *Ad Age*. "As far as I'm concerned, we have one brand, one brand strategy, and will speak with only one voice to our customers." She was determined to see that all the businesses followed a unified strategy to restore an AT&T brand that had been bruised and bloodied over the previous two years. And she thought she could do it while cutting costs. "Currently, each product has its own direct mail and own advertising supporting it. Those efforts will soon be consolidated," she told *Ad Age*. "This year it's our hope to spend less money on advertising for the same or greater impact as last year. I'll know we're doing our jobs well when we see an actual connection between our brand and our revenue growth."

She said she found the move from PR to marketing invigorating. "I'll no longer be so concerned with how AT&T's actions are interpreted by the media," she said. "Now I'm simply focused on

---

[113] "Could AT&T Rule the World?" (*Fortune*, May 17, 1993), and "1 800-GUTS: AT&T's Bob Allen has transformed his company into a world-class risk taker" (*Businessweek*, Aug. 30, 1993).

[114] "Why AT&T's Latest Plan Won't Work" (*Fortune*, June. 23, 1997), and "AT&T: When Will the Bad News End?" (*Businessweek*, Oct. 7, 1996).

leading this category, leading it now, leading it in the future, and resurrecting one of the great brands of our time."[115]

She had rows of binders on her shelves documenting the work of countless high-level task forces she had led or participated in, trying to define the essence of the AT&T brand. But however lofty the brand definition, it was swamped by a torrent of tacky price wars and complicated calling plans. In many ways, AT&T and its competitors were ruining the category, making long distance telephone calls a commodity. Of more than 90 commercials rated by *USA Today* since 1995, phone company commercials ranked among the least popular and most disliked. Consumers complained they were confusing and meanspirited. But now Marilyn was the closest AT&T had ever come to a chief marketing officer. In AT&T parlance, the business unit advertising directors would report to her on a "dotted-line basis." And she was determined to restore the company's emotional connection with its customers by focusing on their hearts rather than their wallets.

Marilyn pressed the Y&R advertising agency into service with the charge of defining the company's ultimate promise to all its customers, using the intelligence gathered when she and Alex Kroll had dug deeply into AT&T's mission back in 1987 and '88. Except this time, they would translate the power of that promise into advertising that would resonate with all its constituencies. She wanted to stop competing solely on the basis of price and go beyond selling specific products to fostering enduring relationships with customers. She wanted to redefine what AT&T meant to people, in their gut as well as in their brain.

The campaign Y&R developed took an emotional slice-of-life approach, matched to familiar pop songs, performed by artists like

---

[115] K. Cleland, *Ad Age*, Mar. 17, 1997.

Elton John, Cindy Lauper, and Crosby, Stills, and Nash. As in the case of the previous "You Will" campaign, the commercials showed how AT&T helped people connect to each other and to the information they need, but *now* rather than in some distant future.

For example, "Teen Date" showed a teenage girl coming home from a date and continuing her budding flirtations with the boy online. Another spot, "Beaches," showed a working mother who played hooky from work to take her young daughters to the beach, where she could take an important conference call from her cellphone. "Long Time Gone" showed a young soldier use his AT&T calling card to phone his father from Vietnam, where he had fought a generation earlier. Each commercial ended with the tagline, "It's All Within Your Reach."

USA Today's advertising critic said, "AT&T's latest corporate ad campaign has achieved the near-impossible in the telecom industry."[116] Almost a third of consumers polled said that they liked the campaign. Forty-one percent of women said they liked the ads very much. Almost 40 percent of consumers from 18-to-24 years old said the campaign was effective. Advertising experts also liked the commercials. The campaign piled up awards, including a Gold EFFIE for its effectiveness in the category of corporate reputation, image, and identity. Indeed, the summary accompanying the EFFIE award read as if it had been pulled directly from Marilyn's brand strategy:[117]

> "Brand AT&T breaks away from the competition by personalizing and differentiating itself in a commodity market. The brand campaign is

---

[116] Dottie Enrico, "AT&T Makes Connection with Ad Campaign," *USA Today*, May 19, 1997.

[117] In the American Advertising Awards (ADDYs) national competition, AT&T received an ADDY for the "Beaches," "Rocket Man," and "Teen Date" trio. At the New York Festival's International Television Advertising Competition, the campaign won Best of Show and Best Campaign for Telecommunications.

designed to showcase AT&T as the company that understands life today and assures telecom users that 'it's all within your reach.' [The commercials] succeed in presenting a fun, different, and caring AT&T."

The campaign ran a little more than a full year, outlasting Marilyn Laurie herself.

When Marilyn first met with the company's new CEO Mike Armstrong, she was struck by his confidence, the depth of his industry and technical knowledge, and his total misunderstanding of the AT&T brand. He thought of it as a label that could be applied to just about any product, something that simply signaled the source of a product or service. And he thought of the company's consumer long distance business as a wasting asset, like an oil well. He proposed to milk it for as long as he could, then sell it off.

She wasn't particularly concerned. She had educated other senior executives on the central importance of brands in general and AT&T's in particular. While Armstrong's assessment of consumer long distance was technically correct, he was underestimating how much the company's other consumer services, such as its internet and wireless offerings, leveraged the franchise built in consumer calling. That too was something he would realize over time.

Over the next few months, she had relatively little contact with Armstrong, though she knew he was holding all-day meetings in the boardroom just across from her office every Monday, as he did a "deep dive" into each of the company's businesses and the corporate staff organizations. But when she heard he had asked Burlingame to find a chief marketing officer for the company, she decided it was time to leave.

Marilyn went to Burlingame's office and, like many before her, she closed the door. She had had a good, if not close relationship with him ever since the 1980s. They had been peers for years, and then she had reported to him for five months before he moved to human resources and she replaced him as head of public relations. In fact, he had made it a point to ensure that she was always paid as much as he was. The only time he failed was when he and she were tied as the company's fifth highest paid officers, the mandated cut off for publication in the company's annual 10K report. They had had a long discussion about the trade-offs between revealing that the fifth highest paid employee was a woman who ran public relations or a man who ran human resources. They decided to have him paid $50 more in return for the invasion of privacy.

"Hal," she said. "I hear you're looking for a chief marketing officer. When you find one, it will make my job redundant. And I wanted you to know if you want to offer me a separation package, I'm prepared to leave." Burlingame did his usual dance around the subject, but he didn't try to change her mind. Within a few days, his staff had pulled the separation package together and she announced her retirement from AT&T in the spring of 1998.

Although the "It's All Within Your Reach" tagline remained in place through 2000, AT&T relapsed into focusing its marketing resources on individual business segments. Actor Paul Reiser touted the company's long distance rates and the comedian Carrot Top pitched a dial-around service. In May 2000, the Boston market research firm Yankee Group, chided the company for failing to create a consistent brand image and warned it risked becoming irrelevant in the internet age. A new chief marketing officer came in, lasted about a year, and left to be replaced by two lower-level executives who split the duties of running consumer long distance during the day, while they huddled with consultants at night looking for ways to sell it.

Ultimately, the whole company would be sold off in pieces with one of the former Bell phone companies buying what was left, principally to get its brand.

CHAPTER TWENTY-THREE

A CURIOSITY, A THREAT, AND A PUZZLE

Marilyn's professional life spanned more than four decades and three distinct waves of the feminist movement.[118] The wave of the 1960s and 1970s, that brought women some measure of equality in workplace and home, arguably propelled her career. Though it was less than a smooth ride. In addition to the inherent challenges of practicing public relations in turbulent times and coping with C-suite politics that can be thorny in the best of times, Marilyn also had to deal with implicit gender biases that survived all four feminist waves, from the first wave that won women the right to vote in the 19th century to the "call out" culture of the fourth wave in the 21st.

In psychological terms, we all exhibit elements of masculine "agency" and feminine "communality." It's simply an accident of our patriarchal history that leadership qualities have become associated with stereotypical masculine traits such as confidence, decisiveness, and ambition. A 2018 study revealed that communality is still widely considered a "nice, but expendable trait in leaders, a frill."[119]

---

[118] Some feminist historians distinguish four waves of feminism. The first, in the 19th century, sought political equality characterized by women's right to vote. The second, in the 1960s and '70s, sought social equality in areas such as employment, divorce, and reproductive rights. The third wave, which began in the 1990s, embraced intersectionality and challenged traditional concepts of femininity and beauty. The fourth wave of the 2000s uses digital technology to bring discussion of such topics as body positivity and sexual harassment into the public square. See, for example, Rampton, M., "Four Waves of Feminism," *Pacific* magazine, Fall 2008. http://bit.ly/38afGbZ.

[119] A. C. Vice, J. L. Napier, "Unnecessary Skills: Communality as a Nice (But Expendable) Trait in Leaders," *Frontiers in Psychology*, Oct. 15, 2018; 9: 1866. See: http://bit.ly/2SbrWU5.

Historian and political scientist James MacGregor Burns believes this pervasive male bias is ultimately doomed. "As leadership comes properly to be seen as a process of leaders engaging and mobilizing the human needs and aspirations of followers," he writes, "women will be more readily recognized as leaders and men will change their own leadership styles."[120] Sadly, that day had not yet come in Marilyn's time.

Social science has shown that women still pay a price for exhibiting the same drive that makes men successful. Some weird and obsolete evolutionary adaptation causes girls in middle school to sit on their hands when teachers ask questions for fear of what the boys will think.[121] It continues even into graduate school. A 2017 study of Harvard MBA students found that the women among them intentionally played down their professional ambitions because they thought it would jeopardize relationships with classmates.[122]

An experiment conducted at Columbia University and New York University showed the price women pay when they violate the standards of gender stereotypes, even when they are equally competent.[123] A group of business school students were asked to read someone's resume and rate them on a range of qualities, including whether they would like to work with the person described.

The resumes were identical, except the name at the top of half was Heidi; on the other half, Howard. The business students rated

[120] James MacGregor Burns, *Leadership*. (New York: Harper Collins, 1978), p. 14.

[121] J. Davies, (2005). "Expressions of gender: An analysis of pupils' gendered discourse styles in small group classroom discussions." *Discourse and Society*, 14(2), pp. 115–132.

[122] L. Bursztyn, T. Fujiwara, A. Pallais, "Acting Wife: Marriage Market Incentives and Labor Market Investments," *American Economic Review*; 107 (2017), no. 11:3288–3319.

[123] F. Flynn, C. Anderson, "Heidi vs. Howard: An Examination of Success and Likeability," Columbia Business School and New York University, (2003).

them both as equally competent. But Howard was judged a more likable and good colleague to have, while Heidi was considered aggressive, selfish, and not someone they'd like to work with. As pop star Taylor Swift learned in her own career, "A man can be 'strategic,' but a woman doing the same thing is 'calculating.' Men can 'react,' but women can only 'overreact'."[124] Part of the problem is semantical confusion. Expressing an opinion while being respectful of others' is assertive; promoting an opinion by belittling those of other people is aggressive. Gender stereotypes often muddle those distinctions.

We expect ambition and drive of men; but women are supposed to be warm, friendly, and nurturing. To be otherwise is to be abnormal. Powerful women are still uncommon enough, even in our enlightened times. But in the 1970s and '80s, they were essentially unicorns, attracting attention wherever they popped up. And that attention was not always benign. Even today, women who violate gender stereotypes are penalized by being shunned, the subject of whisper campaigns, or simply disliked. A 2018 Pew study shows that two-thirds of Americans think "powerful man" is a compliment; nine out of ten, think "powerful woman" is an insult.[125]

So throughout her career, Marilyn had to deal with being both a curiosity and a threat.

But most of all, she was her own woman, which made her a puzzle to many. "At a time when 'Ms.' was the politically correct form of address for women managers, she stuck with 'Mrs.'," her Bell Labs colleague Bill Weiss notes. "And, even though no ambitious female manager would dare be seen at the office in anything other than a boxy 'power suit,' Marilyn invariably wore dresses or skirts."

---

[124] Ms. Swift was interviewed by Tracy Smith on the CBS program *Sunday Morning* on Oct. 23, 2019.

[125] K. Walker, K. Bialik and P. van Kessel, "Strong Men, Caring Women," Pew Research Center (July 24, 2018). https://pewrsr.ch/39iqd4Z.

When Marilyn started her career, only about half the U.S. workforce was female. Today, more women than men work outside the home.[126] But they almost all struggle with the same two problems—balancing the demands of work and family and breaking through a glass ceiling into management's upper ranks. Marilyn solved the second problem, but struggled with the first, just as most women did then and still do now.

She worked long hours and valued other people who did, characterizing them as "high-energy." It was her default setting. She could do that because, like Barnard College's president, Mrs. Mac, she had resources unavailable to most working women. Her husband Bob ran a thriving business and was proud of her success, even as he was sometimes frustrated by her preoccupation with work. As an AT&T officer, she could afford to outsource housework and childcare. But giving equal balance to work and family simply wasn't a realistic option for someone with her aspirations to make a difference on a grand scale. And she didn't believe she should abandon those aspirations simply because she was a woman.

Ultimately, her daughters shared that belief but they didn't always feel that way at the time. One daughter remembers that Marilyn seldom spoke of her job when at home, paradoxically giving her the impression she wasn't sharing her life's greatest passion with them. The other remembers blaming her for moving them to New Jersey just as she was entering high school. And they both remember that the stay-at-home "PTA" moms resented Marilyn's inability to

---

126 "U.S. nonfarm employment by gender," U.S. Bureau of Labor Statistics. In December 2019, the nonfarm workforce consisted of 76.2 million women and 76.1 million men. In 1971, 22 million women and 44 million men were in the nonfarm workforce. The grey cloud in these sunny statistics is that job growth has been concentrated in predominantly "female" occupations such as education and healthcare. Also, "women's jobs" pay so little that women are more likely than men to hold multiple jobs.

"pitch in" at school. Looking back, even Marilyn chided herself for "less than skillful motherhood capacities," and her husband's "problems" with her near total engagement with her job.

Marilyn never tried to fool herself into thinking her daughters were entirely happy having a working mother. As her friend Eve Preminger put it, "She knew the girls felt neglected, but she said she had to make a choice and, having made it, she saw no point in crying about it. She didn't regret her choice, but she was unhappy it caused her girls unhappiness."

But as adults, both daughters can look back and say, "when she was there, she was totally there." Marilyn took to heart advice she was given when she took her younger daughter Lisa to a spa in Arizona. "Balance is something you have and lose all the time," the spa therapist said. "Your goal should be to *find* balance, not to *be* in balance." She worked hard to find time to be "there," whether by traveling to exotic places with Bob and their daughters, carving time out of a weekend of conference calls and deskwork for a game of tennis, or spending long weekends at their farm.

Sunday nights were sacrosanct, when the whole family would watch a movie on TV and eat take-out Chinese food. When she had a free weekend, Marilyn led "expeditions" into New York to explore the Museum of Natural History or to ice skate in Central Park. And when she was able to get home at a reasonable hour, she stopped by the local fish market or supermarket to pull together dinner. Broiled scallops and something called "Chicken Marilyn" were favorites.[127]

After retiring, when time became more fully her own, she reveled in her teenage grandchildren. "Babies are cute," she said, "But they're more interesting as they get older." As a grandparent, she may

---

[127] The official recipe for "Chicken Marilyn" was lost, but it seems to have consisted of chicken parts, button mushrooms, and pearl onions braised in tomato sauce.

have developed a keener sense of what she had missed, but it came with little regret. Marilyn had taught her girls to take charge of their own lives, free of the straitjacket of gender stereotypes.

To be fair, Marilyn's job was not only time consuming, it was intellectually and emotionally exhausting. Things might have been different if she had worked for a company with fewer problems or if women had not faced so many hurdles to advancement in her day. But she was a woman of her time, and AT&T was the place she found meaning despite its problems. Indeed, balancing work and family, along with career advancement, remain the two dominant symptoms of "the problem with no name" even today.

While employers increasingly recognize the value women bring to the workplace, few have figured out how to make work work for parents—fathers as well as mothers. While some companies now offer their employees paid family leave, day-to-day childcare is often unaffordable, inadequate or unavailable, and hours spent working are unpredictable. In 28 states and the District of Columbia, infant day care costs more than in-state tuition at a public university. More than half of Americans—51 percent—live in neighborhoods classified as "childcare deserts," meaning there is either no daycare close by or only one opening for every three children needing it.[128]

Meanwhile, technology has turned white collar jobs into 24/7 commitments for both men and women. Management people are expected to work around the clock, answering emails and joining conference calls at all hours.[129] Long hours are so expected in

---

[128] Child Care Aware of America, "The US and the High Cost of Child Care," 2018 Report, http://bit.ly/2UyboHf.

[129] Kim A. Weeden, Youngjoo Cha, Mauricio Bucca, "Long Work Hours, Part-Time Work, and Trends in the Gender Gap in Pay, the Motherhood Wage Penalty, and the Fatherhood Wage Premium," *The Russell Sage Foundation Journal of the Social Sciences*, Vol. 2, No. 4, Aug. 2016, pp. 71–102.

industries such as consulting, law, accounting, advertising, and public relations, one sociologist termed them "greedy institutions."[130] In lower paid occupations, blue collar workers increasingly work unpredictable schedules. In the food and service industries, two-thirds of workers have less than two-weeks' notice of their schedules. Four out of ten have had shifts canceled in the last month.[131]

And while women have greater representation in management, they continue to be underrepresented at every level, especially in the C-suite, where the glass ceiling is thickest.[132] The durability of that ceiling used to be blamed on stereotyping, discrimination, an empty pipeline of qualified women, or the machinations of "the old boys' network." But since around 2001, the reigning explanation has been "work-family conflict"—the notion that women's childrearing and household responsibilities hamper their career advancement.[133] But that explanation is in lockstep with a deeper problem—the cultural belief that a woman's place is in the home. After all, being a father doesn't seem to have interfered with men's careers. We expect men to be devoted to their work; women, to their family.[134] When a man leaves the office at 5:00 p.m., everyone assumes he has a dinner

---

[130] See Lewis Closer, "Greedy Institutions: Patterns of Undivided Commitment," *Free Press*, 1974.

[131] Daniel Schneider and Kristen Harknett, "It's About Time," *The Shift Project Research Brief*, October 2019. http://bit.ly/379PVHn.

[132] LeanIn.org and McKinsey & Company, "Women in the Workplace," 2019, p. 8–9. See: https://go.aws/.

[133] I. Padavic, R. J. Ely, and E. M. Reid: "Explaining the Persistence of Gender Inequality: The Work-family Narrative as a Social Defense Against the 24/7 Work Culture," *Administrative Science Quarterly*, Feb. 14, 2019. DOI link: http://bit.ly/2w1eoBV.

[134] M. Blair-Loy, "Cultural Constructions of Family Schemas: The Case of Women Finance Executives Author(s)," *Gender and Society*, Vol. 15, No. 5 (Oct. 2001), pp. 687–709.

meeting with a client. When a woman does, people assume she has to care for her child or make dinner for her family.

In families without stay-at-home dads or the resources to hire help, that may indeed be the case. But settling for the proposition that husbands and wives need to pick between home and career is a false choice. The real answer is to organize work so both fathers and mothers—and people without children, for that matter—can balance their work and personal lives. And in the process free women from the "mommy track."

Marilyn was early through the glass ceiling. But it came at a cost. She endured a long period of suspicion and distrust. Her assertiveness, directness, and drive gave her a reputation among her peers for reckless ambition. They simply didn't find her likable. In retirement, Marilyn could only cringe looking back at her early days in the company.

> I was reckless and foolhardy. I overdid
> everything. I was disliked and rejected by
> everyone. I bungled because I was ignorant about
> the organization's [established] mechanisms. I
> was told [by peers] that I would not last long.

She not only lasted, she thrived because she never followed the expected path in any job—she took more risks, finding a new way to do every assignment because she didn't know the established way. "If I had done what everyone else was doing," she later admitted, "I probably would have failed." She was seldom popular among her peers, but most of the people who actually worked for her respected her. The people for whom *she* worked, with very few exceptions, valued and trusted her.

Trust, after all, is the real goal. According to historian Claire Bond Potter, "likability" was invented by men as a shortcut to gaining people's trust.[135] For businesswomen, likability was a potential trap. As Potter put it, likability is "nebulous, arbitrary, and meaningless, yet inescapable."[136] It's an imaginary emotional attachment that only exists in the receiver's mind and follows the easy path of gender stereotypes. A man is likable if he's "someone you'd like to have a beer with." What makes women likable runs in another direction, certainly not that of self-confidence, intelligence, and competence. In fact, as writer John Devore points out, for a woman to be "likable," she must "accept that men are in charge." Beer after all is a man's drink and "sharing a few with the guys" is a time-honored male stereotype.[137] The woman who delivers the beer without spilling any and smilingly takes the empties away is "likeable." In practice, likability means conforming to gender stereotypes. And as a practical matter, for women, there is an inverse relationship between promotions and likability.

One female CEO described her own technique for dealing with the likability trap as a kind of gender judo. "I'm warm Ms. Mother 95 percent of the time, so that the five percent of the time when I need to be tough, I can be."[138] Decades of social research reveal why such tactics are necessary. Americans expect women to be helpful, modest, and nice. But the ideal man is direct, assertive, and ambitious. What's "leadership" in a man is "bossy" in a woman.

Marilyn refused to play that game. She simply never thought in terms of gender. "I grew up all the way throughout [school and first

---

[135] Claire Bond Potter, "Men Invented Likability: Guess Who Profits," *New York Times,* May 4, 2019.

[136] Potter, *New York Times,* May 4, 2019.

[137] John DeVore, "What's Behind Our Obsession With 'Likability': On sexism and the politics of beer," *Medium,* Jan. 6. See: bit.ly/2uwzRlN.

[138] Joan C. Williams, "How Women Escape the Likability Trap," Sunday *New York Times,* Aug. 18, 2019.

jobs] with men as friends and I thought of them as friends," she once said. "And I didn't live my life here as a female. I lived my life as a PR person who was a New Yorker. At some point, I woke up and realized I was the senior woman at AT&T and wondered how that happened."

When pressed, she even claimed her gender was an advantage rather than an obstacle in her advancement. "I think maybe I was always able to speak my mind without fear, and with less repercussion, because I was less threatening as a woman, and it was clear that I was not competing for the top-line job," she once said.

That's not to say Marilyn was oblivious to the negative side of being a woman working in a patriarchy. She always claimed to have a collegial and friendly—even warm—relationship with many of her male colleagues. But in retirement, she realized something. She had never been invited into their social circles or homes.

"Looking back, there were negative effects. I see them now," she said late in her career. "I didn't have the same kind of social relationships. Guys never invited me to lunch—you know, one on one. I came to attribute it to the fact that men didn't want to be seen eating at a restaurant alone with a woman from work. I think they were nervous about it when they were married. I think they were nervous about it if they weren't married."

For their part, her colleagues didn't consider her a "clubby" person. John Zeglis was general counsel during all the years Marilyn led public relations. They and their organizations worked hand and glove. Yet, "she never came into my office just to shoot the breeze," he remembers. "She was always working her thing."

Being the only woman in the room through a series of high-level positions undoubtedly had other negative effects. A 2019 McKinsey study found that women who are the only female at their level have a particularly difficult experience:

More than half have to provide more evidence of their competence than others do. Nearly half have their judgment questioned in their area of competence, and nearly a quarter hear demeaning remarks about themselves or other women.[139]

We will never know whether Marilyn escaped such slights, ignored them, or fought back. We do know her direct and assertive manner challenged the popular notion of femininity requiring demure and self-effacing behavior. But she was careful not to come off as a feminist firebrand storming the executive suites.

The higher she went, the more composed she became, careful how she carried herself. It was only when she had achieved a seat at the policy-making table that she publicly embraced feminism, not as an effort to make women more like herself—or worse, like men—but as an attack on a patriarchy that saw the world through gender stereotypes and confused femininity with weakness.

In C-suite discussions, she was direct and tenacious. She meant what she said and did what she promised. Her colleagues learned to trust her. And in the end, she cleared a path that other women could follow, without raising as many eyebrows or putting as many necks out of joint.

---

[139] LeanIn.org and McKinsey & Company, "Women in the Workplace," 2019, pp. 52–53. See: https://go.aws/2OBkYVU.

CHAPTER TWENTY-FOUR

LIFE AFTER AT&T

After their two girls were on their own in the 1980s, Marilyn and her husband decided to move back into New York City. She was entitled to a driver, which would make the commute essentially a moving office for her. And Bob's studio was in Midtown, just off Fifth Avenue. He could finally give up his monthly commuter ticket on New Jersey Transit for a subway MetroCard.

They found a place in a pre-war co-op apartment on Central Park West by responding to an ad in the real estate section of the *New York Times*. The Majestic is a twin-towered, 29-floor skyscraper between 71st and 72nd Street. Designed in the Art Deco style, it must have reminded Marilyn of her childhood home on the Grand Concourse in the Bronx.

The apartment they bought was on the ninth floor and featured a sun-filled corner solarium overlooking Central Park. Marilyn set up shop at a small desk there, and it became an extension of her offices in Basking Ridge and in AT&T's official headquarters in an old Long Lines building downtown. After retiring, the solarium became the headquarters of Laurie Consulting. Save for a part-time assistant, Marilyn was the consultancy's sole employee. Her business niche was developing brand and public relations strategies for corporations and non-profit organizations. She only worked as much as she wanted, and she was careful to stay in the lane of offering advice and strategies to be implemented by someone else. She had spent enough of her life with a knot in her stomach every time the phone rang.

Her friend, Nobel prize-winner Arno Penzias, whom she had known at Bell Labs, lined her up to provide counsel to some small technology startups, which was fun. She did work for her friends Tim and Nina Zagat, founders of the eponymous restaurant guide, which was not only fun, but also fed her appetite for fine dining. She also helped former colleagues who were now running the public relations departments at other corporations and who occasionally asked her to speak to their staffs or to help wrestle a tricky public relations issue.

One engagement was somewhat typical. A former member of Marilyn's leadership team at AT&T had become the chief communications officer of a global industrial company. Like Marilyn had been, she was the highest-ranking woman in a company that was deep in testosterone. The company had several well-known brands, but they had been allowed to lie fallow. Part of her job was to help the marketing staff revitalize them. She asked Marilyn to join her in coaching an executive who was developing a particularly critical marketing plan. Unfortunately, the plan was long on strategy and short on detail. After listening carefully to his vision, Marilyn summed the problem up with a smile and just nine words. "You're at 50,000 feet," she said. "You gotta land the plane."

The executive—a rather confident sort—set his deck of papers aside and just looked at her. He clearly got the point. Then they all got down to business on the real issues of the marketing plan. "To me, that story is so Marilyn," her former colleague later said, "Super smart, with great wit, a fearless attitude, and an unfailing ability to get right to the heart of an issue."

Marilyn had twelve good, productive years following her AT&T career. Even though she had enjoyed a seven-figure salary as the head of AT&T's public relations organization, she admitted to experiencing an unusual frisson of excitement when her first check for consulting arrived. She got to spend more time at the family's farm in upstate New York, she was active on the boards of the New York City Ballet, Columbia University, New Visions for New York's Public Schools, and New York-Presbyterian Hospital. She traveled to exotic locales with Bob and supported his burgeoning career as a fine artist at shows in New York and upstate. And she got to spend more uninterrupted time with her daughters and grandchildren.

One afternoon, on her way to Lincoln Center for a meeting, Marilyn bumped into someone she hadn't seen since they were both pushing baby carriages in Central Park some thirty years earlier. Eve Preminger was now a Manhattan surrogate court judge, but they both instantly recognized each other and made a date to reconnect over lunch. When they did, they picked up just where they had left off decades earlier, taking about their kids and husbands and whatever was in the news.

"I remember the *Times* had written about some big DNA discovery and we both wished we knew more about genetics," Preminger said. "I had heard about an exhibit at the Natural History Museum and suggested it might help us better understand the subject, so we trotted off to see it." Unfortunately, the exhibit didn't amount to much. So Marilyn decided to pull together her own syllabus of reading. "She went on to ace the topic," Preminger says. "And I began to realize that my job was to make her stop working and have fun."

The two of them did have fun, going to theater together, visiting museums, and sharing long lunches with conversations that extended into the waitstaff's family meal before dinner service. But that didn't stop Marilyn from auditing biology courses at Columbia University.

Marilyn received a slew of awards in her time,[140] but the recognition that meant most to her was her induction into the Page

---

[140] Among the awards and recognition Marilyn received were the Women in Communications Matrix Award, the Tribute to Women in International Industry Award, the Human Relations Award of the American Jewish Committee, and the Women's Equity Action League Award. She was admitted to the YWCA Academy of Women Achievers and the National Honor Roll of Women in Public Relations.

Society's Hall of Fame in 2002. That was a particularly significant honor for her because the organization was named after Arthur W. Page, one of her AT&T predecessors, who had positioned public relations as a key management function and not simply a matter of wordsmithing and party planning.

Page, in fact, was eventually put on AT&T's board of directors and saw to it that his people had a seat at the table wherever policy and operating decisions were made in the company. He drove that model deep into the company's culture, adhered to by a long succession of CEOs. And each of Page's successors, up to and including Marilyn and her immediate successor, was a member of the company's senior leadership.

The acceptance speech she delivered focused not on her many accomplishments, but on her three worst failures, described earlier in this book:

> In thinking about what was relevant to the
> challenges in front of businesses today, perhaps
> surprisingly, I didn't remember the best of my
> times at AT&T. I remembered the three worst
> moments of those 25 years . . . three personally
> miserable, rotten, lousy experiences. They were
> all tests of corporate character -- which I
> believe is the core of every crisis that
> actually threatens the existence and credibility
> of a company.
>
> I'm not one of the people who likes to suggest
> PR should be the "conscience" of the
> corporation. I don't understand setting us up as
> holding moral standards that are above our
> colleagues. But one of our jobs as senior
> managers is to examine and make explicit the
> real rules of our corporate culture. While of

course we must be key members of the management policymaking team, some part of us must remain the eternal outsider -- fighting total absorption into the culture, retaining a clear eye and the ability to challenge the way things are done.

We learn again and again in our lives that people seem to have an infinite capacity for self-delusion . . . to see reality not as it is, but as we wish it was. That's our job: to keep a firm grip on reality as it is . . . to keep our grip on the employee's view of reality -- on the public's view of reality. Our job is to bring that news to every policy and decision. That's our contribution to protecting corporate integrity.

I don't think it takes an MBA ethics course to know right from wrong. But it takes guts to wrestle many of these problems to the ground and do the right thing.

Arthur Page was that kind of businessman. He was that kind of public relations counselor. And I know of no honor I would rather have than to be part of the Hall of Fame that bears his name.

Four years later, in 2006, Marilyn received the Alexander Hamilton Award for Lifetime Achievement in Public Relations. The award was given by the Institute for Public Relations, an organization that fosters greater use of research-based knowledge in PR. Marilyn wasn't the main speaker on the agenda. She was allotted five minutes for acceptance remarks and could have easily spoken off the cuff, said "thank you," and sat down to finish her dessert. One past award recipient had literally phoned in his acceptance.

But that wasn't Marilyn. With a remarkable economy of words, she put the award in a historical context, referencing both Hamilton's time, when "the colonies struggled with new ideas about liberty, security, and nationhood," and our own, "when America the superpower is dealing with these same ideas—under the pressures of globalization." And then she teed up the challenge facing our political and business leaders at the dawn of a new century:

> As a result of the United States' immense political, military and economic power, we have inherited enormous responsibilities for global leadership. A tough challenge for exercising that leadership is to grow our capacity to deal with the "other" -- the immigrant at home, the stranger abroad.

> I don't know about you, but I've become obsessed with the concern that if we don't educate ourselves in a hurry about the rest of the world -- and understand how they see issues that are critical to us -- we will keep stumbling into the kind of messes that our self-centered attitudes got us into the last few years.

It wasn't all high-altitude philosophy. Marilyn ended by suggesting that the times call for a new approach to the management function for which she was being recognized. "When we talk about what we do in PR," she said, "the focus is usually on advocacy." But maybe it's time, she suggested, to put more emphasis on "the other side of what we do—the listening and analysis that helps put decisions into a sound context.... We need to step up and utilize our public relations skills as citizens."

Then she listed what she had personally resolved to do, from reading more international media to contributing to organizations that teach young people tolerance and conflict resolution.

The fellow who organized the award program later told me he felt bad "for the guy who had to follow her." He meant the next speaker. But I had to smile because he had also described me, since I followed Marilyn as executive vice president of public relations and brand management at AT&T. She was indeed a tough act to follow. She was also a generous sounding board and an endless source of intellectual stimulation. After my AT&T career, when I started writing more or less full-time, I turned to her for help and advice.

In mid-2010, I told her that I had been mulling over her Hamilton speech ever since she gave it. I was fascinated by her belief that we need "to grow our capacity to deal with the 'Other'." But I thought that challenge encompassed even more than immigrants and global customers. To many Americans, the "Other" are not only people of color or who speak a different language, they are also non-traditional families born of continuing sexual and cultural changes. They are men in turbans or yarmulkes, women in saris or hijabs. They are single-issue activists, passionate about rights they believe are being trampled or groups they consider ill served.

"There's a book in all this," I told Marilyn. "And I'd like you to help me write it."[141] At about this point, I paused for breath, and a long silence followed.

Then Marilyn said, "I seem to have had a greater influence on you than I thought."

Talk about understatement.

---

[141] The book that resulted, *OtherWise: The Wisdom You Need To Succeed In A Diverse and Divisive World,* was dedicated to "Marilyn Laurie, friend, colleague, and inspiration."

We agreed to talk further about the project, and I made a mental note to spend more time on receive than transmit next time. Sadly, that's not what we talked about at our next meeting.

*   *   *

In 2009, Marilyn turned 70. She and Bob still enjoyed hiking in places like the Swiss Alps or the glaciers of Patagonia. But they really loved living in New York City. There was always something to do. And since they lived across the street from one of the greatest public parks in the country, if not the world, they spent a fair amount of time outdoors, riding their bikes past the memorial to John Lennon at Strawberry Fields and climbing Cherry Hill or heading south past the Sheep Meadow.

One day in June 2009, as Marilyn and Bob biked under a brilliant blue sky, she suddenly struggled to keep her balance and found herself swerving into the path of bikers coming from the other direction. She overcorrected and fell off her bike. Slightly bruised and a little dizzy, she and Bob decided to walk their bikes home.

The next day, Marilyn and Bob went to their farm in upstate New York, about two-and-a-half hours from Manhattan. Marilyn uncharacteristically dozed all the way up and awakened with a piercing headache. Instead of going to the supermarket for provisions, they decided to make a stop at the local hospital emergency room. The doctor there examined her and, based on her symptoms of dizziness and headache so severe she was nauseated, he diagnosed possible meningitis. She was admitted and immediately given a heavy dose of antibiotics intravenously. She was kept in the hospital for three days and then sent home with an IV still in her arm.

Back in New York, friends chided her for entrusting her care to a country hospital upstate. She was on the board of trustees of New York-Presbyterian Hospital. Why on earth wouldn't she at least consult them? Whomever she called at New York-Presbyterian told her to put herself in a taxi and get to the emergency room *stat*. An hour after she got there, she found out she had a brain tumor, and it had to come out.

She had the surgery about a month later and went home, determined to lead as normal a life as possible. In a matter of weeks, she was in chemotherapy, but often well enough to attend board meetings at Columbia University and at the New York City Ballet. She had lunch with former colleagues, went out with friends to some of her favorite restaurants. But sometimes she would lose her balance, just for a moment, and she'd have to reach out to a wall for support. Her speech sometimes faltered. Friends began to notice she was not herself—conversation with her became "nonlinear," jumping from topic to topic. She began to have trouble seeing clearly.

```
So I'm pretty severely visually impaired.
Driving is over. And yet, each time I walk down
the street, left arm up in front to keep from
banging into something, I'm overwhelmingly
grateful I can see [anything at all]. Happier
than when I took in routine vistas without
another thought.

How do people born into darkness manage? How
tragic is their state compared to my lifetime of
visual experience, joy and cues that now help me
navigate around this minor obstacle? Ok, I'm no
longer the intended audience for a Jerry
Bruckheimer film -- I lose about 30 percent of
the action because I can't process it. This
qualifies as a problem? Not.
```

I first became aware of Marilyn's health problems in December of 2009 and sent her an email expressing my concern and support. I told her how much I had learned from her, through good times and bad. "For some reason, the disasters are more vivid than the successes though there were plenty of those too," I wrote. "I think that's because you were always at your best when times were tough." I then reminded her, in some detail, of what we had gone through together—good, bad, and ugly. "You were always steady, supportive, positive, and caring," I continued. "That reflects a truth about you— an unhesitating willingness to tackle any challenge that matters. Your current challenge may matter more than any you've taken on. You should know that you don't face it alone."

Marilyn's reply was typically optimistic and cheery:

```
Dick,

Thanks for the kind words, the entertaining --
if catastrophe-strewn -- memories and the
personal concern. Look forward to staying in
touch.

-- Marilyn
```

When I saw Marilyn for the last time, six months later, she was quite frail. Curled up at the end of a couch in her New York City apartment, surrounded by pillows, with a blanket over her lap, and a sailor hat on her head to hide the hair loss, she looked even smaller than I remembered. But her first words reassured me that her spirit had not been worn down. "Mortality sucks," she said. "It. Really. Does. Suck."

She was never someone to beat around the bush. She had disposed of the one topic that hung over every conversation she probably had in those days, and the one that everyone feared the most. And with that out of the way, we could share old memories, especially those of things that went awry, because that's where all the laughs were.

It would take a little more than a year for a malignant brain tumor and the subsequent surgery and chemotherapy to wear this indomitable woman down. And through it all—through the procedures, the hair loss, the vision loss, the loss of balance, the nausea, the weakness, the fatigue, the moments of disorientation—through it all, she did what she had always done. She wrote down what she was experiencing and thinking in her cursive handwriting.

In the hospital:

A rangy, attractive, well-dressed gentleman approaches the piano and begins to play. Lush arpeggios roll through the space as he rambles through classic piano bar tunes from my youth, starting with "The Last Time I Saw Paris." My heart was young as I remember [my sister] Lois singing that from my childhood. It's the early '50s suddenly, and there are still echoes of the War in the room. The tears begin to roll.

I'm crying for my youth . . . , for always being the youngest in the room . . . , for the precocity of early achievement . . . , for the forever promise of the next challenge, the next idea, the next, the next . . . and here, here in this uniformly-lit, timeless void on the ninth floor of the hospital with the songs of World War II washing over me, I'm the wizened old lady on the sofa with a plastic cup of tea in front of her . . . , brown and chemical-yellow hair plastered to her head in a post-operative cloche . . . , softly crying to the familiar strains -- or at least familiar then -- before rock, before rap. From the era of American optimism and hope and belief.

My sister Lois says none of us get out of this
life alive. True. True. But up to a point, it
doesn't apply to us personally. And then one
day, it does.

Home after surgery:

I'm snuggled in deep within the folds of the
crisp, soft duvet, legs askew. The surgical area
is completely healed so I can put my head
anywhere on the puffy set of pillows. It's a
decadent state of peace and rest. Absolutely no
pain. No anxiety. Everything is preternaturally
quiet: no fire engines screaming down Central
Park West . . . , not even the hum of nighttime
traffic. Everything slowed from the normal pace
of time. Sleep comes . . . , sleep
leaves . . . , profound feelings of rest
permeate every molecule of my body. Who knew the
nights could be so fine?

Her last days at home:

They say it's better to give than receive. And I
generally agree with that, since engagement is
one of the greatest joys of my life. But I'm
receiving now and damn it's good too. The steady
hand from Bob, or Amy, or Lisa as I walk or
reach for anything. Taking turns to help me give
up control . . . , not exactly my strong suit.
But as I experiment with it . . . it's, it's OK,
and the gentle support returning to me is
energizing and warming to the core. Lisa strokes
my arm . . . , Amy softly clasps my hand . . . ,
Bob hugs gently. Wherever my skin itches,
someone rubs in lotion. Our family was not into

touching a lot before. We are now. No wonder
cats purr.

How crazy is it that I actually feel euphoric
some of the time as a result of this
catastrophe? All those bestsellers about the
power of love and the religious experience and
the "lift" from love and caring. Turns out
there's some truth to that.

If I said my 70th year was going, by god, to be
the best of my life in some way . . . , and that
was the breakthrough concept that I was aiming
for . . . , it happened. The experience of deep
and unconditional love from the girls and Bob
has been so beyond any emotion I have ever
experienced, that it has lifted me to a giddy
state of euphoria, quite independent of
everything going on inside of me. Who knew what
exalted emotional joy could be generated by the
simple daily motions of hanging out together
exchanging looks of love and a hand to hold
onto? Learning late. But lesson learned.

Asked where people find meaning in old age, gerontologist
Thomas Cole said, "From loving and being loved. Their world and
aspirations shrink a little bit. Love takes on larger meaning."[142]
Marilyn was still relatively young in her final days, but her world had
shrunk to a sofa piled with pillows and a rented hospital bed. And
this woman who, in one daughter's words was "never uncomfortable
being uncomfortable" finally allowed herself to be comforted.

---

[142] Thomas Cole was quoted by Clare Ansberry, "What Men in Their 80s Can Teach Us
About Aging," *Wall Street Journal*, Jan. 13, 2020. See: https://on.wsj.com/2SKIPpQ.

In July, 2010, Marilyn slipped into a coma. She died peacefully at home in Manhattan just a few days later, early on the morning of July 14, with her husband and two daughters at her bedside.

She was 71.

CHAPTER TWENTY-FIVE

LEGACY

Philosopher Søren Kierkegaard once noted that life must be lived forward but can only be understood looking backward.[143] So Marilyn never understood the full meaning of her life, because she didn't see all the ripples she set in motion.

Some of us leave an organization with vivid memories of our time there. A few leave a memory of their tenure in those they left behind. And a very few leave a legacy that endures through successive generations of those who follow them. Marilyn was in the latter category. She left us her understanding of public relations' purpose and the values that should guide its practice. Her story made it a little easier for the women who followed her—at AT&T and in other companies. She gave those of us with a Y chromosome a model to emulate, too.

It started with the way she defined "great public relations":

```
Great public relations is making sure you do the
right thing, not that you have the right thing
to say. You will always have the right thing to
say, if you've done the right thing.
```

This wasn't a slap at her internal clients. Nor did she use it as an escape hatch to separate herself from mistakes made deep in her own organization. Marilyn was very aware of the wrong things her organization did (like the racist cartoon in the company magazine), as well as the things it did wrongly (like the way the company tried to

---

[143] This is a paraphrase of Kierkegaard's original observation: "It is really true what philosophy tells us, that life must be understood backwards. But with this, one forgets the second proposition, that it must be lived forwards." Søren Kierkegaard, Journalen JJ:167 (1843), *Søren Kierkegaards Skrifter*, Søren Kierkegaard Research Center, Copenhagen, 1997, volume 18, p. 306.

extract itself from the abortion debate). She took personal accountability, learned from every mistake, and did her best to get her people to do the same.

But she also knew that the company's policies and actions would be the ultimate driver of the company's reputation. Arthur Page had won her a seat at the policymaking table, but she had to continually earn her right to stay there by bringing added value to the discussions. "You need to know the business as well as the people running it do," she told her PR people. "And you have to know the outside world *better* than they do. The first gives you credibility; the second will make you valuable." Reading the trades and business papers is not enough. "If you aren't curious about what's going on in the world . . . you're not going to be able to make the connections it's your job to bring to the table," she warned. "Listen deeply to all kinds of audiences—through all kinds of media—so you bring a convincing, uniquely 'outside' perspective to the table. A broad understanding of public opinion and trends will bring authority to your advice."

But providing that advice required one more thing—courage. "You cannot be afraid because we have to constantly be trying to affect policy, trying to deal with actions that come up, trying to be there before decisions are final—and sometimes change decisions even after they are final," she warned, "so the capacity to relate to operational leaders without fear, as a peer, as a colleague, is very important." She didn't think public relations people should have an inferiority complex. "I think we add as much value—if we do what we do well—as anybody else at the table and we deserve to be heard," she said. "But you have to believe that to be heard."

Al Partoll, the executive responsible for representing the company's interests in the regulatory agencies of all 50 states for much of Marilyn's career, was one senior executive willing to listen.

He claimed one of Marilyn's greatest contributions to the company was sensitizing it to the external environment.

"Although the Bell System dissolved in 1984," he said. "AT&T was still an insular and insulated organization, driven by internal indices rather than by the outside world. Rule One was to please your boss by achieving whatever the Green Book or the Red Book or some other color book said was your goal. Marilyn helped us all understand that wasn't enough. She brought outside issues to the table and helped me get my job done."

Partoll's boss General Counsel John Zeglis agrees. "Marilyn had a bigger idea of public policy than those of us in the law department," he said. "To her, public policy was made by the public, not by legislatures. And she considered it her job to make sure we understood what the public demanded of us, even when we weren't particularly interested in hearing it."

Not that her advice was always sought nor, when given, followed. In retirement, she had to admit that, "when I was in charge [of public relations], the very, very largest challenges were trying to help senior management adapt to the various things that those of us who have a broad view of the world could see needed to be done—outside the technical and financial aspects of the business."

They were challenges she was willing to tackle. "She had no problem standing in front of a group of men, hands on hips, and saying what she had to say, even if not welcome," Partoll remembers. "She confronted males on equal terms and didn't take any of their bull. She wanted to be valued for *who* she was, not *what* she was."

Some resented her refusal to stay in the lane supposedly assigned to her by function and gender. But she had a more expansive view of public relations than wordsmithing and party planning. And although she knew some people thought she got to the top because of her gender rather than merit, she had enough confidence to realize that was their problem, not hers.

One of the secrets to Marilyn's success was her ability to come at problems from the perspective of all those affected, as well as the public interest. It was a way of thinking that does not come naturally to most businesspeople whose success depends on being laser focused on a small number of goals.

"All large bureaucracies are defensive, self-absorbed, constantly in denial, and rarely care about the outside world," she once said. In many ways, she was the company's peripheral vision. In fact, she saw it as her role to be a voice in the boardroom for the company's employees, customers, and the communities where it operated.

That was the value she could bring to the decision making table and it was the foundation of how she explained public relations' purpose to others:

The purpose of public relations is to bring the policies and practices of an institution into harmony with the needs and expectations of the public.

Sometimes that means persuading the public that the institution is doing the right thing; sometimes it means persuading the institution to change its behavior.

But as Marilyn added, somewhat prophetically for AT&T as it turned out, "When the company's practices fall out of alignment with the public's expectations, there is almost always hell to pay." As Marilyn moved from one internal client to another through the 1980s and '90s, she used that definition to help her colleagues and peers understand how she viewed the practice. "It seemed to me this was how Arthur Page had defined public relations 60 years earlier," she said. "After using that quote in a talk when Ian Ross was in the room, and another when Bob Allen was there, each of them told me they thought that definition was spot on . . . . Not that you could tell from what followed."

Marilyn was the ultimate insider who still knew what it felt like to be an outsider. Ironically, that feeling didn't come from frequently being the only woman in the room as she progressed in her career. What made Marilyn feel like an outsider was more a matter of geography and values than of gender. Although, when she worked for the company, AT&T's headquarters had been in New York for nearly a century, it was as Midwestern as a cornfield. Most of the company's senior executives—and all its recent CEOs—went to school, married, raised their kids, and spent much of their careers in the big square states in the middle of the country. Marilyn was born, bred, and educated in New York City. She spoke with the flat accents and directness of the cabdrivers and beat cops in her native Bronx. Some of her colleagues felt she brought "a New York edge" to every discussion, though they admit her tone carried no meanness, simply a passion to get things done.

But Marilyn wasn't totally blind to the sexism that bookended her career. In retirement, she did allow, "If I had so much talent, why didn't they put me in the line somewhere? Probably it was because I was woman." She racked it up to "puts and takes." In reality, it was because she had not been preceded by someone like herself, who broke through the glass ceiling through dint of creativity, intellect, and courage, paving the way for others.

Gail McGovern was one of the women who benefited from Marilyn's plea that female candidates for promotion to officer be given the same benefit of the doubt as the men. She was the first woman at AT&T to be given profit and loss responsibility for a line of business, and a few years later became president of AT&T's largest and most profitable business—consumer long distance service.

Although Marilyn played no direct role in that part of her career, McGovern credits her with setting an example and preparing the way. "She was quietly supportive of women, but never shrill, never loud about gender," McGovern says. "But she set a model of how to behave in a room of all men."

That model was sorely tested when McGovern was invited to a high-level review of the company's diversity profile. In addition to Marilyn and Mirian Graddick-Weir, the human resources executive who was giving the presentation, McGovern was the only other woman in the meeting, which said a lot in itself. But when a very senior executive asked Graddick-Weir why she bothered to keep statistics on women at higher levels since they would all just get pregnant and leave, McGovern felt as if all eyes were on her, waiting for an eruption. She kept her cool. But after the meeting, Marilyn caught up with her in the hallway and quietly suggested that she get her resume in circulation. It was as if Sisyphus had let go of his rock. Within months, McGovern left to take a high-level job at Fidelity Investments and she ultimately became CEO of the American Red Cross. Marilyn announced her retirement around the same time.

Marilyn may have known when to cut bait, but she was no pushover. She knew that an organization of 500 people develops its own ecology, following ruts worn into daily life by simple repetition. "There's a tension in any large organization between self-actualization and achieving common goals," she told her direct reports. "Our job is to get everyone aligned behind the few critical issues most important to the executive committee, the business unit presidents, key external stakeholders, and our own people's professional development."

That would not be easy in an organization so heavily matrixed. Each of the public relations vice presidents who reported to her led teams serving different business units and geographical areas, as well as different corporate headquarters' functions. They each had dual reporting relationships to her and to internal clients. Nevertheless, she made it clear, in writing yet, that she expected them to "set the standard for cooperation, working together to resolve impasses that develop between groups, stamping out backbiting and turfism." Most of all, she expected her direct reports to "leave a footprint" outside the organization's well-worn ruts. And she believed the best way to do that was to come up with a small number of "Big Ideas" the whole decentralized organization could embrace and that could serve as the creative backbone for business-specific projects.

Marilyn was always chasing big ideas she could put into the PR wind machine. Not everyone was immediately on board. Kathy Fitzgerald was one of the women who rose through the ranks in Marilyn's wake, ultimately becoming the chief communication officer at Lucent Technologies when it was launched and later assuming the same role at the KPMG accounting firm and still later at the New Jersey utility PSE&G. She had Marilyn's quick mind and rock-solid judgment, but while Marilyn had never written a news release, Fitzgerald had ink and its digital equivalent in her veins. "While I often thought our focus should be on PR blocking and tackling to get the job done, [Marilyn's] constant exhortation to look for the 'big idea' made me stretch," she said, "almost as much as it made me crazy at times."

Stretch Marilyn's people did. One team came up with the idea of announcing a "Telecommuting Day," on which the company would encourage employees who could to work from home, phoning in to meetings as necessary. What was admittedly a stunt helped turn the then arcane concept of telecommuting into a workplace trend of the 1990s. The promotion caught the media's attention and showed how telecommuting cut corporate expenses, helped employees better balance their work and family responsibilities, and addressed societal problems such as crowded highways and pollution. And it led to even more ambitious projects in partnership with agencies such as the Department of Labor, the Department of Transportation, and the Environmental Protection Agency.

Marilyn's search for similar big ideas extended beyond the borders of her own organization. She hired an outside agency to place stories about AT&T's products and services in consumer media. And she gave the same assignment to a small team of her own people. The agency came up with a long list of editors, mostly in print media, to whom they sent pitch letters and made follow-up phone calls. Nothing much happened. The internal team got on the highest-rated TV afternoon talk show by offering "communications makeovers" to Oprah Winfrey's studio audience. The internal team obviously had deeper knowledge of the company's products and services. But they also had a big idea. Point made. Maybe two points.

Marilyn didn't only operate at 50,000 feet; she also paid attention to the nuts and bolts of the PR practice. Bruce Brackett, who did some speechwriting for Bob Allen, remembers what it was like to have Marilyn as an editor. "I had prepared press conference remarks to promote a new service," he said. "Marilyn reviewed the draft and circled one colorful phrase with the dismissive comment, 'That's rhetoric.' I countered with: 'It's a sound bite.' She gave an ambivalent shrug of her shoulders, which I interpreted to mean I could keep that line. As luck would have it, that line was prominently quoted in media coverage of the event. And when she saw me later, she said, 'Aren't you glad you pushed back?' That little incident told me Marilyn was both willing to admit she was wrong and ready to use any opportunity to help develop subordinates."

Many of us walk around with pockets full of good intentions we never tap. Marilyn spent hers. When I managed my first large team, I had so much trouble finding the right balance between abdication and meddling, I got in people's way. Marilyn called me into her office one day and, after the usual pleasantries, she told me she had received an anonymous letter about me. Somewhat creatively, I thought, the writer called me a "martinet." To be honest, I wasn't surprised, but I was deeply embarrassed. Marilyn said she understood how tricky it is to suddenly supervise people who were your peers just a week earlier. She said she also knew that it's difficult to shake an organization out of complacency without upsetting people. And that getting people to strive for higher standards invites challenge. "But sometimes managers get too controlling," she told me, "because they're scared. You have no reason to be scared—you're talented and so are the people who report to you."

It was a long time before I realized she was, at least in part, recounting her own experience—the appetite for accomplishment hamstrung by the fear of failure when you're so dependent on others. And that may be why she was so fearless in running interference between the occasionally overreacting C-suite and her team on the front lines. As one PR colleague said, "We will probably never know the full extent of her support."

This is not to suggest she was perfect. She was, like all of us, a flawed human being. She could be encouraging and supportive as well as jealous and guarded. As a colleague, she could be searingly intense. One senior executive who worked closely with her said, "You wouldn't want to take her on a long canoe trip."

"I feel very strongly about the winning value of always striving to do better," she once confessed to an interviewer. "It doesn't matter what I do, I'm constantly looking for better performance."[144] That also applied to her staff. "She was always telling me how to do things

---

[144] L. J. McFarland, L. E. Senn, and J. R. Childress, *21st Century Leadership: Dialogues With 100 Top Leaders*, p. 126.

better," Kathy Fitzgerald remembers. "Once, I said, 'Jesus, was I that bad?' And she said, 'Oh, no. You were excellent. I just want you to be as good as you can be. And you can be even better'."

On the other hand, when her organization delivered the goods, she was not embarrassed to walk up and down the halls ringing a corny brass bell and cheering her people on. Adele Donohue who went on to become the chief communications officer at AT&T Wireless and later at the Merck & Company pharmaceutical company, received such a bell. "I thought the whole bell thing was kind of hokey and I'm pretty sure I made fun of it at the time," Donohue says, "but when I retired years later and cleaned out my office, I was surprised to find that little bell on one of the bookshelves. I have changed companies twice and offices at least four times. But I still have that little brass bell."

Marilyn could be confident in one moment and insecure in another. I once complimented her on a talk she gave to an audience of factory workers. "Oh yeah?" she said. "If it was so good, why weren't there any questions?" She would have preferred challenge to silence because then she would have known she reached them.

Her career mirrored the times in which she lived. It began in environmentalism, one of the great social movements of the 1960s. It was bookended by systemic sexism and the gender stereotyping in which it flourished. It was caught in the legal, technological, and financial cross-currents that brought down AT&T, one of the nation's premiere corporations. Change was the medium in which Marilyn flourished. In fact, she once compared AT&T to a masonry building, and said her whole career was dealing with bricks falling off. "But for me each change was exciting, new things to think about, new problems," she said. She liked to quote her friend Arno Penzias as saying, "That's what's important, finding good problems to work on."

Marilyn leaned into problems when others looked away. She was intellectually curious, open-minded in exploring an issue, but assertive when she formed a view, and clear in articulating it. She was creative, whip-smart, and an unusual mix of toughness and caring.

She may not have always represented the new style of nurturing, communal leadership James MacGregor Burns envisioned. She broke through the glass ceiling using the same tools of advancement men had used for generations. She was assertive, cunning, and competitive, all in service of making a difference on a grand scale. We will never know the true cost to Marilyn and her family of that driving aspiration. Her protest that "she wouldn't do it any other way," really meant that in her day, there *was* no other way.

In her final days, as she sat quietly in the hospital chemo department, poison dripping into her veins, she filled more than a page of lined paper with goals. No one knows whether they were the goals she had tried to achieve, felt she *had* achieved, *wished* she had given more attention, or a final instruction to her daughters and grandchildren . . . and us:

Make waves.

Find time to bond with friends and family.

Take time to be still and notice the beauty around you.

Explore new places and inspiring things.

Have the ambition to influence the future, the courage to stand up for your ideas, and the stamina to make yourself heard.

Nurture your dreams and the dreams of those you love.

Call up the energy and creativity to break out of your box.

Have the courage to pursue your passions.

Maintain defiant belief in new possibilities.

Develop the toughness to reject the cacophony of
competing demands and the wisdom to choose
meaning over busyness.

May you experience the joy of finding peace.

In her job, Marilyn had to be sensitive to self-delusion. The worst client was one who suffered from it. They could not be reasoned out of their misbelief. A web of mental biases protected them from reality—confirmation bias, anchoring effects, cognitive dissonance, the lists in psychology texts seem to go on forever. But Marilyn seldom engaged in magical thinking just to ease some anxiety. Given a choice between fight and flight, she invariably chose fight. But even she understood when fight was futile. And she had reached that point medically. Comfort was the goal now. Death was close. Her response was to pose three existential questions:

Isn't right now forever?

Don't we all die -- not that it's particularly
relevant throughout our lives -- but the issue,
the panic is how much we know in advance about
when and how.

If you are standing in the tall grass of the
Serengeti and there's a full-grown lion only
three feet away and you cannot see him, is that
how much we know about when and how? You know
he's there -- the guide has said he's
there . . . and you cannot see him. Is this a
visual impairment? Or an act of evolution?

Is it possible to get tired of Dulce de Leche
ice cream?

The first question explained how she lived her life—fearlessly and passionately. The second acknowledged her state at the time. She was in the tall grass, and she not only knew the lion was there, she knew he was about to pounce. And the third question simply said, "Don't waste time worrying about when." She had better things to do. One of them was to describe what she hoped would be her legacy:

    I would like to think I changed a few things
    along the way. I'd like to think that I caused a
    fair number of people to care about the
    environment at a time when it was not an issue.
    I'd like to think I helped AT&T be more
    successful in the era when it was of great
    service to the world.

    I would hope I caused some people, who do what
    we do, to think that you can do it with
    integrity and with courage.

    I've tried to work with entities that I think
    make the world a better place, and I've tried to
    help them be more successful at what they do
    well. It's so important that what you do when
    you go to work in the morning matters to you.
    And I hope the people who worked for me felt
    that way.

With more than a decade's hindsight, we can say she taught generations of public relations people how to practice PR and cleared a path through the glass ceiling for many women, directly and by example. She demonstrated how we can take charge of our own lives to find meaning in our work. She showed us how to handle days of heady highs, and humbling lows, with grace and resilience.

And she changed a few lives along the way.

INDEX

CPSIA information can be obtained
at www.ICGtesting.com
Printed in the USA
BVHW070723040820
585326BV00005B/16